POEMS:
AMERICAN
THEMES

BOOKS BY WILBERT J. LEVY

More Powerful Reading

Poems: American Themes

Reading and Growing

Sentence Play

Wordplay

Paragraph Play

Amsco Literature Program

The Red Badge of Courage With Reader's Guide

Treasure Island With Reader's Guide

Amsco Writing English Series

Writing English: Foundations

Paragraph Power

Sense of Sentences

Composition: Prewriting, Response, Revision

Dedicated to serving

AMSCO

our nation's youth

*When ordering this book, please specify:
either* **N 399 W** *or Poems: American Themes*

POEMS: AMERICAN THEMES

WILBERT J. LEVY

AMSCO SCHOOL PUBLICATIONS, INC.
315 Hudson Street, New York, N.Y. 10013

ACKNOWLEDGMENTS

Grateful acknowledgment is made to the following sources for permission to use copyrighted materials.

Samuel Allen: "To Satch" by Samuel Allen.

Brandt & Brandt Literary Agency, Inc.: From *John Brown's Body* by Stephen Vincent Benét, Holt, Rinehart and Winston, Inc., copyright 1927, 1928 by Stephen Vincent Benét, copyright renewed © 1955, 1956 by Rosemary Carr Benét.

Cherokee Publishing Company: "Machines" by Daniel Whitehead Hicky.

Mrs. Gwendolyn Crosscup: "To James" by Frank Horne.

Curtis Brown, Ltd.: "Dick Szymanski," copyright © 1968 by Ogden Nash.

Babette Deutsch: "Morning Work-out" by Babette Deutsch.

Dodd, Mead & Company, Inc.: "The Skater of Ghost Lake" from *Golden Fleece* by William Rose Benét, copyright 1933, 1935 by Dodd, Mead & Company, Inc., copyright renewed.

Doubleday & Company, Inc.: "I See a Star" by Alonzo Lopez from the book *The Whispering Wind* by Terry Allen, copyright © 1972 by The Institute of American Indian Arts. "My Papa's Waltz," copyright 1942 by Hearst Magazines, Inc., and "Night Journey," copyright 1940 by Theodore Roethke, both from the book *The Collected Poems of Theodore Roethke.*

Dufour Editions, Inc.: "Underwater" by Michael Schmidt.

E. P. Dutton: "America, the Beautiful" from *Poems* by Katharine Lee Bates.

Norma Millay Ellis: Excerpt from *Epitaph for the Race of Man*, "God's World," "Lament," "Love Is Not All," "On Hearing a Symphony of Beethoven," "Pity Me Not," "Recuerdo" from *Collected Poems*, Harper & Row, copyright 1917, 1921, 1922, 1923, 1928, 1931, 1934, 1945, 1948, 1950, 1951, 1955, 1958, 1962 by Edna St. Vincent Millay and Norma Millay Ellis.

Dave Etter: "The Fact" from *The Last Train to Prophetstown* by Dave Etter, University of Nebraska Press, 1968.

Mari Evans: "When in Rome" from *I Am a Black Woman*, published by William Morrow & Company, 1970.

Farrar, Straus & Giroux, Inc.: "Losses" from *The Complete Poems* by Randall Jarrell, copyright 1948 by Mrs. Randall Jarrell, renewed copyright © 1975 by Mary von Schrader Jarrell. "Water" from *For the Union Dead* by Robert Lowell, copyright © 1962, 1964 by Robert Lowell.

Harcourt Brace Jovanovich, Inc.: "plato told," copyright 1944 by E. E. Cummings, renewed 1972 by Nancy T. Andrews, reprinted from *Complete Poems, 1913-1962* by E. E. Cummings. "Fueled" from *Serve Me a Slice of Moon* © 1965 by Marcie Hans. "Chicago" from *Chicago Poems* by Carl Sandburg, copyright 1916 by Holt, Rinehart and Winston, Inc., copyright 1944 by Carl Sandburg. "Mr. Attila" from *The Complete Poems of Carl Sandburg*, copyright 1950 by Carl Sandburg. Three excerpts from *The People, Yes* by Carl Sandburg, copyright 1936 by Harcourt Brace Jovanovich, Inc., copyright 1964 by Carl Sandburg. "Smoke Rose Gold" and "Jazz Fantasia" from *Smoke and Steel* by Carl Sandburg, copyright 1920 by Harcourt Brace Jovanovich, Inc., copyright 1948 by Carl Sandburg.

Harper & Row, Publishers, Inc.: "Truth" from *The World of Gwendolyn Brooks* by Gwendolyn Brooks, copyright 1945 by Gwendolyn Brooks Blakely. From *On These I Stand* by Countee Cullen: "Any Human to Another," copyright 1935 by Harper & Row, Publishers, Inc., renewed 1963 by Ida M. Cullen; "Incident," copyright 1925 by Harper & Row, Publishers, Inc., renewed 1953 by Ida M. Cullen. "Mirror" from *Crossing the Water* by Sylvia Plath, copyright © 1963 by Ted Hughes, originally appeared in *The New Yorker*. "Ex-Basketball Player" from *The Carpentered Hen* by John Updike, copyright © 1957 by John Updike, originally appeared in *The New Yorker*.

Holt, Rinehart and Winston: "The Gift Outright," "Mending Wall," "Out, Out—," "Stopping by Woods on a Snowy Evening," and "The Telephone" from *The Poetry of Robert Frost* edited by Edward Connery Lathem, copyright 1916, 1923, 1930, 1939, © 1969 by Holt, Rinehart and Winston, copyright 1942, 1944, 1951, © 1958 by Robert Frost, copyright © 1967, 1970 by Lesley Frost Ballantine.

Houghton Mifflin Company: "Lilacs," "Meeting-House Hill," "Patterns," and "Trades" from *The*

To the Teacher

Since the *Teacher's Manual* for this book affords full discussion, no elaborate introduction is necessary here. However, one urgent point is appropriate.

Our time is afflicted by a widespread impoverishment of the ability to perceive experience sensitively and a corollary impoverishment of language to articulate experience, acting together in a vicious cycle.

To the English educator, and to the general public as well, this underlying malaise shows itself variously. It is felt that students can't read well, write well, or speak well. Scores on standardized verbal tests have declined. More important than such quantifiable phenomena are evidences of a general stifling of personal development. There seems to be a spreading mode of existence that is inane and herdlike, devoid of self-activation, critical perception, enriching enthusiasms, healthful pleasures, uplifting values. These conditions are a threat to our political democracy, our economic well-being, our ideal of individuality.

We are not clear about the causes of the malaise. It is my own belief that the commercial television tube is a major contributing element, far more potent than is realized in its capacity to reduce individuals to a robot mass. Yet it is less important to agree on causes than it is to see the problem clearly and to mobilize countermeasures.

Again, the problem is impoverishment of the ability to perceive experience sensitively and impoverishment of language to articulate experience. Poetry is the antithesis. Poetry is the keenest perception of experience and the rendering of that perception in the most richly articulate language. The teaching of poetry, therefore, offers itself as a strong, direct counterthrust. It has always been important that poetry be taught. Today, it is critically important.

What is more, poetry must be taught boldly and completely, with an unmitigated aspiration toward its niceties, subtleties, and artistry. Yes, the student must be given every help, every encouragement. Yes, every stroke in the art of the teacher should be applied. But the thrust toward bringing the student as far as possible along the road to learning the perceptions and articulations of poetry must be sure and strong. In teaching poetry, it will serve well to remember the poetic words that Browning had Andrea del Sarto speak:

> "Ah, but a man's reach should exceed his grasp,
>   Or what's a heaven for?"

Briefly, that is the matrix of thought that has led to the putting together of this book. In that putting together, the insights and creativity of my editorial consultant, Nora E. Johnston, presently of Bath, England, have been of enormous help. I thank her.

Wilbert J. Levy

Contents

Reading Poetry: A Short Introduction

It is best to start by being quite honest. Poetry-reading is different from all other reading. Learning to read poetry with understanding and enjoyment is not simple or easy; on the contrary, it requires special effort and application. It requires learning the necessary techniques.

The effort is well rewarded. Poetry is consciousness-raising. Through poetry, you can know yourself better, know all people better, know the world better. Through poetry, you, all people, and the world become better worth knowing.

Learning to read poetry requires hard work. The first steps—and they are important ones—are, however, easy. Let us have a beginning look at two sides of poetry: the stuff of poetry—what poems are written about—and the language of poetry. You already know a good deal about both.

First, what is the stuff, the subject matter, about which poems are written? Is it unfamiliar or unusual? The opposite is true. There is nothing closer or more familiar to you than the stuff of poetry.

Have you ever seen a terrible auto accident the sight of which has haunted you with feelings of dread and horror? Have you jogged or swum or danced and experienced inexpressible delight in the feel of your muscles in well-coordinated action? Have you ever felt that the daily routine of your life was unbearably monotonous and meaningless? Have you enjoyed the smell of freshly cut grass in spring? Have you yearned for love until it hurt beyond words? Have you laughed? Have you shed tears? Have you felt uplifted, ecstatic, confident, hopeful, guilty, worried, insecure?

Of course, your answer to most of these questions will be yes! These basic feelings that we all share and these common experiences are the stuff of poetry. You know them as well as you know your own face in the mirror, the pulse of your own blood. The stuff of poetry is you. You have expert knowledge of the stuff of poetry.

At a beginning level, you also know something about the language of poetry. In fact, a little baby instinctively speaks the language of poetry. Picture a baby in its mother's arms. It has had a good long nap and has been bathed and dressed. It has just been fed. The mother is holding the baby, warmly and securely. The father is looking at it with adoration. The baby opens and closes its fists, waves its arms and legs, feels the wonderful feeling of its muscles in action. The baby gurgles and coos, says "ma-ma-ma-ma, da-da-da-da." Those rhythmically repeated musical sounds express far better than ordinary language ever could the blood-muscle-bone-skin-eye-mouth-tummy feelings of the baby, the deep sense of delight the baby feels in being alive, in being itself, in its joy with the world! Those sounds express to the hearer precisely and clearly the otherwise inexpressible feelings of the baby. Those sounds are a natural, primitive form of poetry.

Traces of the language of poetry appear also in the familiar language of the adult world. This is especially true when expression of or appeal to emotions is involved, as in sports, entertainment, or selling.

At football games, we chant:

"Rah-rah-rah
Sis-boom-bah!"

At baseball games, we shout:

"Up the river, down the lake
The pitcher has a bellyache!"

In these wild expressions of enthusiasm, we are not interested in using words only for their dictionary meanings. We use other qualities of words—rhythm, rhyme, repetition, figurative language (the pitcher doesn't really have a bellyache)—to convey our emotions and whip up everybody else's emotions.

We use images and symbols and sound repetitions in some of the names we give our teams and athletes, our entertainments and entertainers, our automobiles. You can probably add many examples of your own to the following: the Bronx Bombers, the Philadelphia Flyers, the Detroit Lions, the Sultan of Swat, Mean Joe Greene, the Human Eraser, the Juice, Wonder Woman, Mod Squad, Woody Woodpecker, The Brady Bunch, the King of Swing, Old Blue Eyes, Thunderbird, Skylark, Cougar.

As these examples illustrate, there are special qualities of words other than literal, dictionary meanings that we sometimes use even in ordinary language to express ourselves. These special qualities have technical names—such as rhyme, alliteration, image, metaphor, symbol, connotation—terms you will learn more about as you go on.

You are already acquainted with the use of these special qualities of words because they are occasionally made use of in ordinary language to lend interest or color to what is being said. This is a helpful beginning, but it is only a beginning.

Ordinary language is one-dimensional. The purpose of ordinary language is to confine meaning, to pin it down, to make "perfectly clear" things that can be made perfectly clear. However, the most important things about us as human beings are not at all perfectly clear. They are complex, murky, contradictory, uncontainable. To express this stuff that poetry is about, the poet makes use of all the qualities of words in subtle, complex ways. The poet artistically combines the dictionary meanings of words with such devices as rhythm, metaphor, and symbol to capture the stuff of human experiences and human feelings. Therefore, the language of poetry is "thick," multidimensional, suggestive. The meaning created by this language can be compared to the rings of ripples created by a stone thrown into a pond. The ripples move outward in circles in all directions at once and end no one knows where. This kind of language must be studied and learned.

You can begin to learn some simple but all-important basics of the art of poetry-reading from a nursery poem you enjoyed in your childhood.

"Hey diddle, diddle
The cat and the fiddle
The cow jumped over the moon;
The little dog laughed
To see such sport,
And the dish ran away with the spoon."

There are three key points to learn from "Hey Diddle, Diddle" about reading poetry.

WORD SOUNDS

The first key point is that this nursery poem is meant to be read aloud, and this is the way every child naturally learns it. The sounds of the words are an important element in the enjoyment of the poem. There is a happy, energetic, carefree feeling in the sounds of the opening nonsense words, "Hey diddle, diddle." The same feeling is expressed in the lively rhythm of the other lines and in the repetition of sounds in the rhymes of "diddle"–"fiddle" and "moon"–"spoon."

In poetry, the sound qualities of words are used to help express meaning and feeling. Poems should always be read aloud and this is a good time to begin to put that rule into practice. Read "Hey Diddle, Diddle" aloud right now and enjoy its happy sounds. No, wait! Before you read, remember this. Do not read any poem in a singsong rhythm. Do not pause at the end of each line. Read the poem for the meaning of the words, adjusting your pauses and your rhythm to the meaning, not to the sound of the words, the line endings, or the rhymes. The sound effects will come through naturally, by themselves, and enrich the meaning. If you read to emphasize sounds, the meaning will tend to get lost. *Now* read "Hey Diddle, Diddle" aloud.

WORD PICTURES

Besides word sounds, what is in this nursery poem? It consists almost entirely of a series of word pictures. The reader, whether a child or a mature person, sees in the mind's eye pictures of a cat playing a fiddle, of a cow jumping over the moon, of a dog laughing at the whole happening, and of a dish running away with a spoon. All of these pictures are full of fun and energy just as the word sounds of the poem are. The second key point is that word pictures, or images, are an important element of poetry. Good readers of poetry look for these images, see them in their minds' eyes, and react to them.

SUGGESTED MEANING

We like to know just what the meaning is of anything we read. What is the meaning of "Hey Diddle, Diddle"? In the ordinary sense, it doesn't seem to have any direct meaning at all. It consists of a series of very lively, funny images against a background of lively, carefree sounds. The images and the sounds combine to express a *suggested* meaning. There are in the world about us and in the world within us comedy and liveliness. We all have in our blood a sense of this comedy and liveliness and we enjoy it. One of the first things a little baby does is to smile happily and wave its legs and arms energetically. The "meaning" of "Hey Diddle, Diddle" is the recognition and expression of the comedy and liveliness in human experience. Of course, we could just say, "Comedy and liveliness are part of me and I like them." But you will surely agree that "Hey Diddle, Diddle" does a much better job because it *is* the feeling, not just a statement about it.

The third key point is that the meaning of a poem is the capturing—largely through suggestion—of a feeling, a mood, an understanding, an event that is part of the world of human experience. This meaning is often suggested through images and sounds.

Meaning in a poem is also suggested through other qualities of words. As one example, think about the word "fiddle" in this poem. A synonym for "fiddle" is "violin." Why did the anonymous poet use "fiddle" instead of "violin"? Of course, "fiddle" makes a nice rhyme, but that is far from the whole reason. The word "fiddle" is associated in our minds with energetic, comic dancing music. This suggested meaning, or connotation, of the word is exactly right for the poem and its whole suggested meaning. The synonym "violin" has entirely different connotations and would be all wrong for the whole poem. The poet carefully chooses words so that their connotations, as well as their direct meanings, or denotations, contribute to the suggested meaning of the whole poem.

From the nursery poem, you have learned three key points of poetry reading: Word Sounds, Word Pictures, Suggested Meaning. Each of these three characteristics of poetry occurs in the form of a variety of devices that have technical names.

Word Sounds may be shaped through **alliteration, assonance, cacophony, consonance, euphony, meter, onomatopoeia, repetition, rhyme, rhythm.**

Word Pictures can occur in the form of **analogy, imagery, metaphor, metonymy, personification, simile, synecdoche.**

Suggested Meaning can be achieved by **allusion, ambiguity, anticlimax, antithesis, apostrophe, connotation, diction, hyperbole, irony, paradox, understatement.**

The STUDY QUESTIONS for each poem will help you to see how these and other devices are used to help make meaning in each poem. The GLOSSARY OF TERMS IN POETRY (pages 293–313) gives you clear explanations of these and other terms. Refer to the GLOSSARY as you need to and as often as you need to while studying each poem. You may wish to spend a few minutes now looking up some of the terms that have been listed above.

Next, let us look at another familiar rhyme to learn a fourth important point about poetry-reading.

"Bye, baby bunting,
Daddy's gone a-hunting
To get a little rabbit skin,
To wrap the baby bunting in."

This verse was written a long time ago and the original writer of the words is unknown. However, there was a definite person who originally put these words together as we know them now. Let us call that unknown, original writer "Mr. Ecks." Who is speaking the words of the poem, under what circumstances? Is it Mr. Ecks? No, it is definitely not

Mr. Ecks. Again, then, who is it and what are the circumstances?

The speaker is the mother of the little baby, not the poet Mr. Ecks. As soon as we recognize this important fact, look closely at the meaning of the words from that point of view, and ask ourselves what the circumstances are under which the speaker speaks her words, then whole new worlds of meaning open up that we would otherwise miss.

We see that the speaker is the mother of a little baby. She speaks warmly and soothingly to the baby as she lulls it to sleep. She says that Daddy has gone hunting for rabbits so that a warm cover can be made for the baby out of the rabbit skins. The baby is soothed by the sound of the words. However, the baby cannot understand the meaning of the mother's words. The mother is probably speaking them for her own comfort, while anticipating the return of the husband with the rabbits—the skins of which she will make into a covering to protect the baby from the cold and the flesh of which will provide food as well!

If we look closely, more is suggested. This is a long time ago, for nowadays people do not hunt to provide food and clothing. The diction, especially the word "a-hunting," also suggests the language forms of a time gone by. The family must live in the country, probably in a small cold cottage, inadequately warmed by a little fire. Life is probably a hard struggle for basic necessities. Yet the family keeps up the struggle and is sustained by warm love and courage.

All this meaning is suggested in this simple four-line verse. The key to unlocking the meaning is to look closely and carefully at the words of the poem to answer the question, "Who is the speaker and what are the circumstances?" Sometimes, it is true, the words of the poem represent the poet speaking directly to us as a fellow human being. More often, however, the speaker is a fictional person speaking in fictional circumstances. It is essential to grasping the poem that we learn from it all we can about that person and those circumstances.

Try this technique out on another familiar children's rhyme, one written a long time ago by Jane Taylor. Who is the speaker and what are the circumstances in this verse? Answer as fully as you can.

"Twinkle, twinkle, little star.
How I wonder what you are.
Up above the world so high,
Like a diamond in the sky!
Twinkle, twinkle, little star.
How I wonder what you are."

Now go a few steps further. What word sounds help to express the meaning? What word pictures occur? What is the suggested meaning?

You have learned four key points of poetry-reading.

1. Read the poem for word sounds. To do this, read the poem aloud, not once but several times.

2. Read the poem for word pictures. To do this, read the poem several times so that the pictures become clearer and clearer.

3. Read the poem for rich, suggested meaning, realizing that the meaning of a poem is the capturing of a feeling, a mood, an understanding, an event that is part of your own familiar experience as a human being. To do this, read the poem several times.

4. Read the poem closely to answer the question, "Who is the speaker and what are the circumstances?" To get the richest answer to this question, read the poem several times.

To these four key points, we can add a fifth.

5. A poem must be read not once but many times for you to achieve fullest understanding and appreciation of it.

You now have a working knowledge of five important techniques for poetry-reading. You are ready to study the poems in this book, enjoy them for themselves, and become a better and better poetry reader as you go along.

In the book, you will find a number of aids to your reading of the poems. Here is an explanation of the best way to use these aids.

THEMES The poems are arranged in units according to themes, or large ideas, that will be familiar to you and whose importance you will recognize. The seven themes are SPORTS, LIB, THE HUMAN FAMILY, ECOLOGY, VALUES, THE GIFT OUTRIGHT, GOOD TIMES—BAD TIMES. Each theme is introduced by a discussion that will set the poems of the unit in a broad framework and give you some starting points for getting into the poems. Read each of these introductions carefully and react to them with your own thinking. Of course, our human experiences and poems about them don't occur under the headings of themes. Themes are tools of our minds that help us organize and interpret experiences and poems in a particular way.

POEM INTRODUCTIONS Each poem is accompanied by a short introductory discussion to provide you with helpful background information that you may not have, or to direct your attention to a problem or question that will lead into the poem, or to give you some other help in getting started on a successful reading.

DEFINITIONS AND EXPLANATIONS Most poems are accompanied by a set of notes about words and phrases in the poem with which you may need assistance. These notes offer various kinds of important help. Remember that the language of poetry is "thick"; words are used in the richest way, and you must try to have the richest understanding of them. The stone thrown into the pond makes an initial splash and then the rings of ripples move out in ever-widening circles. The words of the poem should have a similar effect as they splash on your understanding. The notes will help you react to the words in this way.

Sometimes the notes will simply give you a definition of a word with which you may not be familiar. The definition will be one that fits the particular shade of meaning intended by the poet. For example, in the first poem, the notes define "undulates" and "distended" as these words are used in the poem.

Sometimes the notes will help you in the important step of visualizing specifically and more fully picture-making words and phrases used in the poem. Examples are the notes given for the first poem on "V's of geese," "mare's-tails," and "fairway."

Sometimes the notes will help you with the fullest comprehension of a specific reference used in the poem. For example, the first poem begins with the following lines:

> "Playing golf on Cape Ann in October,
> I saw something to remember."

You can read the words "Cape Ann" as simply a place name and let it go at that. The poem intends a richer, more specific meaning. As the notes explain, Cape Ann is a narrow New England peninsula jutting into the ocean. The historic, colorful fishing town of Gloucester is on Cape Ann. The sea makes its salty presence felt everywhere on the land and in the air. When the words "Cape Ann" mean all this to you and your senses, and more that you may add, then you will have gotten well started on reading the poem the way a poem should be read.

Before you read each poem, study the notes of the DEFINITIONS AND EXPLANATIONS. Use the line reference to pick out the word or phrase in the poem and look at it in its context. When you get to reading the poem, glance at the notes whenever necessary.

STUDY QUESTIONS After you have read the poem itself several times with the aids that have been mentioned, you will understand the poem at a satisfactory level and you will enjoy it. But that is not enough. You will want to go further to realize the fullest comprehension and know the deepest pleasure of the poem. You will want to explore its meaning in greater depth and to react more fully to its meaning for *you*. You will want to have a fuller appreciation of the art of the poem, of the way its sounds and pictures and other language devices work. The STUDY QUESTIONS will help you to achieve these goals, to make you an expert reader of the poem. In answering the STUDY QUESTIONS, you will sometimes want to make use of the GLOSSARY OF TERMS IN POETRY. When you come across such terms as **metaphor, synecdoche,** and **assonance** printed in bold type in the questions, refer to the GLOSSARY as you need to for explanations. After a while you *won't* need to, and you will have a real, working understanding of the meaning of these terms, not just memorized definitions.

UNIT REVIEWS You know that some of the childhood rhymes, such as those we have discussed, have stayed with you. They have become a permanent part of your life and you will probably pass them along to your children. Certain songs that you heard a long time ago may also have stayed with you and will do so for years. In the same way, you will want some of these poems and some of the things that you have learned from the poems to stay with you, to give you memories and renewed pleasure in years to come. Each section of the book concludes with a UNIT REVIEW. The exercises of the UNIT REVIEW are designed to reinforce and perhaps make permanent the strong memories of some of the poems you will have read.

You are ready to begin your studies in this book. You may well find it one of the most important books you have ever read.

SPORTS

*Among our greatest national events are the World Series of baseball,
the Superbowl of football, the playoffs of basketball, the U.S.
Open of tennis, the Master's Tournament of golf, the Kentucky
Derby of horse racing, and the heavyweight championship of
boxing. We celebrate almost as enthusiastically various competitions
of track and field, swimming, ice skating, and auto racing. Our
national heroes have included Babe Ruth, Babe Didrikson, Willie
Mays, Althea Gibson, Jim Thorpe, Jack Dempsey, Nancy Lopez,
Jack Nicklaus, Willie Shoemaker, Muhammad Ali, and Pelé.
We pay our top professional athletes more than we pay many
doctors, lawyers, scientists, artists, writers, and business leaders,
and even more than our President. We shout ourselves hoarse for
our high school and college athletic stars.*

*Sports are the center of life for the youngster desperately competing
in the local little league and for the grownup glued to the TV
watching the action and catching the pearls of wisdom dropping
from a favorite sports announcer's lips. Sports are recreation,
relaxation, discipline, health, comradeship, warfare, patriotism,
and big business. For better or for worse, sports are a central part
of the American experience.*

*It is the calling of poets to capture experience and the meaning of
experience. Various faces of the experience of sports have commanded
our poets' attention.*

Why are so many people attracted to such outdoor sports as golf, swimming, surfing, skating, cycling, jogging? Of course, they are attracted by the fun and challenge of the sport itself. However, as you undoubtedly know from your own experience, the outdoor setting is an important part of the pleasure. In this poem, a player is inspired to write about an October day on the golf course.

DEFINITIONS AND EXPLANATIONS

Cape Ann (line 1) Cape Ann is a picturesque peninsula on the northern coast of Massachusetts, on which the historic fishing town of Gloucester is located. The sea makes its presence felt everywhere on Cape Ann.

V's of geese (lines 9–10) In the autumn, wild geese migrate from northern Canada to the south. In vast numbers, they fly established routes that carry them over the New England coast. They travel at altitudes as high as 9,000 feet above sea level, in V-shaped formations, the leader at the point. They fly rapidly, and they sound wild honks and cackles as they knife across the sky.

mare's-tails (line 10) Long, narrow formations of clouds, appearing very high in the sky and resembling a horse's flying tail in shape. They belong to the type of cloud called cirrus.

undulates (line 18) Moves in waves; pulsates.

compressed (line 20) Pressed together; compact.

distended (line 20) Stretched out.

starlings (line 22) These black birds travel in flocks consisting of enormous numbers of birds.

legible (line 26) Readable; able to be made out easily.

Lot's wife (line 29) In the Bible, Lot's wife was turned into a pillar of salt as punishment when she defied the command not to turn and look at the wicked cities of Sodom and Gomorrah, which were being destroyed by the angels of God.

fairway (line 33) The long grassy stretch of a golf course between the tee and the green. The golfer tries to keep the ball in play along the fairway.

casual (line 43) Unplanned; unpredictable.

billow (line 43) A great surge or swelling.

negligently (line 47) Carelessly.

STUDY QUESTIONS

1. The golfer describes the colorful autumn setting in striking **imagery**. How does he picture the apples in the trees? How does this **simile** reinforce the setting suggested in lines 1 and 12? Why does the golfer say the elm trees are "transparent" (line 7)? What are the elm trees compared to? Describe the smell and feel of the air suggested to you by these and other images in the poem.

continued

The Great Scarf of Birds

JOHN UPDIKE

Playing golf on Cape Ann in October,
I saw something to remember.

Ripe apples were caught like red fish in the nets
of their branches. The maples
were colored like apples,   5
part orange and red, part green.
The elms, already transparent trees,
seemed swaying vases full of sky. The sky
was dramatic with great straggling V's
of geese streaming south, mare's-tails above them.   10
Their trumpeting made us look up and around.
The course sloped into salt marshes,
and this seemed to cause the abundance of birds.

As if out of the Bible
or science fiction,   15
a cloud appeared, a cloud of dots
like iron filings which a magnet
underneath the paper undulates.
It dartingly darkened in spots,
paled, pulsed, compressed, distended, yet   20
held an identity firm: a flock
of starlings, as much one thing as a rock.
One will moved above the trees
the liquid and hesitant drift.

Come nearer, it became less marvellous,   25
more legible, and merely huge.
"I never saw so many birds!" my friend exclaimed.
We returned our eyes to the game.
Later, as Lot's wife must have done,
in a pause of walking, not thinking   30

continued

The Great Scarf of Birds

2. When the golfer first sees the flock of birds, he says they appeared "As if out of the Bible/or science fiction." What effect of the flock on the golfer is suggested by these two **allusions?** What other Biblical allusion appears in the poem? Why do you think the Bible suggests itself to the golfer's mind as he walks the course?

3.   "It dartingly darkened in spots,
        paled, pulsed, compressed,
                distended, yet
     held an identity firm . . ."
        (lines 19–21)

The words "paled" and "distended" get at the same meaning in two different ways. Explain. Read the lines aloud. How do the **sound effects** reinforce the description of the flock? Give two examples of **alliteration** that are part of the sound effects of these lines.

4. Explain the comparison of iron filings in the **simile** in lines 16–17. Explain the phrase "One will" (line 23).

5. When the flock comes closer, the golfer says it becomes "more legible, and merely huge" (line 26). What exactly is meant? How does the **connotation,** or suggested meaning, of these words contrast with the connotation of the words the golfer uses when he first sees the flock?

6. The flock is compared to a scarf (lines 40–48). Read the lines in which this **simile** occurs. Of what sort of material must the scarf be made? What quality of the movement of the flock is emphasized by the **image?**

7. What was the effect on the golfer of seeing the flock lift and ascend? Can you explain this feeling? In your opinion, is this a common or uncommon kind of experience?

8. Briefly discuss another sport in which the natural setting may be an important attraction to the participant.

of calling down a consequence,
I lazily looked around.

The rise of the fairway above us was tinted,
so evenly tinted I might not have noticed
but that at the rim of the delicate shadow   35
the starlings were thicker and outlined the flock
as an inkstain in drying pronounces its edges.
The gradual rise of green was vastly covered;
I had thought nothing in nature could be so broad
    but grass.

And as   40
I watched, one bird,
prompted by accident or will to lead,
ceased resting; and, lifting in a casual billow,
the flock ascended as a lady's scarf,
transparent, of gray, might be twitched   45
by one corner, drawn upward and then,
decided against, negligently tossed toward a chair:
the southward cloud withdrew into the air.

Long had it been since my heart
had been lifted as it was by the lifting of that scarf.   50

Professional sports have attracted the greatest of athletes. But, even among the pros, there are standouts—stars, superstars, and, finally, a select group whose unique careers and personalities have made them legendary figures. Leroy "Satchelfoot" Paige is a legend of baseball. "Satch" is thought by some observers to be the greatest baseball pitcher of his time. But the amazing thing is that he began his major league career at an age when most athletes have long retired from the playing field.

Paige, a black athlete, was at the peak of his powers when the major leagues were open to whites only. So, for twenty years, he performed brilliant and dazzling feats on the mound in the organized Negro leagues. Of course, he received little of the media coverage that his achievements might have earned had he been in the big leagues. Yet, somehow, by word of mouth, his reputation grew until he became a living legend. Finally, major league baseball was integrated, and Satch became a big league pitcher. How would this elderly man do in the big time? Well, he not only showed how great he was, but he went on and on, until the fans began to wonder how old that man on the mound really was—fifty? sixty? seventy? Eventually, he was given the place he had earned among the immortals in the Baseball Hall of Fame. Samuel Allen captures the spirit of the career of Satchelfoot Paige in his short poem.

STUDY QUESTIONS

1. In this tribute to Satch, the poet makes Satch himself the speaker instead of a number of other possible choices. Why do you think the poet makes this choice?

2. What single aspect of Satch's career receives the greatest emphasis?

3. What qualities of Satch's personality and character are brought out? (Bear in mind the frustrations he knew.)

4. In what ways are the **diction** and the **rhythms** of the poem true to the speaker?

5. In what "league" is Satch going to do his final pitching?

6. Why is a legendary sports hero like Satch an inspiration to most people?

7. Do you know of any other athletes who have continued activity in a sport into their later years? What special appeal do such athletes have for you?

To Satch

SAMUEL ALLEN

Sometimes I feel like I will *never* stop
Just go on forever
Till one fine mornin
I'm gonna reach up and grab me a handfulla stars
Throw out my long lean leg   5
And whip three hot strikes burnin down the heavens
And look over at God and say
How about that!

odern technology and new equipment have given us some relatively new sports, of which scuba diving and snorkeling are among the most popular. How do you account for the appeal of these underwater sports? Particularly, what is the unique attraction of the setting of these sports as compared with other outdoor sports? What contrasts can you make between the feelings created by the setting in which a golfer plays and the setting around the scuba diver? The haunting and powerful poem "Underwater" will give you some answers to these questions and will bring you very close to the scuba diving experience, even if you have never been there yourself.

DEFINITIONS AND EXPLANATIONS

cathedral (line 1)   The great Gothic cathedrals of Europe are among the most notable of all human structures. Their majestic, soaring interiors were designed to express the deep religious spirit of the Middle Ages. Great blocks of stone were used to create reaches of horizontal and vertical spaces that spread outward and upward in splendid archways. Stained glass windows filled the reaches of space with special and appropriate qualities of light and color.

perspective (line 5)   A particular point of view from which a scene is observed.

translucency (line 8)   The quality of letting just enough light through so that objects are seen as shadowy and dim.

vermilion (line 12)   Bright, yellowish red.

paunches (line 14)   Protruding bellies.

timorous (line 17)   Timid; afraid.

tenement (line 19)   A building with many apartments, usually overcrowded and run-down.

conflagration (line 26)   A big, destructive fire.

sanctuary (line 31)   Any place of refuge or protection; a holy place. (At one time, fugitives were immune from arrest or punishment in a church or other sacred place and were said to have "sanctuary" when so protected.)

bland (line 34)   Soft; mild.

STUDY QUESTIONS

1. Who is the speaker in this poem? Who is the "you" (line 24)?

2. The underwater setting is compared in a **metaphor** to a cathedral (lines 1–2). In what ways is this an appropriate comparison? (Think of qualities of space, light, sound, and movement.)

3. How does the scuba diver extend the cathedral **metaphor** with respect to prayers, heaven, the worshippers, sanctuary? What do the words "ceiling" and "air" (line 7) actually refer to?

4. In the "cathedral sea," the divers commit a sin or desecration. Describe in your

continued

Underwater
MICHAEL SCHMIDT

Underwater, this is the cathedral
sea. Diving, our bubbles rise
as prayers are said to do, and burst
into our natural atmosphere—
occupying, from this perspective,   5
the position of a heaven.

The ceiling is silver, and the air
deep green translucency. The worshippers
pray quietly, wave their fins.
You can see the color of their prayer   10
deep within their throats: scarlet, some,
and some fine-scaled vermilion; others

pass tight-lipped with moustaches
trailing and long paunches, though
they are almost wafer-thin seen sideways,   15
or unseen except for whiskers.
Further down, timorous sea-spiders
slam their doors, shy fish disappear

into their tenement of holes, and eels
warn that they have serpent tails.   20
Deep is wild, with beasts one meets
usually in dreams. Here the giant octopus
drags in its arms. We meet it.
We are hungry in the upper air, and you

have the sea-spear that shoots deep;   25
you fire accurately, raising a conflagration
of black ink. The animal grabs stone
in slow motion, pulls far under a ledge

continued

Underwater

own words what they do and what happens. Why do they commit this act and what is the result? What is the special emotional impact of the crime of murder in a cathedral?

5. At what line does there occur a sudden change in the mood of the poem from a feeling of mystical peace and order to a feeling of chaotic danger, violence, and guilt? In your judgment, why did the poet include these two clashing, contradictory feelings in the poem?

6. T. S. Eliot wrote a play called *Murder in the Cathedral.* In your opinion, how suitable would that title be for this poem? Would you prefer it to "Underwater"? Why or why not?

7. Using as a basis any personal experience with snorkeling and scuba diving or films you have seen, comment on the accuracy of descriptions and feelings expressed in the poem. What would you add from your own experience or knowledge?

and piles the loose rock there as if
to hide might be enough. It holds tight,   30

builds sanctuary, and I think cries
"sanctuary!"—it dies at your second shot.
We come aboveboard then, with our eight-armed
dinner and no hunger left, pursued by the bland
eyes of fish who couldn't care, by black   35
water and the death we made there.

Football, basketball, and baseball are our popular team-spectator sports. From little leagues to the pros, these sports are big-time, complex, highly organized, expensive. The wild enthusiasm and fanaticism of millions of spectators; the pressures of owners, alumni, managers, and coaches; the outpourings of sportswriters and commentators swirl like gales around the athletes. Questions have been raised about the effect of all this on the athlete as a person. For some it may be a rich and rewarding life. For others it may be punishing and destructive. Think specifically about high school athletic stars who for one reason or another go no further with their education or their sport. What happens to the youth who, after four years of experiencing hero-worship, honor, and glory, suddenly finds it all gone? "Ex-Basketball Player" tells about such a case.

DEFINITIONS AND EXPLANATIONS

Flick (line 6)   The word "flick" means a light, quick movement.

coiled (line 26)   Tensed as though ready to leap or spring.

tiers (line 29)   Rows of seats.

Necco Wafers, Nibs, and Juju Beads (line 30)   These are the brand names of small candies that come in a mixture of bright colors.

STUDY QUESTIONS

1. Describe Flick Webb's achievements and status as a high school basketball player. Why was he given the nickname Flick?

2. What is meant by the **personification** "The ball loved Flick" (line 16) and the **simile** "His hands were like wild birds" (line 18)?

3. What are Flick's job and status now?

4. Note the description of Pearl Avenue, the street on which Flick works. How is Pearl Avenue a **symbol** of Flick's life?

5. Read the description of the gasoline pumps in the second **stanza**. With what in Flick's past life are "the idiot pumps/Five on a side" connected? How do the pumps ironically contrast Flick's old life and his present one?

6. Perhaps the strongest and most important part of this poem is what it suggests or tells indirectly about Flick's inner life, his feelings about himself now. What does each of the following lines suggest to you about Flick: lines 19–21 (Is it really a gag, or only a pretended gag expressing an inner despair?); lines 23–24 (What unhappy contrast must Flick be feeling?); lines 25–26 (Why is he "coiled"?); lines 28–30 (Consider Flick's behavior and the phrase "bright applauding tiers." What is going on in his mind? What terrible **irony** is there in the last line?) Now, summarize Flick's mental state and comment on it.

7. Do you think Flick might have been better off if he hadn't been a star athlete? Which line in the poem suggests an answer to this question?

Ex-Basketball Player

JOHN UPDIKE

Pearl Avenue runs past the high-school lot,
Bends with the trolley tracks, and stops, cut off
Before it has a chance to go two blocks,
At Colonel McComsky Plaza. Berth's Garage
Is on the corner facing west, and there,   5
Most days, you'll find Flick Webb, who helps Berth out.

Flick stands tall among the idiot pumps—
Five on a side, the old bubble-head style,
Their rubber elbows hanging loose and low.
One's nostrils are two S's, and his eyes   10
An E and O. And one is squat, without
A head at all—more of a football type.

Once Flick played for the high-school team, the Wizards.
He was good: in fact, the best. In '46
He bucketed three hundred ninety points,   15
A county record still. The ball loved Flick.
I saw him rack up thirty-eight or forty
In one home game. His hands were like wild birds.

He never learned a trade, he just sells gas,
Checks oil, and changes flats. Once in a while,   20
As a gag, he dribbles an inner tube,
But most of us remember anyway.
His hands are fine and nervous on the lug wrench.
It makes no difference to the lug wrench, though.

Off work, he hangs around Mae's Luncheonette.   25
Grease-gray and kind of coiled, he plays pinball,
Sips lemon cokes, and smokes those thin cigars;
Flick seldom speaks to Mae, just sits and nods
Beyond her face toward bright applauding tiers
Of Necco Wafers, Nibs, and Juju Beads.   30

E very adult knows that sports can add to the zest and fun of life. Quite naturally, adults, whether parents or not, want to introduce children to the enjoyment of sports as soon as possible with swimming lessons, tennis lessons, little league activities, and so on. Do adults sometimes begin too early or press too hard, thus doing more harm than good? "The Swimming Lesson" has something to say about this question.

DEFINITIONS AND EXPLANATIONS

medieval (line 5) Belonging to the Middle Ages. The word sometimes has the meaning of lacking knowledge, understanding, or enlightenment.

maxim (line 5) A rule or principle of conduct.

frenzied (line 9) Excited and fearful; frantic.

STUDY QUESTIONS

1. Who might the "somebody" (line 4) have been?

2. The alliterative phrase "medieval maxim" (line 5) is used to describe one method some people believe in to teach a little child to swim. What is the method? In her use of the phrase "medieval maxim," what does the speaker tell us she thinks of this method? What do you think of the method?

3. In the first three lines, an adult remembers an early childhood experience. Is the memory clear and vivid or dim and vague? Justify your answer from the words of the poem. What, then, is suggested to you about the effect that the original experience had on the young child? In the context of these lines, what is meant by the phrase "Reaching around my life"?

4. As a result of the shock of being thrown into the water, what view of life did the child grow up with? Explain as fully as you can how this view resulted from the experience. In your explanation, take into account the child's feelings toward the adult "somebody" as well as the experience itself. On the basis of your explanation, is it more likely that the "somebody" was a parent or other adult that the child loved and depended on, or that the "somebody" was not particularly close?

5. In all probability, what were the feelings and intentions of the adult in tossing the child into the water? How did the child herself view the act? From this contrast, what wisdom do you learn about the relationship between adults—parents, older brothers and sisters, teachers—and the children they care for?

6. What examples can you give of other experiences children may have in their relationship with adults that may involve the same or similar problems?

The Swimming Lesson

MARY OLIVER

Feeling the icy kick, the endless waves
Reaching around my life, I moved my arms
And coughed, and in the end saw land.

Somebody, I suppose,
Remembering the medieval maxim,   5
Had tossed me in,
Had wanted me to learn to swim,

Not knowing that none of us, who ever came back
From that long lonely fall and frenzied rising,
Ever learned anything at all   10
About swimming, but only
How to put off, one by one,
Dreams and pity, love and grace—
How to survive in any place.

Hunting was once a necessity for life, later the sport of the nobility. Today, hunting is a controversial sport, enjoyed by many, but opposed by environmentalists, conservationists, and humane groups. "Bert Kessler," a poem about the fate of one hunter, seems to express the poet's own feelings about hunting, and, at the same time, raises some interesting psychological questions.

DEFINITIONS AND EXPLANATIONS

Bert Kessler (title) This poem comes from a collection of short, interrelated poems called the *Spoon River Anthology*. Each poem deals with a particular person who lived in a typical small Midwestern town called Spoon River, located in western Illinois. In each poem, the person named in the title tells his or her own story. However, the story is told from an unusual perspective, for each person is dead and is speaking from the grave. All the poems together give the reader a realistic cross section of the people of heartland America.

Spoon River Anthology is one of the great achievements of American literature.

I winged my bird (line 1) I wounded the bird in the wing while he was in flight.

soared (line 3) Rose high in the air.

down (line 6) Soft, fine feathers.

plummet (line 7) A lead weight.

quail (line 10) A game bird.

brier (line 11) A plant full of sharp thorns.

STUDY QUESTIONS

1. In the first six lines, the hunter describes his shooting of the bird. The description makes the event seem glorious and beautiful. For example, the hunter says "I winged my bird" instead of "I shot the bird." What other words or phrases in lines 1–6 suggest glory and beauty, as seen from the hunter's point of view?

2. In line 7, as the hunter comes close to direct contact with the death of the bird, the mood begins to change. What words or phrases in lines 7–10 build up a **connotation** of the unpleasantness of death close at hand, as contrasted with the earlier feelings of glory and beauty in the shooting of the distant bird?

3. "I reached my hand, but saw no brier" (line 11). What has the hunter felt to make him say that he saw no brier? What did the hunter realize then?

4. There is a reversal of roles in the poem.

The hunter-slayer becomes the hunted-slain. When he shot the bird, Bert Kessler saw glory and beauty. How does Kessler now see the hunter—the rattlesnake—that has bitten him? What are some of the words and phrases that express his feelings? Notice the unusual **diction** in line 15: "The head of him" and "the rings of him" (instead of "his head" and "his rings"). What is the effect of this unnatural diction?

5. In reading the poem aloud, how would you say the last word, "grass," for fullest dramatic effect?

6. Think about death as it is presented in this poem. Is there any truth in the notion that some people may take a certain relish in death when it is distant, but feel differently when it is close to home? Do you see any connection here with violence in spectator sports, in the movies, on television? What conclusions do you draw?

Bert Kessler

EDGAR LEE MASTERS

I winged my bird,
Though he flew toward the setting sun;
But just as the shot rang out, he soared
Up and up through the splinters of golden light,
Till he turned right over, feathers ruffled,   5
With some of the down of him floating near,
And fell like a plummet into the grass.
I tramped about, parting the tangles,
Till I saw a splash of blood on a stump,
And the quail lying close to the rotten roots.   10
I reached my hand, but saw no brier,
But something pricked and stung and numbed it.
And then, in a second, I spied the rattler—
The shutters wide in his yellow eyes,
The head of him arched, sunk back in the rings of him,   15
A circle of filth, the color of ashes,
Or oak leaves bleached under layers of leaves.
I stood like a stone as he shrank and uncoiled
And started to crawl beneath the stump,
When I fell limp in the grass.   20

Have you ever gone ice skating on a pond or lake on a clear, crisp winter night? What sights stand out in your mind? What sounds? What sensations? What do you remember as the dominant mood of the experience? Is night skating an ideal romantic setting for two sweethearts? This is a story poem about two night skaters, a poem that will haunt your memory for a long time.

DEFINITIONS AND EXPLANATIONS

ebony (line 2)   A hard, black wood.

scrolled (line 2)   Etched or carved with curved designs.

sentineled (line 4)   Standing like guards.

firs (line 4)   Tall, straight evergreen trees.

reel (line 25)   A dance characterized by circular and gliding movements.

skurr (line 26)   This is an **onomatopoeic** word imitating the sound of skate blades on ice.

lacquered (line 29)   Having a highly polished, smooth surface.

bound (line 35)   Edge; boundary.

veers (line 43)   Changes direction.

STUDY QUESTIONS

1. As the reader of the poem, you are an invisible witness to the events at Ghost Lake, where no one usually comes "late after dark." What is the first indication you have of the presence of a human being? Describe Jeremy's appearance and movements as you first see him. Describe Cecily's movements on her way to Ghost Lake. Why does Cecily kneel "in snow by the still lake side" (line 19)? In what sense are her feet "winged" (line 20)?

2. Was this meeting accidental or prearranged? What do Cecily and Jeremy say when they first meet? What do they do? What do they seem to be expressing in their actions? What is the first warning of danger and who is first aware of the danger? What is the sound that pursues Jeremy and Cecily as they race away? What happens to the lovers?

3. Two lovers meet late at night to skate on a dark, lonely, and dangerous lake. From the beginning, suspense and danger are in the air and seem to lead inevitably to the sudden tragedy. You have to use your imagination to complete this story, of which you know only this one incident. Who are Jeremy and Cecily? Why do you think they meet at such a time and place? Why does danger seem to surround them?

4. Mystery, suspense, and danger are suggested by the name of the lake itself—Ghost Lake. The tall fir trees around the lake are described in line 4 as standing like sentinels, as though alert and on guard. Mention a number of other words and phrases whose **connotation** is of mystery, suspense, and danger.

5. **Sound effects** play an important part in the action and mood of this story poem. What movement of the characters do the **rhythm** of the lines and the **rhyme scheme** musically reinforce? What are the sounds that break the silence of the lake at night? The sounds of the letters *s* and *z* predominate in the words of this poem. Why? Give several examples of **alliteration** and **onomatopoeia** that contribute to the total impact of the poem.

The Skater of Ghost Lake

WILLIAM ROSE BENÉT

Ghost Lake's a dark lake, a deep lake and cold:
Ice black as ebony, frostily scrolled;
Far in its shadows a faint sound whirrs;
Steep stand the sentineled deep, dark firs.

A brisk sound, a swift sound, a ring-tinkle-ring;   5
Flit-flit,—a shadow, with a stoop and a swing,
Flies from a shadow through the crackling cold.
Ghost Lake's a deep lake, a dark lake and old!

Leaning and leaning, with a stride and a stride,
Hands locked behind him, scarf blowing wide,   10
Jeremy Randall skates, skates late,
Star for a candle, moon for a mate.

Black is the clear glass now that he glides,
Crisp is the whisper of long lean strides,
Swift is his swaying,—but pricked ears hark.   15
None comes to Ghost Lake late after dark!

Cecily only,—yes, it is she!
Stealing to Ghost Lake, tree after tree,
Kneeling in snow by the still lake side,
Rising with feet winged, gleaming, to glide.   20

Dust of the ice swirls. Here is his hand.
Brilliant his eyes burn. Now, as was planned,
Arm across arm twined, laced to his side,
Out on the dark lake lightly they glide.

Dance of the dim moon, a rhythmical reel,   25
A swaying, a swift tune,—skurr of the steel;

continued

Moon for a candle, maid for a mate,
Jeremy Randall skates, skates late.

Black as if lacquered the wide lake lies;
Breath is a frost-fume, eyes seek eyes;   30
Souls are a sword-edge tasting the cold.
Ghost Lake's a deep lake, a dark lake and old!

Far in the shadows hear faintly begin
Like a string pluck-plucked of a violin,
Muffled in mist on the lake's far bound,   35
Swifter and swifter, a low singing sound!

Far in the shadows and faint on the verge
Of blue cloudy moonlight, see it emerge,
Flit-flit,—a phantom, with a stoop and a swing . . .
Ah, it's a night bird, burdened of wing!   40

Pressed close to Jeremy, laced to his side,
Cecily Culver, dizzy you glide.
Jeremy Randall sweepingly veers
Out on the dark ice far from the piers.

"Jeremy!" "Sweetheart?" "What do you fear?"   45
"Nothing, my darling,—nothing is here!"
"Jeremy?" "Sweetheart?" "What do you flee?"
"Something—I know not; something I see!"

Swayed to a swift stride, brisker of pace,
Leaning and leaning, they race and they race;   50
Ever that whirring, that crisp sound thin
Like a string pluck-plucked of a violin;

Ever that swifter and low singing sound
Sweeping behind them, winding them round;
Gasp of their breath now that chill flakes fret;   55
Ice black as ebony,—blacker—like jet!

Ice shooting fangs forth—sudden—like spears;
Crackling of lightning,—a roar in their ears!
Shadowy, a phantom swerves off from its prey . . .
No, it's a night bird flit-flits away!   60

Low-winging moth-owl, home to your sleep!
Ghost Lake's a still lake, a cold lake and deep.
Faint in its shadows a far sound whirrs.
Black stand the ranks of its sentinel firs.

You have probably heard the expression "poetry in motion." It might be used to describe the flight of a gull, the movements of an athlete, the performance of a dancer. The phrase "poetry in motion" expresses the deeply felt thrill aroused by the beauty of perfect grace, coordination, and timing. "The Double Play" is inspired by poetry in motion on the baseball diamond.

DEFINITIONS AND EXPLANATIONS

banks of arc lights (line 6) Clusters of powerful artificial lights used in night games to light the field.

invisible shadows (lines 9–10) The artificial lights are positioned so that shadows are cancelled out.

poised (line 12) Balanced in position.

pirouettes (line 13) Spins around gracefully; pivots.

casual (line 23) Cool; nonchalant.

STUDY QUESTIONS

1. Who is the speaker of the poem and where is the speaker located?

2. In your own words, describe the sequence of actions of all the players mentioned in the poem as being involved in the double play.

3. How do you know that there was one out before the double play?

4. Notice the phrase "In his sea-lit/distance" (lines 1–2). What is the "distance" referred to here? Can you explain the **metaphor** "sea-lit"? (In what ways may the appearance of the lit-up baseball diamond to the spectator be similar to the appearance of the sea to an underwater diver carrying a powerful lamp?)

5. Notice the **simile** in line 6 in which the ball is said to bound like a vanishing string. How is the moving ball like a vanishing string?

6. To reflect the speed and uninterrupted flow of movement in the double play, the poet uses an unusual language construction. Study these words in the poem: "ball," "shortstop," "second baseman," "first baseman." How are these words used to suggest the unbroken flow of action? How do the line endings reflect the flowing action of the double play? Notice the particularly odd break between lines 16 and 17. What is the effect of this break?

7. The shortstop catches and throws the ball. But, to describe these actions, the poet says "redirects its flight." Why do you think the poet made this choice of words?

8. The double play is likened to a dance in line 17, and this **metaphor** has been suggested earlier in such verbs as "whirling" (line 9) and "poised" (line 12). Give two other verbs that suggest the dance terminology. What kind of dance seems to be suggested.

9. How does most of the team leave the field? How does the pitcher leave? How would you explain the difference?

10. What is "the poem" that "has happened" (line 24)?

11. Choose a sport that you like and know well. What action or play would you like to see described in a poem like this one? (Perhaps you would like to try writing the poem.)

The Double Play

ROBERT WALLACE

In his sea-lit
distance, the pitcher winding
like a clock about to chime comes down with

the ball, hit
sharply, under the artificial   5
banks of arc lights, bounds like a vanishing string

over the green
to the shortstop magically
scoops to his right whirling above his invisible

shadows   10
in the dust redirects
its flight to the running poised second baseman

pirouettes
leaping, above the slide, to throw
from mid-air, across the colored tightened interval,   15

to the leaning-
out first baseman ends the dance
drawing it disappearing into his long brown glove

stretches. What
is too swift for deception   20
is final, lost, among the loosened figures

jogging off the field
(the pitcher walks), casual
in the space where the poem has happened.

Jogging has become very popular today, almost a fad. However, running is the oldest and most natural of all sports. When the Olympic Games first started in ancient Greece, the contests consisted almost entirely of footraces of various distances. Though much has been added to the modern Olympic Games, the track events are still the core of this greatest of all athletic competitions. "To James" is a dramatic poem about a footrace . . . and something more.

DEFINITIONS AND EXPLANATIONS

spikes (line 6)   In outdoor racing, the runners' shoes may be equipped with spikes that can dig into the ground without any slipping and give the athletes the fullest return on their efforts.

cinders (line 7)   The outdoor track is sometimes surfaced with cinders to give the runner a dry, firm foothold.

stretch (line 8)   On a curved track, the stretch is the straight length leading to the finish line. In all cases, the stretch is the final part of the race when runners put forth all the strength and effort left in them.

catapulted (line 9)   Hurled forward with great force.

tape (line 10)   The string stretched across the track at the finish line. The victor breaks the tape with his chest as he crosses the finish line.

lurched (line 13)   Suddenly shot forward.

starting holes (line 14)   At the starting point, the runners are in a tense, crouched position, ready to spring forward at the firing of the starting gun. They lean forward on their fingertips. Their legs are behind them with toes braced into holes for the fastest possible kick from the starting line. Nowadays, special blocks are often used instead of starting holes.

sinews (line 16)   The tough fibers that connect muscle to bone.

STUDY QUESTIONS

1. Who is James? What is the relationship of the speaker to James? What else do lines 12–14, lines 20–22, and lines 29–31 suggest about the speaker?

2. Consider the **line** lengths and the **rhythms** of this poem as well as what the words tell you. Is this a sprint, a middle-distance race, or a long-distance race?

3. The poem is about two races—a real race and a metaphorical one. At what line does the speaker begin to talk about the metaphorical race? In the **metaphor,** what do you think is really meant by each of the following?

"It's a short dash" (line 32)

"Dig your starting holes
Deep and firm" (lines 33–34)

"Think only of the goal" (line 41)

"To victory" (line 51)

continued

To James

FRANK HORNE

Do you remember
How you won
That last race . . . ?
How you flung your body
At the start . . .   5
How your spikes
Ripped the cinders
In the stretch . . .
How you catapulted
Through the tape . . .   10
Do you remember . . . ?
Don't you think
I lurched with you
Out of those starting holes . . . ?
Don't you think   15
My sinews tightened
At those first
Few strides . . .
And when you flew into the stretch
Was not all my thrill   20
Of a thousand races
In your blood . . . ?
At your final drive
Through the finish line
Did not my shout   25
Tell of the
Triumphant ecstasy
Of victory . . . ?
Live
As I have taught you   30
To run, Boy—
It's a short dash

continued

To James

4. Can you think of any reasons why the speaker may have wanted to say the words of this poem to James?

5. Frank Horne is a black poet. Does knowing that fact affect your answer to the previous question in any way?

6. Suppose you wanted to read this poem to an audience as dramatically and effectively as you could. Would you say the words loudly or softly? slowly or rapidly? What one or two emotions would you try to express in your reading?

Dig your starting holes
Deep and firm
Lurch out of them   35
Into the straightaway
With all the power
That is in you
Look straight ahead
To the finish line   40
Think only of the goal
Run straight
Run high
Run hard
Save nothing   45
And finish
With an ecstatic burst
That carries you
Hurtling
Through the tape   50
To victory . . .

re you a football fan? How many outstanding quarterbacks or
running backs can you name? On the other hand, how many offensive linemen, particularly centers, can you name? The sad, sad fact
is that all the fame and glory go to the passers and the runners. The
center, who takes all the fierce crunch of the pileup as the two teams
clash at the line, is unnoticed and unknown, literally and figuratively
buried in the heap. Ogden Nash, our best-known humorous poet, has
a little fun with this fact.

EXPLANATION

Dick Szymanski (title) Szymanski was
one of the outstanding centers in pro football a few years back.

STUDY QUESTIONS

1. Explain the humor of lines 5–6.

2. Why can Szymanski "only wonder" (line 7)?

3. Explain the **anticlimax** in lines 9–10.

4. How does Nash use questions to add to the humor of the poem?

5. Nash is especially known for his clever, funny, often highly inventive **rhymes.** Give one example. Why is it funny?

Dick Szymanski

OGDEN NASH

The life of an offensive center
Is one that few could wish to enter.
You'll note that that of Dick Szymanski
Is not all roses and romanski.
He centers the ball, he hears a roar —   5
Is it a fumble, or a score?
What's happening he can only wonder.
Because he's upside down, down under.
He accomplishes amazing feats.
And what gets photographed? His cleats.   10

All sports participants have a dream of reaching ever greater heights—of hitting the most home runs ever, of running the fastest mile ever, of catching the biggest fish ever. Sometimes these dreams carry the dreamer away and lead to exaggeration of the facts. Fishermen are particularly noted for this tendency when telling of the size of the fish they caught and of the even bigger ones that got away. Here is a humorous look, from the other side of the fishing line, at an exaggerator in action.

EXPLANATION

imitation flies (line 6)   A kind of artificial bait used by the person fishing for trout. Such things as feathers and colored silk are tied together in the hope that they will resemble an insect that looks delicious to a fish.

STUDY QUESTIONS

1. In this poem, the speaker expresses a wish to hear a fish tell its side of the story. What does the talking fish tell the other fish? What is the reaction of the listeners?

2. Why is the reference to the size of the fishermen humorous?

3. Why do you suppose it is the "heartfelt" wish of the speaker to hear this kind of fish tale?

4. This short poem is written in iambic **meter** and a simple **couplet rhyme scheme.** Do you feel this marked rhythm and rhyme help the humorous tone or not? Why?

5. In how many different ways is this poem a "fish story"?

Fish Story

RICHARD ARMOUR

Count this among my heartfelt wishes:
To hear a fish tale told by fishes
And stand among the fish who doubt
The honor of a fellow trout,
And watch the bulging of their eyes   5
To hear of imitation flies
And worms with rather droopy looks
Stuck through with hateful, horrid hooks,
And fishermen they fled all day from
(As big as this) and got away from.   10

The gods and goddesses of the ancient Greeks were a strange lot. They had certain supernatural powers, but in many ways they were as helpless and uncertain as humans. Though immortal, they got frustrated, felt dissatisfied, and had problems as people do. The main character in this poem is a god very much like those Greek gods. The poem tells a story about how baseball began, like the myths that were told about those ancient gods and the beginnings of things.

EXPLANATIONS

General Sherman (line 15) William T. Sherman was a great Union general in the Civil War. He is both famous and notorious for his march through Georgia and his burning of Atlanta.

Elizabeth B. Browning (lines 15–16) A great English poet, known especially for the love sonnets she wrote to her poet-husband, Robert Browning.

STUDY QUESTIONS

1. Who is the "Someone" in line 1? How does he feel about the earth?

2. Who are the "girls" (line 8)? What object do they ask the purpose of? What answer (that does not appear in the poem but is strongly suggested by the context) is given them? What teasing question do the girls then ask? Why is their teasing appropriate?

3. What embarrassingly ungodlike accident happens to the main character? What is his ungodlike reaction? How do the specific mention and pairing of General Sherman and Elizabeth B. Browning add to the effect of this incident?

4. What does the main character finally see that brings his feelings of dissatisfaction and frustration to a peak? What human thing does he want to do? What does he do specifically?

5. Notice the **simile** in lines 13–14. How is this madhouse **image** suggested in the language of the first three lines of the poem? What other specific images and incidents add to the total madhouse image?

6. What does the poem seem to suggest about the role or purpose of baseball in a world that is often frustrating, illogical, and cruel?

The Origin of Baseball

KENNETH PATCHEN

Someone had been walking in and out
Of the world without coming
To much decision about anything.
The sun seemed too hot most of the time.
There weren't enough birds around   5
And the hills had a silly look
When he got on top of one.
The girls in heaven, however, thought
Nothing of asking to see his watch
Like you would want someone to tell   10
A joke—"Time," they'd say, "what's
That mean—time?", laughing with the edges
Of their white mouths, like a flutter of paper
In a madhouse. And he'd stumble over
General Sherman or Elizabeth B.   15
Browning, muttering, "Can't you keep
Your big wings out of the aisle?" But down
Again, there'd be millions of people without
Enough to eat and men with guns just
Standing there shooting each other.   20

So he wanted to throw something
And he picked up a baseball.

Horse racing has been called "the sport of kings and the king of sports." For some the attraction is merely the thrill of gambling, for others the social occasion, for still others the glamour of the race-track setting. For the true lover of the sport, however, the central lure is the spectacle of the animal itself, the pure power and grace of the magnificent thoroughbred in action. This poem, whose setting is the race track during work-out time in the early morning, savors the beauty of the racing thoroughbred.

DEFINITIONS AND EXPLANATIONS

contemplative (line 8) Quietly thoughtful; pensive.

radiance (line 8) Glowing or shining light.

toteboard (line 9) The board that displays in lights the betting status of the horses.

brine (line 12) Salt water; the ocean.

withers (line 20) The highest part of the back of a horse, located between the shoulder biades.

canter (line 22) Move at a slow, easy gallop.

voluptuous (line 22) Giving pleasure to the senses.

Centaur (line 28) In Greek mythology, a creature with a man's head, chest, and arms and a horse's body and legs.

wuthering (line 29) Galloping with the head and neck turned slightly sideways.

unsyllabled (line 31) Unbroken; flowing smoothly.

eloquence (line 31) Verbal expression that is forceful, fluent, and graceful.

girths (line 36) The bands around the bellies of the horses which hold the saddles in place.

haunches (line 36) Hindquarters of the horse.

paradigm (line 38) An example; a perfect model.

azuring (line 41) Turning blue.

STUDY QUESTIONS

1. The opening twelve lines set the scene in sharp, sense-appealing **images**. Give some of the highlights. What is the effect of "For no one" (line 6)?

2. Describe the first appearance of the horses. What activities follow? What relationship between horse and rider is suggested in lines 18–20 and line 28?

continued

Morning Work-out

BABETTE DEUTSCH

The sky unfolding its blanket to free
The morning.
Chill on the air. Clean odor of stables.
The grandstand green as the turf,
The pavilion flaunting its brillance   5
For no one.
Beyond hurdles and hedges, swans, circling, cast
A contemplative radiance over the willow's shadows.
Day pales the toteboard lights,
Gilds the balls, heightens the stripes of the poles.   10
Dirt shines. White glisten of rails.
The track is bright as brine.
Their motion a flowing.
From prick of the ear to thick tail's shimmering drift,
The horses file forth.   15
Pink nostrils quiver, as who know they are showing their colors.
Ankles lift, as who hear without listening.
The bay, the brown, the chestnut, the roan have loaned
Their grace to the riders who rise in the stirrups, or hunch
Over the withers, gentling with mumbled song.   20
A mare ambles past, liquid eye askance.
Three, then four, canter by: voluptuous power
Pours through their muscles,
Dancing in pulse and nerve.
They glide in the stretch as on skis.   25
Two
Are put to a drive:
Centaur energy bounding as the dirt shudders, flies
Under the wuthering pace,
Hushes the hooves' thunders,   30

continued

Morning Work-out

3. Describe the climactic activity of two of the horses on the track. Note line 31. Horses, of course, do not actually speak. Think about the definitions given of "unsyllabled" and "eloquence." Then explain the **metaphor.**

4. Why does the odor of earth enrich the air after the work-out? Note line 41. It is not really the air that is azuring, but something associated with it. What? (This is an example of **metonymy.**)

5. Look at line 38. Do you feel that the human athlete in action is also a perfect model of "innocence, discipline, force," or not? Explain.

The body's unsyllabled eloquence rapidly
Dying away.
Dark-skinned stable-boys, as proud as kin
Of their display of vivacity, elegance,
Walk the racers back.   35
Foam laces the girths, sweaty haunches glow.
Slowly returning from the track, the horse is
Animal paradigm of innocence, discipline, force.
Blanketed, they go in.
Odor of earth   40
Enriches azuring air.

Unit Review : SPORTS

1. Memorable lines Poetry offers the pleasure of memorable or quotable lines. Begin to make your own collection of memorable lines. From the poems in this unit, select two passages of one line or several with which to begin your collection. The basis of your selection may be strength of image, music of line, depth of emotion, appeal of theme, or any combination of these. Write the passages in your notebook with title and author. Memorizing the lines will give you added pleasure.

2. Briefly **review the poems** in this unit. Then answer these questions.

 a. Name a poem that is a tribute to a real sports figure.
 b. Name one poem that deals with violence in sports.
 c. Which poem emphasizes the beauty of the natural setting of a sport?
 d. Which poem delights in "poetry in motion"?
 e. Name two poems that probe a negative aspect of sports other than violence. What is the negative aspect in each case?

3. Show your knowledge of **terms in poetry.** Here are five short passages from the poems in this unit. First, see if you can identify the passage by title and author. Then, choosing from the list of terms below, name the term applicable to the passage.

> **simile**   **onomatopoeia**
> **metaphor**   **anticlimax**
> **alliteration**

 a. "He accomplishes amazing feats.
    And what gets photographed? His cleats."
    (Title? Author? Term?)

 b. ". . . a string pluck-plucked of a violin"
    (Title? Author? Term?)

 c. ". . . at the rim of the delicate shadow
    the starlings were thicker and outlined the flock
    as an inkstain in drying pronounces its edges."
    (Title? Author? Term?)

 d. "Underwater, this is the cathedral/sea."
    (Title? Author? Term?)

 e. "Stuck through with hateful, horrid hooks"
    (Title? Author? Term?)

4. Add to your **vocabulary.** Match the definitions in the right-hand column with the words in the left-hand column.

(1) bland		*a.*	pulsate
(2) casual		*b.*	stretched out
(3) catapult		*c.*	timid
(4) distended		*d.*	safe place
(5) frenzied		*e.*	mild
(6) maxim		*f.*	frantic
(7) pirouette		*g.*	nonchalant
(8) sanctuary		*h.*	hurl forward
(9) timorous		*i.*	pivot
(10) undulate		*j.*	rule

5. Poems and paintings Poets and painters are artists who have much in common. Study each of the reproductions of paintings that follow. Examine the image carefully. Just what do you see? What feelings does the image arouse in you? What mood or idea does the picture suggest? If a person or persons appear, try to flesh out in your mind their background and character. Is rhythm, metaphor, or symbol important in the picture? After you have studied each picture in this way, select the one that you associate most powerfully in your feelings with one of the poems in this unit. Be ready to discuss or write about your choice and the reasons for it.

Optional: Select one picture that inspires you to write your own poem, and write the poem.

Max Schmitt in a Single Scull *Thomas Eakins. 1871. The Metropolitan Museum of Art, Purchase, 1934 Alfred N. Punnett Fund and Gift of George D. Pratt.*

State Park   *Jared French. 1946. Whitney Museum, New York.*

Head of Joan   *Richard Lahey.*
1931. Whitney Museum, New York.

Northeaster   *Winslow Homer. 1895. The Metropolitan Museum of Art, Gift of George A. Hearn, 1910.*

Dempsey and Firpo   *George Bellows. 1924. Whitney Museum, New York.*

LIB

Recently, "lib" movements have been prominent on the American scene. Yet, there is nothing new about "lib." The quest for liberation—freedom, equality, individuality—is as old as our nation. It is the American dream.

However, it is a lot easier to have the dream of liberation than to shape it into reality. The stifling of liberation comes in many forms and shapes—economic, political, social, educational, psychological— not always easy to recognize, never easy to change. Inequality of opportunity for minority groups, secrecy and deception in government, misleading language in business and advertising, conformity for the sake of conformity, bureaucracy, computerization, even the misdirected love of a parent for a child, all can act to deprive individuals of the opportunity to realize their full potential. It must always be asked, as well, whether liberation is entirely a social problem. How important are the individual's own character and personality in the quest for liberation?

Poets have explored the complex problem of liberation. We can gain greater wisdom and understanding by reading their work.

Walt Whitman is thought by many to be the greatest American poet. He is certainly foremost as a champion of the American dream of individuality and liberation. These excerpts from Whitman's long and most famous poem express his highly original thoughts about what it means to be a liberated human being.

DEFINITIONS AND EXPLANATIONS

remembrancer (line 10)   Souvenir; keepsake.

transpire (line 14)   Pass through.

sprout (line 28)   The first shoot of growth from a seed or a branch.

Vivas (line 34)   Cheers.

engagements (line 37)   Battles.

curlacue (line 46)   A line of curves and curls (usually spelled "curlicue").

august (line 47)   Dignified and majestic.

vindicate (line 48)   Justify; prove right.

tenon'd and mortis'd (line 56)   Formed into a very strong joint, as in the joining of two pieces of wood.

dissolution (line 57)   Death; disintegration.

amplitude (line 58)   Great size or extent.

voluptuous (line 64)   Richly and fully satisfying to the senses.

vitreous (line 67)   Glasslike.

limpid (line 69)   Clear.

pismire (line 73)   Ant.

chef-d'oeuvre (line 74)   Masterpiece.

infidels (line 78)   Nonbelievers.

placid (line 79)   Calm.

demented (line 84)   Crazed.

barbaric (line 95)   Wild and unrestrained.

yawp (line 95)   A loud call or cry.

scud (line 96)   Clouds or spray driven by the wind.

STUDY QUESTIONS

1. "I celebrate myself, and sing myself." In this first line, as throughout the poem, Whitman is optimistic, cheerful, and full of a sense of his own individual worth. Give three or four other examples of lines that express these characteristics.

2. Whitman's sense of his individual worth is rooted in larger beliefs. What understanding of those larger beliefs does each of the following passages give you?

Lines 8–10   Lines 33–34

Line 39	Lines 64–71
Lines 44–46	Lines 75–78
Line 53	Lines 86–87

3. This poem is written in **free verse,** without regular **rhythm (meter)**. However, the lines are rich with the music of poetry gained through other devices. On page 46 is a listing of some of those devices, each illustrated by an example from the poem. Read through the list and the examples. Then give a second example of each device from the poem.

continued

from Song of Myself

WALT WHITMAN

1

I celebrate myself, and sing myself,
And what I assume you shall assume,
For every atom belonging to me as good belongs to you.

I loafe and invite my soul,
I lean and loafe at my ease observing a spear of summer
    grass. . . .   5

6

A child said *What is the grass?* fetching it to me with full
    hands;
How could I answer the child? I do not know what it is any
    more than he.

I guess it must be the flag of my disposition, out of hopeful
    green stuff woven.

Or I guess it is the handkerchief of the Lord,
A scented gift and remembrancer designedly dropt,   10
Bearing the owner's name someway in the corners, that we
    may see and remark, and say *Whose?* . . .

And now it seems to me the beautiful uncut hair of graves.

Tenderly will I use you, curling grass.
It may be you transpire from the breasts of young men;
It may be if I had known them I would have loved them;   15
It may be you are from old people, and from women, and
    from offspring taken soon out of their mothers' laps.
And here you are the mothers' laps.

continued

Song of Myself

alliteration

> "A scented gift and remembrancer de-
> signedly dropt" (line 10)

repetition

> "It may be you transpire from the
> breasts of young men;
> It may be if I had known them I
> would have loved them;
> It may be you are from old people, . . ."
> (lines 14–16)

emphatic rhythms

> "With music strong I come, with my
> cornets and my drums" (line 30)

colorful diction

> "Vivas to those who have fail'd!" (line
> 34)

imagery

> ". . . earth of the mountains misty-
> topt!" (line 66)

metaphor

> "I guess it must be the flag of my dis-
> position, out of hopeful green stuff
> woven." (line 8)

personification

> "Press close bare-bosom'd night . . ."
> (line 61)

hyperbole

> "And a mouse is miracle enough to
> stagger sextillions of infidels."
> (line 78)

4. Whitman sings again and again of his feeling of self-importance. Whitman also speaks of death. How does he view his own death? Illustrate with lines from the poem. What underlying idea expressed in the poem explains both these feelings? Support your answer with lines from the poem.

5. Whitman, among all our poets, is the most ardent liberationist, the most enthusiastic champion of free individuality. Many lines from this poem can be cited as examples. Give two examples you especially like.

This grass is very dark to be from the white heads of old
    mothers,
Darker than the colorless beards of old men,
Dark to come from under the faint red roofs of mouths.   20
O I perceive after all so many uttering tongues,
And I perceive they do not come from the roofs of mouths
    for nothing.

I wish I could translate the hints about the dead young men
    and women,
And the hints about old men and mothers, and the offspring
    taken soon out of their laps.

What do you think has become of the young and old men?   25
And what do you think has become of the women and children?

They are alive and well somewhere;
The smallest sprout shows there is really no death, . . .

All goes onward and outward—nothing collapses.

18

With music strong I come, with my cornets and my drums,   30
I play not marches for accepted victors only, I play marches
    for conquer'd and slain persons.

Have you heard that it was good to gain the day?
I also say it is good to fall, battles are lost in the same spirit
    in which they are won.

Vivas to those who have fail'd!
And to those whose war-vessels sank in the sea!   35
And to those themselves who sank in the sea!

continued

And to all generals that lost engagements, and all overcome
    heroes!
And the numberless unknown heroes equal to the greatest
    heroes known!

20

In all people I see myself, none more and not one a barley-
    corn less,
And the good or bad I say of myself I say of them.   40

I know I am solid and sound,
To me the converging objects of the universe perpetually
    flow,
All are written to me, and I must get what the writing means.

I know I am deathless,
I know this orbit of mine cannot be swept by a carpenter's
    compass,   45
I know I shall not pass like a child's curlacue cut with a burnt
    stick at night.

I know I am august,
I do not trouble my spirit to vindicate itself or be understood,
I see that the elementary laws never apologize, . . .

I exist as I am, that is enough,   50
If no other in the world be aware I sit content,
And if each and all be aware I sit content.

One world is aware and by far the largest to me, and that is
    myself,
And whether I come to my own today or in ten thousand or
    ten million years,

I can cheerfully take it now, or with equal cheerfulness I can
    wait.   55

My foothold is tenon'd and mortis'd in granite,
I laugh at what you call dissolution,
And I know the amplitude of time.

21

I am he that walks with the tender and growing night,
I call to the earth and sea half-held by the night.   60

Press close bare-bosom'd night—press close magnetic nourishing
    night!
Night of south winds—night of the large few stars!
Still nodding night—mad naked summer night.

Smile O voluptuous cool-breath'd earth!
Earth of the slumbering and liquid trees!   65
Earth of departed sunset—earth of the mountains misty-topt!
Earth of the vitreous pour of the full moon just tinged with blue!
Earth of shine and dark mottling the tide of the river!
Earth of the limpid gray of clouds brighter and clearer for
    my sake!
Far-swooping elbow'd earth—rich apple-blossom'd earth!   70
Smile, for your lover comes.

31

I believe a leaf of grass is no less than the journeywork of the
    stars,
And the pismire is equally perfect, and a grain of sand, and
    the egg of the wren,

continued

And the tree-toad is a chef-d'œuvre for the highest,
And the running blackberry would adorn the parlors of heaven, 75
And the narrowest hinge in my hand puts to scorn all machinery,
And the cow crunching with depress'd head surpasses any
    statue,
And a mouse is miracle enough to stagger sextillions of infidels.

32

I think I could turn and live with animals, they are so placid
    and self-contain'd,
I stand and look at them long and long. 80

They do not sweat and whine about their condition,
They do not lie awake in the dark and weep for their sins,
They do not make me sick discussing their duty to God,
Not one is dissatisfied, not one is demented with the mania of
    owning things, . . .
Not one is respectable or unhappy over the whole earth. 85

In the faces of men and women I see God, and in my own
    face in the glass,
I find letters from God dropt in the street, and every one is
    sign'd by God's name,
And I leave them where they are, for I know that wheresoe'er
    I go,
Others will punctually come for ever and ever.

51

Do I contradict myself? 90
Very well then I contradict myself,
(I am large, I contain multitudes.)

52

The spotted hawk swoops by and accuses me, he complains of
    my gab and my loitering.

I too am not a bit tamed, I too am untranslatable,
I sound my barbaric yawp over the roofs of the world.   95

The last scud of day holds back for me,
It flings my likeness after the rest and true as any on the
    shadow'd wilds,
It coaxes me to the vapor and the dusk. . . .

I bequeath myself to the dirt to grow from the grass I love;
If you want me again look for me under your boot-soles.   100

You will hardly know who I am or what I mean,
But I shall be good health to you nevertheless,
And filter and fibre your blood.

Failing to fetch me at first keep encouraged,
Missing me one place search another,   105
I stop somewhere waiting for you.

The time is the eighteenth century. The place is the highly formalized gardens of a great house in England. The speaker is a young woman of the aristocracy. For a woman, particularly, of that class at that time in England, the life-style was governed by repressive codes and rules, by patterns that suffocated naturalness and freedom. The poem tells of a dramatic incident in the life of this aristocratic young English woman. Read the poem to see how it becomes a universal cry for the liberation of women—and people—of all times and places.

DEFINITIONS AND EXPLANATIONS

Amy Lowell (1874–1925) came from a distinguished, upper-class New England family. Though she lived and died long before the "lib" movements of today, she was truly liberated in her personal life and in her work. She lived unconventionally and independently, defying the "patterns" of her time and class. In her poetry, she broke with tradition to help establish the Imagist school and to popularize **free verse** as contrasted with the strict **meter** of earlier American poetry.

squills (line 3) A garden plant whose flowers grow on small, stiff spikes. The most common variety, called grape hyacinth, is usually planted in masses.

patterned garden-paths (line 4) Many eighteenth-century English gardens were highly formalized. Geometrically designed plantings were crisscrossed by patterns of geometrically laid-out paths.

brocaded (line 5) Brocade is a rich, thick cloth with a raised design of silk, velvet, gold, or silver woven into it. In a dress, it is stiff, heavy, and not very comfortable.

train (line 11) The part of a formal dress or gown that hangs down at the back and trails behind.

thrift (line 13) A low plant that shoots up small flowers on straight, stiff stems.

whalebone (line 18) Women wore stiff, constricting corsets to help give them a fashionable figure. Whalebone, an elastic material from the upper jaw of the whale, was used to give these corsets their binding power.

passion (line 20) Free and intense emotion.

plashing (line 28) Soft splashing.

sen'night (line 64) A week (seven nights).

footman (line 67) A servant. A household with a footman would be likely to have many servants.

arrayed (line 100) Dressed in fine clothes.

boned and stayed (line 101) Tightly corseted.

loose (line 104) Free.

Flanders (line 105) A region that at the time of the poem was part of France and is now part of Belgium. The Duke of Marlborough, one of the greatest English generals, won a victory in Flanders early in the eighteenth century.

continued

Patterns

AMY LOWELL

I walk down the garden-paths,
And all the daffodils
Are blowing, and the bright blue squills.
I walk down the patterned garden-paths
In my stiff brocaded gown. 5
With my powdered hair and jeweled fan,
I too am a rare
Pattern, as I wander down
The garden-paths.

My dress is richly figured, 10
And the train
Makes a pink and silver stain
On the gravel, and the thrift
Of the borders.
Just a plate of current fashion, 15
Tripping by in high-heeled, ribboned shoes.
Not a softness anywhere about me,
Only whalebone and brocade.
And I sink on a seat in the shade
Of a lime-tree. For my passion 20
Wars against the stiff brocade.
The daffodils and squills
Flutter in the breeze
As they please.
And I weep; 25
For the lime-tree is in blossom
And one small flower has dropped upon my bosom.

And the plashing of waterdrops
In the marble fountain
Comes down the garden-paths. 30
The dripping never stops.

continued

Patterns

_____

1. The young woman who is the speaker in this **dramatic monologue** tells much about the details of her attire and appearance. Describe these as exactly as you can—from head to foot. To what extent have women's fashions changed? What do these changes signify? Why is her attire important literally and symbolically?

2. What does the young woman mean when she says that her "passion/Wars against the stiff brocade" (lines 20–21)? (What news has she received that morning that helps account for her feelings?)

3. Note lines 25–27. Why does the woman weep when a lime-tree blossom falls upon her bosom? (Where is the letter?)

4. What are the young woman's inner imaginings as expressed in lines 32–55? How do these imaginings contrast with her actual behavior?

5. Note the **simile** in line 66. What makes the letters seem to squirm like snakes? Why is this an especially suitable comparison? Note the young woman's remarks to the footman. What contrast is there between her outward behavior and her inner feelings?

6. "For the man who should loose me is dead" (line 104). What had the speaker seen as her one last chance for liberation? What is your comment?

7. Explain the title "Patterns" as fully as you can.

8. What is the effect of the **repetition** of the words about walking down the garden paths in the first **stanza?** Give one other example of effective repetition of a word or phrase in the poem.

9. This poem is a **dramatic monologue** written in **free verse** with an irregular, or free, **rhyme scheme.** Give at least one example of emotional emphasis achieved by a line of contrastingly short length. Give at least one example of emotional emphasis achieved by the use of a **couplet.**

Underneath my stiffened gown
Is the softness of a woman bathing in a marble basin,
A basin in the midst of hedges grown
So thick, she cannot see her lover hiding,   35
But she guesses he is near,
And the sliding of the water
Seems the stroking of a dear
Hand upon her.
What is Summer in a fine brocaded gown!   40
I should like to see it lying in a heap upon the ground.
All the pink and silver crumpled up on the ground.

I would be the pink and silver as I ran along the paths,
And he would stumble after,
Bewildered by my laughter.   45
I should see the sun flashing from his sword-hilt and the
      buckles on his shoes.
I would choose
To lead him in a maze along the patterned paths,
A bright and laughing maze for my heavy-booted lover.
Till he caught me in the shade,   50
And the buttons of his waistcoat bruised my body as he
      clasped me,
Aching, melting, unafraid.
With the shadows of the leaves and the sundrops,
And the plopping of the waterdrops,
All about us in the open afternoon—   55
I am very like to swoon
With the weight of this brocade,
For the sun sifts through the shade.

Underneath the fallen blossom
In my bosom   60

continued

Is a letter I have hid.
It was brought to me this morning by a rider from the Duke.
"Madam, we regret to inform you that Lord Hartwell
Died in action Thursday sen'night."
As I read it in the white, morning sunlight,   65
The letters squirmed like snakes.
"Any answer, Madam?" said my footman.
"No," I told him.
"See that the messenger takes some refreshment.
"No, no answer."   70
And I walked into the garden,
Up and down the patterned paths,
In my stiff, correct brocade.
The blue and yellow flowers stood up proudly in the sun,
Each one.   75
I stood upright too,
Held rigid to the pattern
By the stiffness of my gown.
Up and down I walked,
Up and down.   80

In a month he would have been my husband.
In a month, here, underneath this lime,
We would have broke the pattern;
He for me, and I for him,
He as Colonel, I as Lady,   85
On this shady seat.
He had a whim
That sunlight carried blessing.
And I answered, "It shall be as you have said."
Now he is dead.   90

In Summer and in Winter I shall walk

Up and down
The patterned garden-paths
In my stiff, brocaded gown.
The squills and daffodils   95
Will give place to pillared roses, and to asters, and to snow.
I shall go
Up and down,
In my gown.
Gorgeously arrayed,   100
Boned and stayed.
And the softness of my body will be guarded from embrace
By each button, hook, and lace.
For the man who should loose me is dead,
Fighting with the Duke in Flanders,   105
In a pattern called a war.
Christ! What are patterns for?

The right to dissent, to be a member of the minority, to espouse a new or unpopular idea or cause, is one of the most valued parts of the American dream of freedom and liberation. Yet America is a country of contradictions; its practices are not always in harmony with its ideals. America has not always been kind to its dissenters—the suffragists who first fought for women's right to vote, the "bonus army" of World War I veterans, the early labor organizers, the supporters of Martin Luther King, Jr. This short, powerful poem sums up this American paradox.

DEFINITIONS AND EXPLANATIONS

Emily Dickinson had a fierce independence of mind and spirit. In her physical life, she seemed to express this independence in a negative way, for she withdrew from society, finally becoming an almost total recluse. In the life of the mind and spirit, she gave more positive expression to her independence. She championed the cause of abolition of slavery, for example. Above all, she expressed her devotion to the supreme value of individuality and to freedom in the many hundreds of short, brilliant poems that make her one of our greatest poets.

discerning (line 2) Observing with understanding; clearly recognizing a difference.

starkest (line 3) Most extreme; sheerest.

prevail (line 5) Triumph; be victorious.

assent (line 6) Agree.

demur (line 7) Disagree; object.

STUDY QUESTIONS

1. Emily Dickinson's words are skillfully used to mean something more than appears on the surface. The first line is a **paradox.** The only way "Madness" can be "Sense" is if there are two different points of view about the meanings of these words. Whose definition of "Madness" is used in this line? of "Sense"? In your own words, what does the whole line mean?

2. The third line is the same **paradox** in reverse. In this line, whose definition of "Sense" is used? of "Madness"? In your own words, what does this line mean?

3. Does the word "Eye" (line 2) literally mean "eye"? If not, what does it actually mean? (This use of a part for the whole is called **synecdoche.**)

4. By **denotation,** the word "Majority" (line 4) means simply "the greater number of people." By **connotation,** what additional meaning does the word have as it is used in this poem?

5. The word "Chain" in the last line is another example of **synecdoche.** What larger idea does the word "Chain" suggest to your mind? Name two or three other objects that could be used to suggest the same larger idea that "Chain" represents.

6. What is the poet's viewpoint of much majority opinion? of much minority opinion? of the treatment of the minority by the majority? Do you agree?

7. This poem indirectly suggests a second message about the dangers of unthinking acceptance of word labels, such as "madness" and "sense." Why can words such as "progress," "rights," and "freedom" be misleading?

Much Madness is divinest Sense

EMILY DICKINSON

Much Madness is divinest Sense—
To a discerning Eye—
Much Sense—the starkest Madness—
'Tis the Majority
In this, as All, prevail—   5
Assent—and you are sane—
Demur—you're straightway dangerous—
And handled with a Chain—

D o fathers raise their daughters differently from the way they
raise their sons? If so, in what way and why? Is the daughter
better or worse off than the son? Here a poet-daughter suggests some
answers to these interesting and important questions.

DEFINITIONS AND EXPLANATIONS

dragon-seekers (line 3) During the Age of Chivalry, the fashion was for a knight to have a ladylove, a pure and helpless creature. It was the duty of the knight to devote himself to protecting his ladylove from the dangers and evils of the world. Dragons were mythical beasts—huge, fire-breathing, winged serpents. Besides being quite horrible in and of themselves, dragons were regarded as **symbols** of sin and evil. So, in the tales of those days, knights sought out and slew dragons to protect their ladyloves.

improbable (line 3) Not likely to be true or real.

qualms (line 5) Misgivings; fears.

romantic (line 5) Not realistic.

STUDY QUESTIONS

1. According to the speaker, what are some of the things that fathers worry about where their daughters are concerned? In your opinion, is this a fair and accurate picture?

2. The poet begins by saying, "The thing to remember about fathers is, they're men." What particular meaning is the word "men" given in the rest of the poem? Support your answer by reference to specific lines.

3. What is the "journey" (line 15)?

4. Does the speaker feel that the father's worries reflect the natural concerns of a good parent or not? Why? What larger comment does the poem seem to make about the attitude of society toward the role of women?

5. Might a son write a similar poem about mothers? Explain.

6. Just what is the "first lesson" that has given the poem its title? (*Note:* There is a deliberate **ambiguity** in the title; it has two possible meanings.)

First Lesson

PHYLLIS McGINLEY

The thing to remember about fathers is, they're men.
A girl has to keep it in mind.
They are dragon-seekers, bent on improbable rescues.
Scratch any father, you find
Someone chock-full of qualms and romantic terrors,   5
Believing change is a threat—
Like your first shoes with heels on, like your first bicycle
It took such months to get.

Walk in strange woods, they warn you about the snakes there.
Climb, and they fear you'll fall.   10
Books, angular boys, or swimming in deep water—
Fathers mistrust them all.
Men are the worriers. It is difficult for them
To learn what they must learn:
How you have a journey to take and very likely,   15
For a while, will not return.

As in "First Lesson," the quest for personal liberation sometimes takes the form of a conflict between the older generation and the younger one—the so-called generation gap. Here is another short, highly ironic poem on the same theme.

STUDY QUESTIONS _____

1. What four details of young Grampa Schuler's appearance are given? What do these details suggest about his personality and character?

2. What did Grampa Schuler do as a young man? Why?

3. What happened to him in America?

4. What kind of person is the grandson, Jim?

5. What is the irony of the last two lines?

6. How do you explain the change in Grampa Schuler? In your opinion, to what extent is Grampa Schuler typical of people when they get older?

Grampa Schuler

RUTH SUCKOW

Grampa Schuler, when he was young,
Had a crest of hair, and shining eyes.
He wore red-flowered waistcoats,
Wild Byronic ties.
The whole land of Germany   5
Wasn't wide enough!—
He ran away one night, when winter
Seas were fierce and rough.

He has a sleek farm here
With already a settled air.   10

He's patriarchal, with his sons
And daughters round him everywhere.
His son's son Jim has fiery eyes—
He wants to go where the land is new!
Grampa bitterly wonders: "What are   15
Young fools coming to!"

In a dictatorship or totalitarian nation, individuality and personal independence are secondary to the interests of the state. In our American democracy, the state is supposed to serve the interests of individuality and personal independence. To what extent is this ideal achieved? To what extent is it possible to achieve ideal individuality—personal liberation—in modern, highly organized and industrialized society, a society of mass media, of government bureaus and red tape, of public opinion polls, of uniformity and conformity?

DEFINITIONS AND EXPLANATIONS

The Unknown Citizen (title) The Unknown Soldier is an unidentified soldier killed in World War I. He is honored by a marble monument in Arlington National Cemetery as a **symbol** and representative of all the American soldiers who died in that war and other wars. The title "The Unknown Citizen" is an **allusion** to the concept of The Unknown Soldier.

scab (line 9) A worker who refuses to join a union; a strikebreaker.

Installment Plan (line 19) This is a method of buying on credit. The buyer pays part of the price at the time of sale and the balance in regular installments until the bill is paid in full. The method has been criticized because poorer people are tempted to buy things they cannot afford and build up a heavy burden of debt. Some sellers using the plan reap unfairly large profits by charging a total amount far in excess of the normal price.

Eugenist (line 26) A specialist in the science of improving human beings by controlling heredity.

STUDY QUESTIONS

1. Who is the speaker in this poem? Where has he gotten his information about the Citizen? What is the occasion for the speaker's words? Why does he approve of the Citizen? What is he suggesting to all other citizens who read or hear his message? Cite lines from the poem to support your answers whenever possible.

2. Notice the inscription over the poem "To JS/07/M/378." What does this tell you about the attitude of the state toward the Citizen? Unless you read the whole inscription aloud, you may overlook the **internal rhyme** that occurs in the line. What word in the line rhymes with "state"? What is the emotional tone created by this rhyme?

3. Line 4 reads ". . . in the modern sense of an old-fashioned word, he was a saint." What is a saint in the old-fashioned sense? According to the speaker, what makes a person a "saint" in modern times? Give some specific examples from the poem of the behavior of a modern "saint."

4. "And that his reactions to advertisements were normal in every way" (line 15). In the view of the speaker, what probably were these "normal" reactions?

continued

The Unknown Citizen

W. H. AUDEN

To JS/07/M/378   This Marble Monument Is Erected by the State

He was found by the Bureau of Statistics to be
One against whom there was no official complaint,
And all the reports on his conduct agree
That, in the modern sense of an old-fashioned word, he
    was a saint,
For in everything he did he served the Greater Community.   5
Except for the War till the day he retired
He worked in a factory and never got fired,
But satisfied his employers, Fudge Motors Inc.
Yet he wasn't a scab or odd in his views,
For his Union reports that he paid his dues,   10
(Our report on his Union shows it was sound)
And our Social Psychology workers found
That he was popular with his mates and liked a drink.
The Press are convinced that he bought a paper every day
And that his reactions to advertisements were normal in
    every way.   15
Policies taken out in his name prove that he was fully insured,
And his Health-card shows he was once in hospital but left
    it cured.
Both Producers Research and High-Grade Living declare
He was fully sensible to the advantages of the Installment Plan
And had everything necessary to the Modern Man,   20
A phonograph, a radio, a car and a frigidaire.
Our researchers into Public Opinion are content
That he held the proper opinions for the time of year;

continued

The Unknown Citizen

5. The speaker approves of the fact that the Citizen was "sensible to the advantages of the Installment Plan" (line 19). What opposing point of view might be taken?

6. "When there was peace, he was for peace; when there was war, he went" (line 24). What ironic contrast is there in this line between what the speaker looks for in the Citizen in peacetime and in wartime?

7. What do lines 22–23 tell you about public opinion in this society?

8. What is suggested by the use of the word "their" in line 27?

9. Why is the speaker sure that the Citizen felt free and happy? What does this suggest about the state?

10. What is ironic about the title "The Unknown Citizen," considering all that the speaker has to say about the Citizen? However, may the Citizen be "unknown" in a different sense?

11. Do you feel that Auden intended this poem to represent a typical totalitarian state or one like our own? Explain. To what extent do you feel the poem applies to our own society?

12. Why does Auden use straightforward, "unpoetic" **diction,** as in line 16, "Policies taken out in his name prove that he was fully insured"? Why, too, does he use such obvious, mechanical **rhymes** as "Inc."—"drink," "day"–"way," "plan"–"man"?

When there was peace, he was for peace; when there was
     war, he went.
He was married and added five children to the population,   25
Which our Eugenist says was the right number for a parent of
     his generation,
And our teachers report that he never interfered with
     their education.
Was he free? Was he happy? The question is absurd:
Had anything been wrong, we should certainly have heard.

Liberation is always a struggle for every individual and every group. However, for the black people in America, this struggle has been and is uniquely painful and difficult. The black people were ripped from their ancient homelands, from their roots, and were brought here against their will as slaves. One part of the struggle for black liberation has been the search for roots.

DEFINITIONS AND EXPLANATIONS

Rivers (title) Rivers are important to civilization even today. In ancient times, they were absolutely essential to the growth of great civilizations.

Euphrates (line 4) The Euphrates River rises in the mountains of Turkey, eventually joins the Tigris River, and flows into the Persian Gulf. The ancient civilization of Mesopotamia flourished in the valley between the Tigris and Euphrates.

Congo (line 5) The Congo River, in volume of water, is the greatest river of Africa. Ancient black civilizations flourished on its banks.

Nile (line 6) The great Egyptian civilization grew up 5000 years ago along the particularly fertile lands bordering the Nile.

raised the pyramids (line 6) Egypt depended heavily on slave labor to sustain its wealth and power and build its monuments. Many of these slaves were Nubians, blacks who dwelled to the south of Egypt.

Mississippi (line 7) This great American river was intimately associated with the lives of the black slaves who worked on its levees and on the cotton plantations along its route.

New Orleans (line 7) This city was the capital of the cotton trade. When Abe Lincoln was a very young man, he was hired to take a flatboat loaded with produce from Indiana down the Mississippi to New Orleans. This was the first time that young Lincoln saw something of the world outside the wilderness where he had grown up. Among other things he saw in New Orleans was a slave auction with slaves in shackles and chains.

dusky (line 9) Dark; shadowy.

STUDY QUESTIONS

1. Who is the speaker? Note the title of the poem. How old is the speaker? To whom is the speaker talking?

2. Why did the speaker choose the four rivers mentioned in the poem?

3. Rivers are highly suitable as poetic **symbols.** Why?

4. The phrase "I've known rivers" is repeated at the beginning of the first two lines. What other **repetitions** are there? What is the effect of these repetitions?

5. How is it true that rivers are "older than the flow of human blood in human veins"? Why is this fact important to the speaker?

6. What is meant by the phrase "when dawns were young" (line 4)? The use of the word "dawns" in this phrase is an example of **synecdoche.** Why did the poet make this choice of language?

7. In what ways is the Mississippi described as if it were a person? What does the poet seem to be symbolizing when he says that he has seen the Mississippi's "muddy bosom turn all golden in the sunset"?

8. What two sides of black history does the poem suggest? Does it express defeat or hope?

The Negro Speaks of Rivers

LANGSTON HUGHES

I've known rivers:
I've known rivers ancient as the world and older than the
    flow of human blood in human veins.

My soul has grown deep like the rivers.

I bathed in the Euphrates when dawns were young.
I built my hut near the Congo and it lulled me to sleep.   5
I looked upon the Nile and raised the pyramids above it.
I heard the singing of the Mississippi when Abe Lincoln
    went down to New Orleans, and I've seen its muddy
    bosom turn all golden in the sunset.

I've known rivers:
Ancient, dusky rivers.

My soul has grown deep like the rivers.   10

W hat happens to the individual whose dreams of personal liberation begin to seem hopeless? One of our great black poets gives a few possible answers to this question.

DEFINITIONS AND EXPLANATIONS

Harlem (title) Harlem, in New York City, is the oldest and best known of urban black ghettos. It has been the home of a great number of outstanding black people, composers, musicians, writers, artists, political leaders, athletes, who have managed to rise despite terrible handicaps. Far more commonly, it is the home of people who suffer all the ill effects of such ghettos.

deferred (line 1) Postponed; delayed.

raisin (line 3) Raisins are sweet, juicy grapes that have been dried in the sun.

fester (line 4) Become full of pus and painfully inflamed.

STUDY QUESTIONS

1. Why do you think the poem is called "Harlem"?

2. What is the dream? Suggest a few specifics of the dream.

3. Hughes gives six possible answers to the question "What happens to a dream deferred?" The answers are given in the form of six comparisons—five **similes** and a **metaphor.** What are the five similes? What is the metaphor? What does each comparison mean to you as a description of a personal reaction to a hopeless situation?

4. How has the poet used **rhyme** to emphasize the last line? How else is the last line emphasized? Why does Hughes want to emphasize the last line?

5. Read the following short poem called "Incident" by another black writer, Countee Cullen. In what sense does this poem also deal with a "dream deferred" (notice line 2 and line 12)? Which of the two poems appeals to you more? Why?

Once riding in Old Baltimore,
    Heart-filled, head-filled with glee,
I saw a Baltimorean
    Kept looking straight at me.

Now I was eight and very small,   5
    And he was no whit bigger,
And so I smiled, but he poked out
    His tongue, and called me, "Nigger."

I saw the whole of Baltimore
    From May until December;   10
Of all the things that happened there
    That's all that I remember.

Harlem
LANGSTON HUGHES

What happens to a dream deferred?

Does it dry up
like a raisin in the sun?
Or fester like a sore—
And then run?   5
Does it stink like rotten meat?
Or crust and sugar over—
like a syrupy sweet?

Maybe it just sags
like a heavy load.   10

Or does it explode?

Is there any consolation for those whose dream seems hopeless, anywhere they can turn for comfort? Another important black poet gives one answer to that question in this stirring poem.

EXPLANATION

Call me Death! (line 17)   This line means "Call Death to me."

STUDY QUESTIONS

1. Who is the speaker in this poem? To whom is he talking? What is his purpose? In what region does the poem take place?

2. Cite lines that tell you what kind of person Sister Caroline was and what kind of life she lived.

3. What consolation does the speaker offer to his listeners and to those who are living lives like that of Sister Caroline?

4. How does the speaker picture God?

5. Describe in detail Death and his ride. How is the **image** of Death given here different from the image often given?

6. Look at the **similes** in lines 19, 26, 48, 56, 58, and 61. Why would the comparisons used in all of these similes have meaning to the audience listening to the sermon?

7. The poem has the moving musical qualities of a spiritual or of a reading from the Bible. How does the poet's use of **repetition** (as in line 1), of **rhythm** (as in lines 14–16), of **imagery** (as in lines 22–23), of **diction** (as in the use of the word "And") help to achieve this effect?

8. How does this message compare with the messages the Reverend Martin Luther King, Jr. delivered to his congregations?

9. Suppose you were asked to choose an actor to record a reading of this poem. Whom would you choose? Why?

Go Down Death (A Funeral Sermon)

JAMES WELDON JOHNSON

Weep not, weep not,
She is not dead;
She's resting in the bosom of Jesus.
Heart-broken husband—weep no more;
Grief-stricken son—weep no more;   5
Left-lonesome daughter—weep no more;
She's only just gone home.

Day before yesterday morning,
God was looking down from his great, high heaven,
Looking down on all his children,   10
And his eye fell on Sister Caroline,
Tossing on her bed of pain.
And God's big heart was touched with pity,
With the everlasting pity.

And God sat back on this throne,   15
And he commanded that tall, bright angel standing at
    his right hand:
Call me Death!
And that tall, bright angel cried in a voice
That broke like a clap of thunder:
Call Death!—Call Death!   20
And the echo sounded down the streets of heaven
Till it reached away back to that shadowy place,
Where Death waits with his pale, white horses.

And Death heard the summons,
And he leaped on his fastest horse,   25
Pale as a sheet in the moonlight.
Up the golden street Death galloped,
And the hoofs of his horse struck fire from the gold,
But they didn't make no sound.

continued

Up Death rode to the Great White Throne,   30
And waited for God's command.

And God said: Go down, Death, go down,
Go down to Savannah, Georgia,
Down in Yamacraw,
And find Sister Caroline.   35
She's borne the burden and heat of the day,
She's labored long in my vineyard,
And she's tired—
She's weary—
Go down, Death, and bring her to me.   40

And Death didn't say a word,
But he loosed the reins on his pale, white horse,
And he clamped the spurs to his bloodless sides,
And out and down he rode,
Through heaven's pearly gates,   45
Past suns and moons and stars;
On Death rode,
And the foam from his horse was like a comet in the sky;
On Death rode,
Leaving the lightning's flash behind;   50
Straight on down he came.

While we were watching round her bed,
She turned her eyes and looked away,
She saw what we couldn't see;
She saw Old Death. She saw Old Death   55
Coming like a falling star.
But Death didn't frighten Sister Caroline;
He looked to her like a welcome friend.
And she whispered to us: I'm going home,
And she smiled and closed her eyes.   60

And Death took her up like a baby,
And she lay in his icy arms,
But she didn't feel no chill.
And Death began to ride again—
Up beyond the evening star,   65
Out beyond the morning star,
Into the glittering light of glory,
On to the Great White Throne.
And there he laid Sister Caroline
On the loving breast of Jesus.   70

And Jesus took his own hand and wiped away her tears,
And he smoothed the furrows from her face,
And the angels sang a little song,
And Jesus rocked her in his arms,
And kept a-saying: Take your rest,   75
Take your rest, take your rest.

Weep not—weep not,
She is not dead;
She's resting in the bosom of Jesus.

Here is an entirely different comment on liberation, a comment that raises some interesting questions on the role of individual character in the quest for liberation.

DEFINITIONS

windward (line 5)   The side from which the wind strikes.

rapture (line 7)   Great joy; ecstasy.

STUDY QUESTIONS

1. What poetic device is used to make the title intriguing?

2. What **analogy** is used to explain the theme of victory in defeat?

3. The "mighty rapture" of personal fulfillment is described in two **metaphors.**

What are they? What feelings do these metaphors express to you?

4. How, according to the poem, can we find victory in defeat? In what way does this poem echo the statement of "The Negro Speaks of Rivers"?

Victory in Defeat

EDWIN MARKHAM

Defeat may serve as well as victory
To shake the soul and let the glory out.
When the great oak is straining in the wind,
The boughs drink in new beauty, and the trunk
Sends down a deeper root on the windward side.   5
Only the soul that knows the mighty grief
Can know the mighty rapture. Sorrows come
To stretch out spaces in the heart for joy.

The poem "Victory in Defeat" suggests that an individual can overcome adverse outward circumstances to achieve fulfillment. "George Gray" also suggests the importance of the character of a person in shaping his or her own life.

DEFINITIONS AND EXPLANATIONS

George Gray (title)   This is another poem from *Spoon River Anthology*. Remember that the speaker is looking back on his life from the grave.

marble (line 2)   Gravestone.

furled (line 3)   Rolled up and secured to the mast.

disillusionment (line 6)   Disappointment; disenchantment.

destiny (line 11)   Fate.

STUDY QUESTIONS

1. What picture was carved on the face of George Gray's gravestone? What was the picture intended to represent? Why is this intention ironic, in George Gray's view?

2. The picture on the gravestone becomes a **metaphor** that is extended through the poem. Give the lines that carry the metaphor through the poem.

3. What can you infer about the particulars of George Gray's life? (Was he married? Did he have children? What kind of work did he do? What role did he play in the town?) Essentially, what seemed to be his personality fault?

4. How is sorrow personified in line 7? How is ambition personified in line 8? How do these **personifications** strengthen the force of the poem?

5. Another poet, Alfred, Lord Tennyson, wrote "'Tis better to have loved and lost than never to have loved at all." Would Edgar Lee Masters agree?

6. Explain the last line as fully as you can.

George Gray

EDGAR LEE MASTERS

I have studied many times
The marble which was chiseled for me—
A boat with a furled sail at rest in a harbor.
In truth it pictures not my destination
But my life.   5
For love was offered me and I shrank from its
        disillusionment;
Sorrow knocked at my door, but I was afraid;
Ambition called to me, but I dreaded the chances.
Yet all the while I hungered for meaning in my life.
And now I know that we must lift the sail   10
And catch the winds of destiny
Wherever they drive the boat.
To put meaning in one's life may end in madness,
But life without meaning is the torture
Of restlessness and vague desire—   15
It is a boat longing for the sea and yet afraid.

George Gray is not alone. Probably everybody wonders at one time or another whether his or her life is empty and dull, whether the pattern of daily routines and social relationships is monotonous and meaningless, whether, like the person in this poem, he or she was "born to feel, and do, and be" something different and better.

DEFINITION AND EXPLANATION

Rhapsody (title) A long song or poem, usually expressing enthusiasm or great joy.

table-wit (line 9) Jokes told at the table.

STUDY QUESTIONS

1. In this poem, someone is addressed by the speaker as "you." Could the speaker and the "you" be the same person addressing himself or herself in a **soliloquy,** or interior monologue? If so, why would the person say "you" instead of "I"? Why "baby"? If so, what is the mood or frame of mind of the speaker? What is a likely time and place for the occurrence of such a soliloquy?

2. What do you know about this person? (Is it a man or a woman? of what approximate age? of what marital status? of what socioeconomic class? Where does the person live?)

3. Why would an outsider be likely to consider this person successful and happy?

4. Some of the lines of the poem sketch the life of the person as an outsider would see it. Other lines suggest something of the person's inner feelings. Give examples of how **repetition** is used to suggest the inner feelings of the person. How does line 1 suggest something of what is going on inside the person? What do lines 2 and 13, written in parentheses, tell you of the person's inner feelings?

5. Notice the references to the music in lines 7 and 8. What do the three **metaphors** used to describe the music have in common? What effect of the music on the speaker is suggested by these metaphors?

6. Compare this person to the speaker in "Patterns," to the Unknown Citizen, and to George Gray. What are the similarities? What are the differences?

7. The title of the poem tells us something of the intentions of the poet. What is suggested by his use of the word "American" in the title? Why is "Rhapsody" ironic?

American Rhapsody (4)

KENNETH FEARING

First you bite your fingernails. And then you comb your hair
    again. And then you wait. And wait.
(They say, you know, that first you lie. And then you steal,
    they say. And then, they say, you kill.)

Then the doorbell rings. Then Peg drops in. And Bill. And
    Jane. And Doc.
And first you talk, and smoke, and hear the news and have a
    drink. Then you walk down the stairs.
And you dine, then, and go to a show after that, perhaps, and
    after that a night spot, and after that come home again, and
    climb the stairs again, and again go to bed. 5

But first Peg argues, and Doc replies. First you dance the same
    dance and you drink the same drink you always drank before.
And the piano builds a roof of notes above the world.

And the trumpet weaves a dome of music through space. And
    the drum makes a ceiling over space and time and night.
And then the table-wit. And then the check. Then home again
    to bed.
But first, the stairs. 10

And do you now, baby, as you climb the stairs, do you still
    feel as you felt back there?
Do you feel again as you felt this morning? And the night
    before? And then the night before that?

(They say, you know, that first you hear voices. And then
    you have visions, they say. Then, they say, you kick and
    scream and rave.)

continued

Or do you feel: What is one more night in a lifetime of nights?
What is one more death, or friendship, or divorce out of two,
    or three? Or four? Or five?   15
One more face among so many, many faces, one more life
    among so many million lives?

But first, baby, as you climb and count the stairs (and they
    total the same), did you, sometime or somewhere, have a
    different idea?
Is this, baby, what you were born to feel, and do, and be?

Unit Review : LIB

1. Memorable lines   Continue to add to your collection of memorable or quotable lines. From the poems in this unit, select two passages of one line or several. The basis of your selection may be strength of image, music of line, depth of emotion, appeal of theme, or any combination of these. Write the passages in your notebook with title and author. Memorizing the lines will give you added pleasure.

2. Briefly **review the poems** in this unit. Then answer these questions.

  a. Name one poem that deals with the theme of liberation as it specifically concerns women.
  b. Name one poem that deals with the theme of liberation as it specifically concerns black people.
  c. Name one poem that deals with the theme of liberation as it concerns children in relationship to adults.
  d. Which poem sings the praises of the supreme value of individuality?
  e. Name one poem that emphasizes the importance of the role of character in the pursuit of personal liberation.

3. Show your knowledge of **terms in poetry.** Here are five short passages from the poems in this unit. First, see if you can identify the passage by title and author. Then, choosing from the list of terms below, name the term applicable to the passage.

couplet	**personification**
irony	**synecdoche**
paradox	

  a. "The spotted hawk swoops by and accuses me, he complains of my gab and my loitering."
      (Title? Author? Term?)

  b. "And he would stumble after,
       Bewildered by my laughter."
       (Title? Author? Term?)

  c. "Demur—you're straightway dangerous—
       And handled with a Chain—"
       (Title? Author? Term?)

  d. "Only the soul that knows the mighty grief
       Can know the mighty rapture."
       (Title? Author? Term?)

  e. "Believing change is a threat—
       Like your first shoes with heels on, like your first bicycle"
       (Title? Author? Term?)

4. Add to your **vocabulary.** Match the definitions in the right-hand column with the words in the left-hand column.

(1) arrayed   *a.* observing with understanding
(2) august   *b.* be victorious
(3) defer   *c.* rich in appeal to the senses
(4) discerning   *d.* misgivings
(5) disillusionment   *e.* delay
(6) prevail   *f.* ecstasy
(7) qualms   *g.* dressed in fine clothes
(8) rapture   *h.* disappointment
(9) vindicate   *i.* dignified
(10) voluptuous   *j.* justify

5. Poems and paintings Poets and painters are artists who have much in common. Study each of the reproductions of paintings that follow. Examine the image carefully. Just what do you see? What feelings does the image arouse in you? What mood or idea does the picture suggest? If a person or persons appear, try to flesh out in your mind their background and character. Is rhythm, metaphor, or symbol important in the picture? After you have studied each picture in this way, select the one that you associate most powerfully in your feelings with one of the poems in this unit. Be ready to discuss or write about your choice and the reasons for it.

Optional: Select one picture that inspires you to write your own poem and write the poem.

Tormented Man *Leonard Baskin. 1956. Whitney Museum, New York.*

The Subway   *George Tooker. 1950. Whitney Museum, New York.*

Mirage Le Temps   *Yves Tanguy. 1954. The Metropolitan
Museum of Art, George A. Hearn Fund, 1955.*

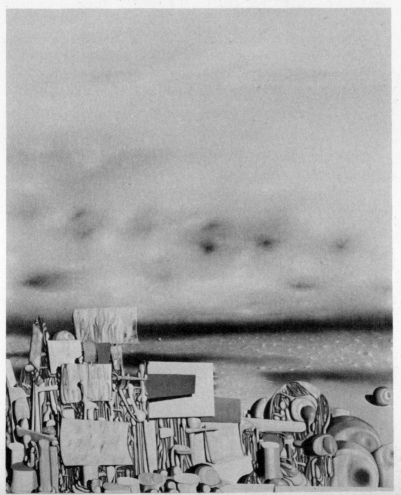

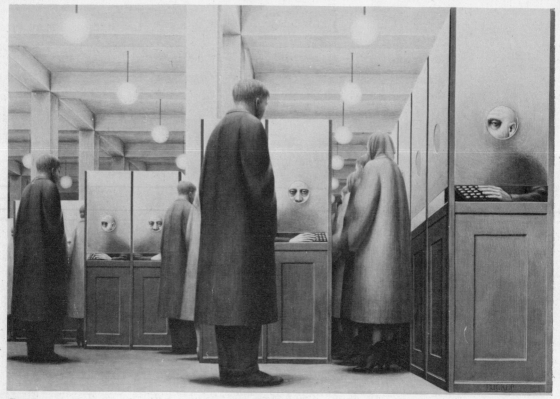

Government Bureau *George Tooker. The Metropolitan Museum of Art, George A. Hearn Fund, 1956.*

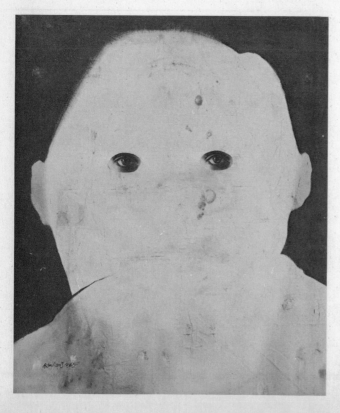

Gazer *Hiram Williams. 1965. Whitney Museum, New York.*

THE HUMAN FAMILY

"Love thy neighbor as thyself."
Old Testament

*"Therefore all things whatsoever ye would that men
should do to you, do you even so to them."*
New Testament

*"No man is an Island, entire of itself.
Every man is a piece of the continent."*
John Donne

*"It's coming yet for a' that,
That man to man the world o'er,
Shall brothers be for a' that."*
Robert Burns

*These well-known quotations, and many more, all express in
different words the same great ideal of love and cooperation among
all members of the human family. In the past, the name "brotherhood" has been given to this ideal. However, despite the good
intentions of the word "brotherhood," today we recognize it as a
sexist word that excludes all the "sisters" of the human family.
We shall, therefore, describe the ideal that was expressed by the
word "brotherhood" with the words "the human family."*

*The human family ideal is as old as civilization. The prophets,
philosophers, and poets of ancient times recognized the interdependence and common lot of all people and incorporated this ideal into
the great religions, philosophies, and poems.*

*The ideal is also as new as American democracy. If we think of our
democracy as a precious golden coin, one side of that coin is
liberation—the recognition of individuality, of the right of every
person to the opportunity for fullest realization of his or her
potential. The other side of that coin is the human family ideal—
the recognition of the interdependence, the oneness, the common
fate of all members of the human race.*

Here are some poems commenting on the human family ideal.

This poem has been set to music, and most of us have sung it many, many times. However, when we sing songs or recite verses automatically as a ritual, we usually mouth the words but don't pay much attention to what they mean. Let's find out what "America, the Beautiful" is saying as a poem.

DEFINITIONS AND EXPLANATIONS

amber (line 2)   Yellow.

pilgrim (line 9)   A pilgrim is a wanderer. More specifically, the American Pilgrims were the band of English Puritans who, seeking religious freedom, came to America and founded the Plymouth Colony in 1620. They surmounted great hardship and deprivation.

impassioned (line 10)   Filled with deep feeling.

stress (line 10)   Struggle against great difficulties.

thoroughfare (line 11)   An unobstructed road; an open passageway.

alabaster (line 27)   A variety of handsome, fine white stone used for sculpture.

STUDY QUESTIONS

1. What physical or natural riches of America are mentioned? Can you add any not mentioned?

2. What element did the Pilgrims add to the natural riches of the country?

3. In what cause, according to the poem, have America's heroes fought? What important characteristic did these heroes have? Name several such heroes.

4. What vision does the speaker foresee of America's cities? (What are the **connotations** of the word "alabaster"?) To what degree has that vision been realized?

5. What is the speaker's definition of "success" for America? Explain what she means as specifically as you can.

6. The speaker suggests that America's natural riches, its history, and its heroes are a kind of foundation, but that America must crown that foundation with the realization of an ideal. What is that ideal? Does America continue to reach for that ideal? How successfully?

7. The poem is an **apostrophe.** Explain.

8. Now that you are fully aware of the meaning of the words of the song, sing it with a full understanding of its feeling.

America, the Beautiful

KATHARINE LEE BATES

O beautiful for spacious skies,
  For amber waves of grain,
For purple mountain majesties
  Above the fruited plain!
America! America!   5
  God shed His grace on thee
And crown thy good with brotherhood
  From sea to shining sea!

O beautiful for pilgrim feet,
  Whose stern, impassioned stress   10
A thoroughfare for freedom beat
  Across the wilderness!
America! America!
  God mend thine every flaw,
Confirm thy soul in self-control,   15
  Thy liberty in law!

O beautiful for heroes proved
  In liberating strife,
Who more than self their country loved,
  And mercy more than life!   20
America! America!
  May God thy gold refine,
Till all success be nobleness
  And every gain divine!

O beautiful for patriot dream   25
  That sees beyond the years
Thine alabaster cities gleam
  Undimmed by human tears!
America! America!
  God shed His grace on thee   30
And crown thy good with brotherhood
  From sea to shining sea!

In a poem called "The Tuft of Flowers," Robert Frost wrote these lines:

> "'Men work together,' I told him from the heart,
> 'Whether they work together or apart.'"

Can you think of some ways in which people work together even though they are apart? After arriving at your own answer to this question, see what Sandburg has to say in the poem that follows.

DEFINITIONS AND EXPLANATIONS

bah-tah-to (line 3) *Batata* is the Spanish word from which our word "potato" is derived. Sandburg's spelling is intended to show the pronunciation.

ponchos (line 4) A poncho is a colorful cloak. It is similar to a blanket with a hole in the middle for the head, the two halves hanging down over shoulders and torso. Ponchos are worn in Spanish-American countries.

aloof (line 23) Holding oneself apart; cold and distant in manner.

pride of distinction (line 23) Sense of being different and superior.

commodious (line 29) Roomy; spacious.

STUDY QUESTIONS

1. In the first eleven lines of the poem, what is the speaker suggesting about our relationship with other peoples of the earth? He mentions mainly items of food, though he could have made other choices. Why does this choice serve his purpose well? Where in these eleven lines does he show a sense of humor?

2. In lines 12–17, the speaker tells us what we have given to the Chinese and what they have given us. What two instances of **irony** does he work into these lines?

3. What are the two possible attitudes toward other peoples that are described in lines 18–30? Which attitude does the speaker favor? How do you know?

4. Why does the speaker describe people as "fellow creepers" (line 29)? What is implied by the use of the word "commodious" to describe the earth?

5. Sandburg writes in **free verse** and in a freewheeling language style that is uniquely his own. He mixes slang and colloquial words and expressions with formal and literary words and expressions. Give an example of such a mixture. What is the effect of this **diction?** He uses two different words for American Indians and three different words for potato. Why? He likes to inventory long lists of items in his poems. What is an example from this poem? What is the effect of such long lists of items?

6. The title of the book-length poem from which this excerpt is taken is *The People, Yes.* What do you think that title means? Suppose this excerpt were a complete poem by itself. What title would you give it?

from *The People, Yes*

CARL SANDBURG

The copperfaces, the red men, handed us tobacco,
the weed for the pipe of friendship,
also the bah-tah-to, the potato, the spud.
Sunflowers came from Peruvians in ponchos.
Early Italians taught us of chestnuts,   5
walnuts and peaches being Persian mementos,
Siberians finding for us what rye might do,
Hindus coming through with the cucumber,
Egyptians giving us the onion, the pea,
Arabians handing advice with one gift: 10
"Some like it, some say it's just spinach."
    To the Chinese we have given
    kerosene, bullets, Bibles
and they have given us radishes, soy beans, silk,
poems, paintings, proverbs, porcelain, egg foo yong,   15
gunpowder, Fourth of July firecrackers, fireworks,
and labor gangs for the first Pacific railways.
    Now we may thank these people
    or reserve our thanks
    and speak of them as outsiders   20
    and imply the request,
"Would you just as soon get off the earth?"
holding ourselves aloof in pride of distinction
saying to ourselves this costs us nothing
as though hate has no cost   25
as though hate ever grew anything worth growing.
Yes we may say this trash is beneath our notice
or we may hold them in respect and affection
as fellow creepers on a commodious planet
saying, "Yes you too you too are people."   30

Scientists study the laws of nature. Poets study the wisdom of nature. In this poem, Emily Dickinson uses nature imagery to make an important statement about human society. Her bare, abbreviated language carries a wealth of meaning.

DEFINITIONS AND EXPLANATIONS

Pedigree (line 1) A written record of ancestry, usually used to prove superiority of breeding and background.

Clover (line 3) The clover is one of the most common of all flowers, growing in practically every meadow, pasture, and lawn. It is not generally considered to be a particularly beautiful or distinguished flower.

Aristocracy (line 4) A privileged or ruling class.

STUDY QUESTIONS

1. Why did the poet choose the clover rather than some other flower, such as the rose, the iris, or the lily? What is the symbolism of the clover?

2. Why does the bee value the clover? Why is the clover "Aristocracy" to the bee?

3. Which two words, especially, suggest that the meaning of this poem is not to be taken literally but is intended metaphorically or symbolically? What is the underlying idea suggested by the **metaphor?**

4. What is the effect of rhyming the long, bookish word "Aristocracy" with the short, common word "Bee"?

The Pedigree of Honey

EMILY DICKINSON

The Pedigree of Honey
Does not concern the Bee—
A Clover, any time, to him,
Is Aristocracy—

One role the black woman has traditionally played in American society is that of maid in a white household. This poem is set against that background.

DEFINITION AND EXPLANATION

When in Rome (title) The expression "When in Rome do as the Romans do" is generally used to mean that visitors or travelers should follow the ways and customs of those around them. In addition, the connotation of "Rome" is of an ancient, superior civilization.

box (line 2) Refrigerator.

STUDY QUESTIONS

1. Identify each of the two speakers. What is the occasion for the "conversation"? Why are the second speaker's words in parentheses? What is the significance of this fact?

2. Judging from her words, how does the first speaker view her own attitude toward the other speaker? Is that view accurate? Explain. How do you account for the kind of food in the refrigerator?

3. Tell everything you know about the second speaker from her words.

4. In this poem, the words of the two speakers are set off against each other in contrast in a kind of musical counterpoint. How is this contrast shown in the way the thoughts of each speaker are expressed, the attitude of each, the **diction** used by each? How are the words of the two speakers tied together in a kind of musical interplay?

5. What do you feel the poem says about the role of the black woman in the American human family? What is the tone of the whole poem—bitter, sorrowful, humorous?

When in Rome

MARI EVANS

Mattie dear
the box is full
take
whatever you like
to eat   5
      (an egg
      or soup
      . . . there ain't no meat)

there's endive there
and   10
cottage cheese
      (whew! if I had some
      black-eyed peas . . .)

there's sardines
on the shelves   15
and such
but
don't
get my anchovies
they cost   20
too much!
      (me get the
      anchovies indeed!
      what she think, she got—
      a bird to feed?)   25

there's plenty in there
to fill you up.
      (yes'm. just the
      sight's
      enough!   30
      Hope I lives till I get
      home
      I'm tired of eatin'
      what they eats in Rome . . .)

O f the various ways we fail to reach the human family ideal, none
shocks us so much as the killing and destruction of war. This
poem tells about the aerial warfare of World War II and its tragedy.

STUDY QUESTIONS

1. Who is the "we" referred to in line 2 and
throughout the poem?

2. Randall Jarrell served as a pilot in the
Air Corps in World War II and writes with
accurate knowledge. What are three ways
the speaker mentions airmen died while
still in training? Why does he say "our
fields" called up the papers, instead of
saying the commanding (or other) officers?
(This figure of speech is called **metonymy**.)
In what way did the airmen die "on the
wrong page of the almanac" (line 6)? Why
do you think the poet says it this way?

3. What other details of the training are
given?

4. "We died like aunts or pets or foreigners" (line 10). The three comparisons in this
simile represent three ways of feeling the
young airmen had about the death of a
comrade during training operations. Explain the feeling represented by each of
these three comparisons. What explanation is offered for such feelings in lines
11–12?

5. Explain the change described in lines
16–17. Which words suggest the dramatic
suddenness of the change?

6. Explain the ironic contrasts in lines
22–23.

7. In the repetition of the phrase "It was
not dying," the speaker suggests that the
idea of dying was acceptable, or at least
bearable. However, in the climactic final
lines, he suggests that the destruction of
the cities, which was the airman's mission
and the purpose for which he risked his life,
was not acceptable or bearable. Why should
this be so? In what sense did the speaker
"die" the night that he dreamed that he was
dead and the cities spoke to him.

8. What is the meaning of the title of the
poem? Why is it a powerful title?

Losses

RANDALL JARRELL

It was not dying: everybody died.
It was not dying: we had died before
In the routine crashes—and our fields
Called up the papers, wrote home to our folks,
And the rates rose, all because of us.   5
We died on the wrong page of the almanac,
Scattered on mountains fifty miles away;
Diving on haystacks, fighting with a friend,
We blazed up on the lines we never saw.
We died like aunts or pets or foreigners.   10
(When we left high school nothing else had died
For us to figure we had died like.)

In our new planes, with our new crews, we bombed
The ranges by the desert or the shore,
Fired at towed targets, waited for our scores—   15
And turned into replacements and woke up
One morning, over England, operational.
It wasn't different: but if we died
It was not an accident but a mistake
(But an easy one for anyone to make).   20
We read our mail and counted up our missions—
In bombers named for girls, we burned
The cities we had learned about in school—
Till our lives wore out; our bodies lay among
The people we had killed and never seen.   25
When we lasted long enough they gave us medals;
When we died they said, "Our casualties were low."
They said, "Here are the maps"; we burned the cities.

It was not dying—no, not ever dying;
But the night I died I dreamed that I was dead,   30
And the cities said to me: "Why are you dying?
We are satisfied, if you are; but why did I die?"

The poet E. E. Cummings developed a unique style that became his personal trademark. He uses no capitals and applies his own unorthodox rules of punctuation. His poetic line, too, is distinctive; he ends his lines in surprising places, sometimes after one word, sometimes even in the middle of a word. He is remarkably successful in these experiments, achieving startling effects of emphasis, humor, and lyric qualities. This poem will look strange and difficult to you at first sight. It isn't! In reading it, forget about the unusual appearance of no capitals, original punctuation, and unusually short line length. Simply read the poem naturally according to the sense of the words. You'll like it.

EXPLANATIONS

plato (line 1) Plato (427?–347 B.C.) was one of the great Greek philosophers. In his work *The Republic*, Plato outlines plans for an ideal society in which human beings live together in perfect harmony. The expression "Platonic love" is derived from Plato's name and his teachings.

lao tsze (lines 6–7) Lao Tsze was a philosopher who founded Taoism, one of the great religions of China. Taoism teaches kindness and love, even the returning of injury with kindness.

general . . . sherman (lines 9 and 12) William Tecumseh Sherman is recognized as one of the great Union generals of the Civil War. However, he is said to have summed up his feelings about war in the famous phrase "War is hell."

nipponized bit of . . . sixth avenue el (lines 21–24) Before World War II, an elevated train ran on Sixth Avenue in New York City. When it was torn down to be replaced by the subway, the scrap iron was sold to Japan (Nippon). This metal was used by Japan for armaments to fight World War II.

STUDY QUESTIONS

1. What is it that Plato, Jesus, Lao Tsze, and General Sherman told? Who are "you" and "I" and "we" who told the same thing? How is this true?

2. Who is the "he" in the poem who was told but "couldn't," "wouldn't," and "didn't" believe?

3. What makes "him" finally believe? What is the actual event that the nipponized bit of the el in the top of his head probably symbolizes?

4. Though dealing with a serious subject, E. E. Cummings prefers a light and humorous touch to a sermonizing or moralizing tone. Give one or two examples.

5. This poem deals with the same theme as "Losses." Do you prefer one of these poems? If so, which one, and why?

plato told

E. E. CUMMINGS

plato told

him:he couldn't
believe it(jesus

told him;he
wouldn't believe   5
it)lao

tsze
certainly told
him,and general
(yes   10

mam)
sherman;
and even
(believe it
or   15

not)you
told him:i told
him;we told him
(he didn't believe it,no

sir)it took   20
a nipponized bit of
the old sixth

avenue
el;in the top of his head:to tell

him   25

The splitting of the atom resulted in a weapon that is viewed as a threat to all humanity. However, this poem points out that the threat does not come from atom-splitting but from another source.

EXPLANATIONS

Empire State (line 7) This building in New York City was for a long time the tallest building in the world.

Parthenon (line 8) The ancient Greeks built the Parthenon, a temple dedicated to their goddess Athena. Many regard it as the most beautiful structure of all time.

STUDY QUESTIONS

1. If the threat does not lie in the atom bomb, where, according to the first **quatrain,** does it lie? How is this true? How great was the threat before the invention of the atomic bomb?

2. Why did the poet refer to the destruction of only two buildings, the Empire State and the Parthenon? Can you suggest any other two buildings that might have been included with equal force?

3. The poet chose to refer to the destruction of cities, statues, and poems. Why do you think he made these choices? How can poems be destroyed?

4. Who or what is the "foe" referred to in the final **quatrain?** What is the **connotation** of the word "curled"? (What animal is suggested?)

5. Which single word in the final **stanza** suggests a sense of urgency or emergency? Which alliterative words add to this sense of urgency by the beat of their sound? How do **line** length and the **rhythm** of the whole poem also add to this sense?

6. What different perspective on war does this poem give you?

7. What are the **connotations** of the title "Atomic"?

Atomic
LOUIS GINSBERG

The splitting apart
    Of man from man
Dooms more than splitting
    The atom can.

In one blaze, will   5
    All things be gone:
The Empire State
    And the Parthenon?

And must the sudden
    Atom's flash   10
Turn cities, statues,
    And poems to ash?

Quick! The foe
    In us is curled,
More fearsome than any   15
    Foe in the world!

ountee Cullen is the black poet who wrote "Incident" (page 70). In
this poem, he writes about the connection between human suffering and the human family ideal.

DEFINITIONS AND EXPLANATIONS ───────────────────────────

marrow (line 4)   The innermost part of
the bone.

diverse (line 11)   Separate; different.

aloes (line 29)   The aloe is a spiny-leaved
plant with a bitter juice.

STUDY QUESTIONS ──────────────────────────────────────

1. According to the poem, what is the
common bond that ties all humans together? Why is this true?

2. In the **simile** in lines 1–6, what, exactly,
is the effect of the ills compared to?

3. What are "Your grief and mine" (line 7)
compared to? In what sense is this idea
true?

4. What mistaken picture of themselves do
"proud" and "confident" people have?

5. What contrast is made between joy and
sorrow in the fourth **stanza?**

6. According to the last stanza, what must
happen to "my sorrow"? What is the
"crown" made of?

7. What plea does the poem seem to be
making?

8. Notice the **diction** used in the title of
the poem. What is suggested by this
wording?

Any Human to Another

COUNTEE CULLEN

The ills I sorrow at
Not me alone
Like an arrow,
Pierce to the marrow,
Through the fat   5
And past the bone.

Your grief and mine
Must intertwine
Like sea and river,
Be fused and mingle,   10
Diverse yet single,
Forever and forever.

Let no man be so proud
And confident,
To think he is allowed   15
A little tent
Pitched in a meadow
Of sun and shadow
All his little own.

Joy may be shy, unique,   20
Friendly to a few,
Sorrow never scorned to speak
To any who
Were false or true.

Your every grief   25
Like a blade
Shining and unsheathed
Must strike me down.
Of bitter aloes wreathed,
My sorrow must be laid   30
On your head like a crown.

How do you fight hatred, divisiveness, and bigotry in the human family? Here is one answer, expressed in few words but saying a lot.

DEFINITIONS AND EXPLANATIONS

Heretic (line 2)   A person whose beliefs and opinions are contrary to established and generally accepted beliefs and opinions.

flout (line 2)   Show contempt or scorn for.

wit (line 3)   Wisdom.

STUDY QUESTIONS

1. Whom do the "he" and "I" represent?

2. What are the names that "he" calls "me" to shut "me" out? In what ways might such names shut "me" out? Why do these names have such an effect? What are some other names that are used with similar effect?

3. Two metaphoric circles are drawn in this poem. Who draws the first circle? What is its purpose? What are some specific real acts this metaphorical circle could represent?

4. Who draws the second circle? How does it compare in size with the first circle? What does the second metaphorical circle represent?

5. Why is the poem called "Outwitted"? Explain the **understatement** of this title.

6. Can you name any leader of modern times who has followed a principle similar to the one expressed in this poem? Was he or she successful? Do you think this principle can work?

7. This speaker expresses thoughts and feelings closely akin to those of the speaker of a poem you read earlier in this unit. What is the poem?

Outwitted

EDWIN MARKHAM

He drew a circle that shut me out—
Heretic, rebel, a thing to flout.
But Love and I had the wit to win:
We drew a circle that took him in!

The culture and traditions of American Indians are steeped in nature. From ancient times, they have lived in a harmonious bond with nature. The rhythms of their lives fluctuated directly with the seasons. Their beloved homes were the sky of day and night, the plains, the rivers, the mountains, the deserts. From nature came their food, clothing, and shelter. Nature provided their industry and the fulfillment of their sense of beauty in their crafts of weaving, basketry, pottery, jewelry-making. Above all, the spiritual life of the Native American people came from their interplay with nature, nurturing their sense of reality and identity. What is the place of such a people in the human family of modern America? Here are the words of a young poet, a Papago of the Southwest.

EXPLANATION

devil's claws (line 9) A shrub of the Southwest whose fibers are used in basket-making.

STUDY QUESTIONS

1. What is the speaker's mother doing? How do you picture the mother in this activity?

2. How do you picture the speaker? What do you imagine are his thoughts and feelings as he watches his mother?

3. Explain the first line. (What do the star and the basket seem to symbolize?)

4. Why do you think the star is black and the sky white (lines 5–6)?

5. Notice the important surprising word used to describe the star—"gentle" in line 7. What meaning is suggested to you by this word choice?

6. Notice the final line. What is the effect of isolating the words "a basket" in this climactic line?

7. What role do you foresee for the speaker as he tries to take his place in the American human family?

8. The cultural traditions of this speaker play a key role in his life. What role have cultural traditions played in your life? Do you feel they have been a help or a handicap?

I See a Star

ALONZO LOPEZ

I see a star
   yet it is day.
The hands of my mother
   make it grow.
It is a black star   5
   set against a white sky.

How gentle that star,
Now that she weaves
devil's claws
Together to make   10
   a basket.

What sort of relationship with neighbors do you favor? Do you prefer to be close and mutually helpful when the need arises, or do you prefer to keep a safe distance to protect yourself from involvement? How close do people have to live to one another to be neighbors? Are people who live in the same town or city neighbors in any way? in the same state? in the same nation? anywhere on the planet earth? This poem, one of the most widely read of all American poems, is about two neighbors. Or is it?

DEFINITIONS AND EXPLANATIONS

Mending Wall (title)   The countryside of New England is crisscrossed with low stone walls. The walls, or fences, are built out of stones of all sizes and shapes that are fitted roughly on top of one another. These walls usually are used to mark the boundaries between properties.

frozen-ground-swell (line 2)   Water expands when it freezes. In the winter, the frozen water in the ground causes the ground to swell and heave upward.

spell (line 18)   Magic formula.

give offense (line 34)   Insult or displease.

old-stone savage (line 40)   A primitive person of the Stone Age.

go behind (line 43)   Look into; think critically about.

STUDY QUESTIONS

1. Who is the speaker? Who is the other person? What are they doing? Give a few details of their work as described by the speaker. What do they actually say to each other in the course of their work?

2. See what you know about the speaker. Which lines show that the speaker has a sense of humor? Which lines show that he likes to think about things and not just accept them because they are customary? Which lines show, however, that the speaker doesn't like to force his thinking on someone else?

3. What is the point of view of the speaker about walls between neighbors? What does the speaker imply about his point of view in lines 1 and 35–36?

4. What is the other person's point of view? How did he arrive at that point of view? What is the meaning of "old-stone savage armed" in line 40 and of "darkness" in line 41?

5. Give examples of "walling in" and "walling out" (line 33). How can walls "give offense"?

6. What larger ideal about human relationships does the poem seem to be suggesting?

7. Although this poem is written in **iambic pentameter,** it has a natural, easygoing, conversational tone. How is that effect achieved?

Mending Wall

ROBERT FROST

Something there is that doesn't love a wall,
That sends the frozen-ground-swell under it
And spills the upper boulders in the sun;
And makes gaps even two can pass abreast.
The work of hunters is another thing: 5
I have come after them and made repair
Where they have left not one stone on a stone,
But they would have the rabbit out of hiding,
To please the yelping dogs. The gaps I mean,
No one has seen them made or heard them made,   10
But at spring mending-time we find them there.
I let my neighbor know beyond the hill;
And on a day we meet to walk the line
And set the wall between us once again.
We keep the wall between us as we go.   15
To each the boulders that have fallen to each.
And some are loaves and some so nearly balls
We have to use a spell to make them balance:
"Stay where you are until our backs are turned!"
We wear our fingers rough with handling them.   20
Oh, just another kind of outdoor game,
One on a side. It comes to little more:
There where it is we do not need the wall:
He is all pine and I am apple orchard.
My apple trees will never get across   25
And eat the cones under his pines, I tell him
He only says, "Good fences make good neighbors."
Spring is the mischief in me, and I wonder
If I could put a notion in his head:
"*Why* do they make good neighbors? Isn't it   30

continued

Where there are cows? But here there are no cows.
Before I built a wall I'd ask to know
What I was walling in or walling out,
And to whom I was like to give offense.
Something there is that doesn't love a wall,   35
That wants it down." I could say "Elves" to him,
But it's not elves exactly, and I'd rather
He said it for himself. I see him there
Bringing a stone grasped firmly by the top
In each hand, like an old-stone savage armed.   40
He moves in darkness as it seems to me,
Not of woods only and the shade of trees
He will not go behind his father's saying,
And he likes having thought of it so well
He says again, "Good fences make good neighbors."   45

Unit Review : THE HUMAN FAMILY

1. Memorable lines   Continue to add to your collection of memorable or quotable lines. From the poems in this unit, select two passages of one line or several. The basis of your selection may be strength of image, music of line, depth of emotion, appeal of theme, or any combination of these. Write the passages in your notebook with title and author. Memorizing the lines will give you added pleasure.

2. Briefly **review the poems** in this unit. Then answer these questions.

    a. Which poem sees in nature a lesson for the human family ideal?

    b. Which poem emphasizes the contributions of many different peoples to American culture?

    c. Which poem sees the destruction of great cities as the most serious loss that comes with war?

    d. Which poem suggests that the "walls" that people construct are against the laws of nature?

    e. Which poem espouses love as the best way of overcoming obstacles to the human family ideal?

3. Show your knowledge of **terms in poetry.** Here are five short passages from the poems in this unit. First, see if you can identify the passage by title and author. Then, choosing from the list of terms below, name the term applicable to the passage.

    alliteration (along with **anticlimax**)   **quatrain**
    iambic pentameter   **simile**
    internal rhyme

    a. "I have come after them and made repair
       Where they have left not one stone on a stone"
       (Title? Author? Term?)

    b. "And crown thy good with brotherhood"
       (Title? Author? Term?)

    c. "poems, paintings, proverbs, porcelain, egg foo yong"
       (Title? Author? Term?)

    d. "Your grief and mine
       Must intertwine
       Like sea and river."
       (Title? Author? Term?)

    e. "In one blaze, will
         All things be gone:
       The Empire State
         And the Parthenon?"
       (Title? Author? Term?)

4. Add to your **vocabulary.** Match the definitions in the right-hand column with the words in the left-hand column.

(1) amber	*a.* spacious
(2) casualties	*b.* magic formula
(3) commodious	*c.* filled with deep feeling
(4) diverse	*d.* cold and distant
(5) flout	*e.* losses in battle
(6) impassioned	*f.* different
(7) heretic	*g.* show contempt for
(8) spell	*h.* yellow
(9) aloof	*i.* struggle against difficulties
(10) stress	*j.* person with dissenting opinions

5. Poems and paintings Poets and painters are artists who have much in common. Study each of the reproductions of paintings that follow. Examine the image carefully. Just what do you see? What feelings does the image arouse in you? What mood or idea does the picture suggest? If a person or persons appear, try to flesh out in your mind their background and character. Is rhythm, metaphor, or symbol important in the picture? After you have studied each picture in this way, select the one that you associate most powerfully in your feelings with one of the poems in this unit. Be ready to discuss or write about your choice and the reasons for it.

Optional: Select one picture that inspires you to write your own poem and write the poem.

Preacher *Charles White. 1952. Whitney Museum, New York.*

To the Lynching! *Paul Cadmus.*
1935. Whitney Museum, New York.

Waving the Flag *George Grosz.*
1947–48. Whitney Museum, New
York.

113

The Emperor   *Abraham Rattner.*
1944. Whitney Museum, New York.

Moonlight   *Joseph Hirsch. 1937.*
Whitney Museum, New York.

114

ECOLOGY

Of all nations, America has been foremost in "progress," and we Americans have been foremost in pride of progress. We have glorified the science, technology, and industry through which we have reshaped the natural environment for the sake of greater comfort and convenience of living. We have exulted in our greater abundance of food, our cars, our planes, our miracle drugs and medical techniques, our plastics and synthetics, our television, our industrial plants, farms, skyscrapers, dams, highways.

However, there has been a jolt. Suddenly we have found that by tinkering with nature, we are tampering with something far more complex and fragile than we realized. We are now faced with appalling ecological crises. Our natural resources are approaching depletion. There is an energy crunch. Our land, our waters, and the very air we breathe are polluted with noxious poisons. The delicate balance of plant and animal life is threatened. Automobiles are causing greater casualties than major wars. Our luxurious foods and our wonderful medicines are damaging our vital organs, our tissues, our cells.

However, nothing is all black or all white. The world is characterized by ambiguity and ambivalence. Yes, nature is beautiful, harmonious, and complex beyond comprehension, but nature is also ruthless and cruel. Nature includes plagues, famines, droughts, floods, earthquakes. Nature is disease and death. Nature is ruled, in part, by the law of brutality, the law of tooth and claw. Yes, science and technology have wrought damage. But few of us would want to go back to cave dwelling; few of us even would want to live in a medieval castle.

As you shall see in the poems of this unit, poets have looked at all sides of the theme of ecology. In their love of the beauty and order of nature, poets have been among the first ecologists. They have long recognized the damage we have done through our science and technology. But poets have also seen the blessings brought by our unique, creative human intelligence as it operates through science and technology.

We have deep feelings about nature. We get pleasure and inspiration from its harmony and beauty. When we can, we go to mountain, to seashore, to lakeside, to bayou, even to the desert to be close to nature's beauty. We try to protect and conserve that beauty in our great parks, and the protection and conservation of that beauty are among the aims of ecology. This poem expresses the writer's intense feelings about the beauty she observes in nature.

DEFINITIONS AND EXPLANATIONS

world (line 1)   The world of nature.

gaunt (line 5)   Bare; grim.

crag (line 5)   A steep, rugged rock mass.

lean (line 6)   Angle; slant.

bluff (line 6)   A cliff.

prithee (line 14)   An archaic word meaning "please" or "I pray thee."

STUDY QUESTIONS

1. What time of year is it? How do you know directly? How do you know by suggestion?

2. Look at the descriptive details of the first **stanza**. In what section of the U. S. is this poem probably set? Why do you think so? To what, in an **apostrophe**, is this stanza addressed?

3. Observing the world about her, the speaker says that she wants to hold it very close, to crush, to lift, and, again, to hold it close. She refers to the woods as aching, almost crying. What **image** does she seem to be suggesting by this **personification?** What is the emotional effect of this image?

4. In what direction does the speaker's emotional state change in the second stanza? (Why does she beg that no burning leaf fall or bird call?) The phrase "burning leaf" is a **metaphor**. Explain why this is so. How is this **image** appropriate to the meaning of the poem? To whom, in an **apostrophe**, is this stanza addressed?

5. Give two examples of **alliteration** from the poem in which the sounds reinforce the emotional force of the words.

6. In each of the stanzas, a pair of relatively short lines are written in a **meter** called **iambic trimeter;** whereas most of the poem is written in a longer line of **iambic pentameter**. What is the effect of the shorter lines?

7. If you were to write a similar poem, what season of the year would you choose and what setting? Why?

God's World

EDNA ST. VINCENT MILLAY

O world, I cannot hold thee close enough!
　　Thy winds, thy wide grey skies!
　　Thy mists, that roll and rise!
Thy woods, this autumn day, that ache and sag
And all but cry with color! That gaunt crag　　　5
To crush! To lift the lean of that black bluff!
World, World, I cannot get thee close enough!

Long have I known a glory in it all,
　　But never knew I this:
　　Here such a passion is　　　10
As stretcheth me apart,—Lord, I do fear
Thou'st made the world too beautiful this year;
My soul is all but out of me,—let fall
No burning leaf; prithee, let no bird call.

Edna St. Vincent Millay responded to the beauty of autumn with almost unbearably intense passion. In this poem, Emily Dickinson writes about exactly the same subject. Her personality was different from Millay's, and her poem makes an interesting contrast with "God's World."

STUDY QUESTIONS _____

1. Explain why "The morns are meeker than they were" (line 1) and why "The Rose is out of town" (line 4).

2. **Personification** is used throughout this poem to describe autumn. Give four examples. What is the general mood conveyed by these descriptions?

3. These **personifications** are used not merely to describe but also to establish a psychological relationship between the speaker and the autumn scene. What is that relationship? What is the effect on the speaker?

4. Emily Dickinson lived much of her life as a recluse, physically isolated from people and society. What does this poem show about the state of mind of the poet in her solitary life?

5. Compare this poem with "God's World." How are they alike? How are they different? Do you prefer one of the poems? If so, which one and why?

The morns are meeker than they were

EMILY DICKINSON

The morns are meeker than they were—
The nuts are getting brown—
The berry's cheek is plumper—
The Rose is out of town.

The Maple wears a gayer scarf—   5
The field a scarlet gown—
Lest I should be old fashioned
I'll put a trinket on.

J ust why does nature move us so deeply with its beauty? In fact, what is beauty? This poem, by one of the giants of American literature, ponders these questions.

DEFINITIONS AND EXPLANATIONS _____

Rhodora (title) A small wild shrub with beautiful purple flowers that bloom in May before the leaves of the plant come out.

nook (line 3) A half-hidden, sheltered spot.

court (line 8) Seek closeness to or the affection of.

sages (line 9) Wise persons.

STUDY QUESTIONS _____

1. How has the speaker been spending his time?

2. Describe the rhodora and the setting in which it is growing. (Give as many visual details as you can. Give sounds, smells, the feel of the air.)

3. How does the rhodora cheapen the array of the red-bird (line 8)?

4. In what sense is the charm of the rhodora "wasted," according to the sages (lines 9–10)?

5. What answer does the speaker give to the question the sages ask?

6. What is the link that brought the speaker and the rhodora together? What bearing does this link have on ecology?

The Rhodora

RALPH WALDO EMERSON

On Being Asked, Whence Is the Flower?

In May, when sea-winds pierced our solitudes,
I found the fresh Rhodora in the woods,
Spreading its leafless blooms in a damp nook,
To please the desert and the sluggish brook.
The purple petals, fallen in the pool,   5
Made the black water with their beauty gay;
Here might the red-bird come his plumes to cool,
And court the flower that cheapens his array.
Rhodora! if the sages ask thee why
This charm is wasted on the earth and sky,   10
Tell them, dear, that if eyes were made for seeing,
Then Beauty is its own excuse for being:
Why thou were there, O rival of the rose!
I never thought to ask, I never knew:
But, in my simple ignorance, suppose   15
The self-same Power that brought me there brought you.

Nature can be seen as having three great divisions: the land, the sea, the sky. Millay, Dickinson, and Emerson wrote mainly about the land in their poems. This short poem is about the sea. The poet paints a picture of a wild sea crashing against a rocky, mountainous shoreline. She sees her picture, however, not with the ordinary eye but with the special vision of the poet.

DEFINITION AND EXPLANATION

Oread (title) In Greek mythology, the realms of nature were guarded by minor goddesses, lovely maidens called nymphs. The Oreads were the nymphs who watched over the mountains. Other nymphs included the Nereids, who protected the Mediterranean Sea, the Naiads, who guarded rivers and streams, and the Dryads, who took care of the trees and forests.

fir (line 6) An evergreen tree similar to a pine.

STUDY QUESTIONS

1. The speaker in this poem is the Oread, the nymph of the mountain against which the stormy sea is raging. How do the great waves appear to her? How do the pools of seawater among the rocks appear?

2. A stormy sea such as this one might be regarded as an alien element, cold and dangerous. What feelings about the sea does this poem evoke? What underlying principle of nature does the poem seem to suggest?

3. This poem is notable for its concise, strong, and singing imagery. Read aloud just the first word of each line of the poem. What is your comment on the **connotation, imagery,** and **sound effects** of these words?

Oread

H. D. (HILDA DOOLITTLE)

Whirl up, sea—
whirl your pointed pines,
splash your great pines
on our rocks,
hurl your green over us,   5
cover us with your pools of fir.

The first and second great divisions of the world of nature are the land and the sea. The third is the sky. In your opinion, which is most strikingly beautiful—the pale blue sky of day with its bright sun and white clouds, the many-colored brilliant sky of sunrise and sunset, or the dark sky of night with its millions of shining stars? This poem is about the night sky.

DEFINITIONS AND EXPLANATIONS

topaz (line 7) A gem of brilliant yellow color.

myriads (line 9) Countless numbers.

aeons (line 11) A period of thousands and thousands of years.

vex (line 12) Annoy; irritate.

stately (line 16) Dignified.

STUDY QUESTIONS

1. The stars have several distinctive characteristics that stir the imagination. Noting these characteristics will help you to understand the spirit of this poem. We usually associate daylight with better vision. How is this reversed in the case of the stars? What does this reversal suggest to you? What quality of the stars is suggested in lines 11 and 12? The stars are so far away that it takes the light from them many years to reach us. Therefore, when we look at the stars, we are bridging the gap of time because we are seeing that which occurred long before we were born. What feelings does this fact stir in you?

2. Where is the speaker standing? What does she see directly around her? What is the quality of the air? Why is the location important? How long does the speaker stand there?

3. Mention several words and phrases that personify the stars. What qualities are given to these "persons" in such words as "Stately" and "majesty"?

4. The speaker chooses a significant word to describe her reaction to the scene she is witnessing. She says she is "honored" (line 18). Why does she make this word choice? In what position does it place the speaker in relation to the scene? What is her state of mind?

5. In what way are the short **stanzas** and **lines,** the simple **rhythms,** and the **alliteration** in lines 4 and 16 appropriate to the mood of this poem? In reading the poem aloud, what voice quality would you use?

6. Grammatically, the whole poem is a single sentence. What is the first main verb and where does it occur? What is the effect of this arrangement?

7. The **diction** of this poem is notable. Can you pick out several words that—perhaps by association, perhaps by sound—make you feel as though you are on that hilltop seeing those stars?

Stars

SARA TEASDALE

Alone in the night
  On a dark hill
With pines around me
  Spicy and still,

And a heaven full of stars   5
  Over my head,
White and topaz
  And misty red;

Myriads with beating
  Hearts of fire   10
That aeons
  Cannot vex or tire;

Up the dome of heaven
  Like a great hill,
I watch them marching   15
  Stately and still,

And I know that I
  Am honored to be
Witness
  Of so much majesty.   20

The American Indian has become an important symbol in our thinking about ecology today. Native Americans are idealized as a people who lived in perfect harmony with their natural environment and were able to satisfy their material needs without despoiling the wealth of the great continent that nourished them. This poem captures the spirit of the traditional relationship between the native American people and their environment.

DEFINITIONS AND EXPLANATIONS

flagons (line 9)   Pitchers; containers for liquid.

cosmetic (line 10)   Beautifying the appearance.

brilliantine (line 11)   An oily hairdressing.

rancid (line 13)   Having the smell of stale oils or fats.

propitiated (line 21)   Sought the good will of; appeased.

martyrs (line 29)   Persons who die for a good cause or principle.

reconciled (line 30)   Made ready to accept or settled differences.

shaman's (line 32)   The shaman is the medicine man. He attempts to influence good and evil spirits.

ritual (line 34)   Performed as a ceremony according to religious law or social custom.

brute (line 34)   Instinctive.

STUDY QUESTIONS

1. The poem names many animal parts and the uses to which Native Americans put them. List as many of these parts as you can and their use.

2. What kind of "music" comes out of the "flute" referred to in line 17? Why did the poet choose this **metaphor?**

3. What is the "need" referred to in line 30? Explain the "shaman's quest" (line 32).

4. What ceremony is described in lines 19–21? What is the purpose of this ceremony? How do Native Americans view their killing of animals as shown by these lines and lines 33–34?

5. Much of this poem is a word painting consisting of various images. Select the **image** that stands out most strikingly to you. Describe it in detail. What colors do you see predominating in this word painting?

6. Suppose this poem were to be read aloud to the accompaniment of music from a single instrument. Which instrument would you choose? Why?

7. How does this traditional Native American society compare with modern, technological society? What are the sharpest differences? What human universals are common to both?

Costume Book
ADRIEN STOUTENBURG

In summer, even chiefs went bare,
though seldom without the pointed jewels
of claws strung into necklaces,
or clacking halos of dead teeth
strung through their black and dancing hair.   5

Beaten hides of bison kept out the cold,
and their swift horns, headgear for warriors,
blazed like new moons turned into bone,
or served as flagons for an antelope's blood,
while the cosmetic bear, crowded with fat,   10
supplied his oozing brilliantine
to blaze on scalps and in a stone lamp's
rancid flame.
                    Oar-shaped, the beaver's tail
flapped from the jerking hems of shirts,   15
while the eagle's hollowed wings
became a puffing painter's flute,
tube for pigments blown like colored smoke
against the borrowed skins of elk and deer
coaxed into shuffling, human shapes—   20
    but all forgiving, propitiated by prayer,
    their furless spirits tumbling in the palm
    of a great father overhead;
    even the fawn, weeping;
    even the caribou, his sinews stretched   25
    through a harsh needle's eye; even the parrot
    plucked of his gaudy sleeves,
    the puma stripped down to her steaming heart,
    the ornamental porcupine—martyrs,
    but reconciled, knowing the need   30
    of naked Sioux and shivering Cherokee,
    the shaman's quest of rattle, pouch, and rib,
    and hearing always, above the arrow's gasp,
    the ritual grunt of brute apology.

We human beings have been proud of our human intelligence. We have been proud of our progress in science, technology, and industry. We have been proud of our ability to change the natural environment to suit our own convenience and purposes. More recently, we have begun to question the wisdom of the changes we have made and are continuing to make. Concern for ecology has grown strong and influential. This poem was written a good many years ago. By contrasting two different kinds of machines, it expresses an early awareness of the ecological problem.

DEFINITIONS AND EXPLANATIONS

gaunt (line 2) Thin and bony, as from starvation.

raucous (line 7) Making a harsh, unpleasant sound.

cleaving (line 10) Splitting apart.

rasping (line 11) Making an unpleasant, grating sound.

turbine (line 25) An engine driven by steam, water, or air.

STUDY QUESTIONS

1. What are the "machines" described in the first **stanza** (lines 1–14)? When are they in operation? Where are they located?

2. Notice the words "gaunt" (line 2) and "muscled" (line 3). What **figure of speech** is the poet using? Give one or two other words or phrases that develop this same figure of speech. What is the total effect of this figure of speech?

3. In the description of these "machines," what sounds are heard? What colors and hues are named? What is the effect of the total **image** on the speaker? What effects on the local environment are mentioned?

4. What is the "machine" described in the second stanza?

5. In the description of the second "machine," what sounds are heard? How do you explain the "whir and beat" mentioned in the last line? What colors are included in this description? How many times does the word "no" occur in this description? What idea is suggested by the use of this negative word? What is the effect of the total **image** on the speaker?

6. What can you infer about the speaker's viewpoint on "machines"?

Machines

DANIEL WHITEHEAD HICKY

I hear them grinding, grinding, through the night,
The gaunt machines with arteries of fire,
Muscled with iron, boweled with smoldering light;
I watch them pulsing, swinging, climbing higher,
Derrick on derrick, wheel on rhythmic wheel,   5
Swift band on whirring band, lever on lever,
Shouting their songs in raucous notes of steel,
Blinding a village with light, damming a river.
I hear them grinding, grinding, hour on hour,
Cleaving the night in twain, shattering the dark   10
With all the rasping torrents of their power,
Groaning and belching spark on crimson spark.
I cannot hear my voice above their cry
Shaking the earth and thundering to the sky.

Slowly the dawn comes up. No motors stir   15
The brightening hilltops as the sunrise flows
In yellow tides where daybreak's lavender
Clings to a waiting valley. No derrick throws
The sun into the heavens and no pulley
Unfolds the wildflowers thirsting for the day;   20
No wheel unravels ferns deep in a gulley;
No engine starts the brook upon its way.
The butterflies drift idly, wing to wing,
Knowing no measured rhythm they must follow;
No turbine drives the white clouds as they swing   25
Across the cool blue meadows of the swallow.
With all the feathered silence of a swan
They whirr and beat—the engines of the dawn.

The literal machines of human science and technology and the metaphorical "machines" of nature are a fertile subject for the imagination of the poet. This poem offers an interesting contrast in content and style to "Machines."

STUDY QUESTIONS

1. What is the first machine described in the poem? How is it fueled? How does it act?

2. What is the second "machine"? How is it fueled? How does it act?

3. What is everybody's reaction to the first machine? to the second?

4. Nowhere does the speaker directly give her own reaction to the two machines or to everybody else's reactions to them. What are her reactions? How do you know?

5. Look at the appearance of the poem on the printed page. What connection do you see between that appearance and the subject matter of the poem?

6. Why do you think the poem is called "Fueled"? Why is this a good title?

7. Although "Machines" and "Fueled" are similar in basic theme, the poets have differed in choice of specific **images,** in choice of language, and in **rhythms.** Do you prefer one of the poems? Why?

8. Hicky and Hans each wrote a poem based on a contrast between a literal, human-made machine and a metaphorical "machine" of nature. Can you suggest another pair of such machines that might make a suitable subject for a poem?

Fueled
MARCIE HANS

Fueled
by a million
man-made
wings of fire—
the rocket tore a tunnel   5
through the sky—
and everybody cheered.
Fueled
only by a thought from God—
the seedling   10
urged its way
through the thicknesses of black—
and as it pierced
the heavy ceiling of the soil—
and launched itself   15
up into outer space—
no
one
even
clapped.   20

The automobile is one of the marvels of the modern age. With its enormous drain on natural resources, its concrete highways, its pollution of the air, and its terrible toll in accidents, the automobile is also one of the foremost ecological problems created by technology. As the title tells you, this poem focuses sharply and dramatically on the last of these problems—automobile accidents. Illness and death are natural. They are as much a part of life as life itself, and, in this sense, are "logical." But, there seems to be something in the killing and maiming caused by auto accidents that is dreadful and unacceptable to most of us. Where there is an auto accident on the open road, a long line of slowed traffic is created merely by the "rubbernecking" of drivers who are stunned and mesmerized by the sight. In the streets, a crowd of pedestrians will quickly gather around the scene of any dreadful accident. The twisted metal and broken glass, the blood and torn flesh will rivet the attention and shrivel the spirits of the beholder in a way different from that of any other disaster. Why?

DEFINITIONS AND EXPLANATIONS

beacons (line 5)   Lights.

deranged (line 15)   Made insane.

douches (line 18)   Washes.

husks (line 21)   Dry, rough, useless outside coverings, as husks of corn.

convalescents (line 24)   People gradually recovering health after an illness.

intimate (line 24)   Close and friendly.

gauche (line 24)   Awkward; lacking poise.

saw (line 26)   Saying; proverb.

banal (line 27)   Commonplace; hackneyed.

resolution (line 27)   A decision to do something.

stillbirth (line 34)   A birth in which the baby is born dead.

occult (line 36)   Beyond understanding; mysterious.

denouement (line 38)   Outcome or solution of the problem of a story.

expedient (line 39)   Convenient; suitable to the circumstances.

STUDY QUESTIONS

1. Who are the speakers (the "we") in this poem?

2. Briefly describe each step in the approach of the ambulance as perceived by the crowd. Why does its bell sound "quick" and "soft"? What makes the crowd see the ambulance "Pulsing out red light like an artery" (line 3)?

3. Who are the "mangled"? What mental effect has the scene had on the crowd? By contrast, how do the cops behave? Why do they behave in this manner?

continued

Auto Wreck

KARL SHAPIRO

Its quick soft silver bell beating, beating,
And down the dark one ruby flare
Pulsing out red light like an artery,
The ambulance at top speed floating down
Past beacons and illuminated clocks   5
Wings in a heavy curve, dips down,
And brakes speed, entering the crowd.
The doors leap open, emptying light;
Stretchers are laid out, the mangled lifted
And stowed into the little hospital.   10
Then the bell, breaking the hush, tolls once,
And the ambulance with its terrible cargo
Rocking, slightly rocking, moves away,
As the doors, an afterthought, are closed.

We are deranged, walking among the cops   15
Who sweep glass and are large and composed.
One is still making notes under the light.
One with a bucket douches ponds of blood
Into the street and gutter.
One hangs lanterns on the wrecks that cling,   20
Empty husks of locusts, to iron poles.

Our throats were tight as tourniquets,
Our feet were bound with splints, but now,
Like convalescents intimate and gauche,
We speak through sickly smiles and warn   25

continued

Auto Wreck

4. Why are the wrecked automobiles described metaphorically as "Empty husks of locusts" (line 21)?

5. How has the scene made the spectators feel physically? How do you explain this? What kinds of remarks do they make as they begin to recover? Can you give a possible example?

6. What do the last seven lines suggest about the differences between death in an auto accident and other ways of dying? Notice the **metaphor** in the last two lines. What has been literally spattered on the stones of the street? What has been figuratively spattered?

7. Have you ever been a close witness to a terrible auto accident? What were your reactions? How long did they last?

With the stubborn saw of common sense,
The grim joke and the banal resolution.
The traffic moves around with care,
But we remain, touching a wound
That opens to our richest horror.   30
Already old, the question Who shall die?
Becomes unspoken Who is innocent?
For death in war is done by hands;
Suicide has cause and stillbirth, logic;
And cancer, simple as a flower, blooms.   35
But this invites the occult mind,
Cancels our physics with a sneer,
And spatters all we knew of denouement
Across the expedient and wicked stones.

We have begun to learn that the "miracles" of science and technology are a mixed blessing. We have learned this lesson in the field of medicine and health where it has become increasingly clear that for the benefits of medicine we pay the price of harmful side effects, sometimes very serious, even life-threatening ones. We have begun to learn that the advantages of such tools as X rays must be weighed against the serious damage they can do. We have begun to recognize that surgeons may have been too ready to perform operations that were neither necessary nor advantageous. More broadly, we have learned that when we tinker with people because of illness, we are at the same time tampering with the underlying processes of life, which are more complicated than we have recognized. In this typically short and brilliant poem, Emily Dickinson shows she recognized all this a long time ago.

DEFINITIONS

incisions (line 3)   Cuts made by a surgeon into tissues and organs.

culprit (line 4)   Guilty person.

STUDY QUESTIONS

1. Read the whole poem aloud, and then close your eyes. What **image** do you see? Describe the picture in every detail. What single line in the poem has played the greatest part in suggesting to you the image you have described?

2. A key word in the meaning of this poem is "Culprit." In what way is "Life" the culprit in this case?

3. What does the speaker really think of the surgeon's "fine incisions"?

4. What relationship between "Life" and illness is the speaker pointing out? What warning does she give to the surgeons, and, by implication, to doctors in general? Do you agree?

Surgeons must be very careful

EMILY DICKINSON

> Surgeons must be very careful
> When they take the knife!
> Underneath their fine incisions
> Stirs the Culprit—*Life!*

The ecological problem of pollution takes many different forms, some less obvious than others. More and more attention is being given to the problem of pollution of the mind, particularly as it results from commercial television, another "blessing" of science and technology. Commercial television is a great pipeline of programs and commercials that pours its contents into virtually every American home and into the minds of the occupants. There is good reason to believe that commercial television is our most important educational force, playing a far more important role than our schools in shaping the mind and character of the American people. Some experts believe that commercial television tends to reduce the habitual viewer to a robotlike creature, whose capacity for thinking and feeling has been reduced to subnormal levels. Practically everybody recognizes the ways in which commercials, with their repetitious deceptions, brainwash viewers. The programs themselves brainwash viewers in somewhat less obvious ways that are alarming more and more concerned people. Howard Nemerov writes about the programs, the commercials, and one television viewer.

DEFINITIONS AND EXPLANATIONS

existential (line 15)   Living without purpose or meaning.

expound (line 20)   Explain; interpret.

global hats (line 26)   Space helmets.

depilatory (line 38)   A commercial product, used by women mainly, for removing unwanted hair from such areas as legs and upper lips.

STUDY QUESTIONS

1. What episode from a television program is described in the first **stanza?** Why do you suppose the viewer sees the incident "rather as normal than sad" (line 7)? There are two instances of **anticlimax** that add to the **irony** of this stanza. What is the anticlimactic reaction of the viewer to the violent smacking down of the "buddy"? What is the anticlimactic reaction of the viewer to the whole scene?

2. What scene, following the commercial, is described in the second stanza? What commercial then follows in the third stanza? How does the viewer feel about the commercial?

continued

A Way of Life

HOWARD NEMEROV

It's been going on a long time.
For instance, these two guys, not saying much, who slog
Through sun and sand, fleeing the scene of their crime,
Till one turns, without a word, and smacks
His buddy flat with the flat of an axe,   5
Which cuts down on the dialogue
Some, but is viewed rather as normal than sad
By me, as I wait for the next ad.

It seems to me it's been quite a while
Since the last vision of blonde loveliness   10
Vanished, her shampoo and shower and general style
Replaced by this lean young lunk-
head parading along with a gun in his back to confess
How yestereve, being drunk
And in a state of existential despair,   15
He beat up his grandma and pawned her invalid chair.

But here at last is a pale beauty
Smoking a filter beside a mountain stream,
Brief interlude, before the conflict of love and duty
Gets moving again, as sheriff and posse expound,   20
Between jail and saloon, the American Dream
Where Justice, after considerable horsing around,
Turns out to be Mercy; when the villain is knocked off,
A kindly uncle offers syrup for my cough.

And now these clean-cut athletic types   25
In global hats are having a nervous debate

continued

A Way of Life

3. What scene is described in the third stanza? What commercial follows?

4. What scene is described in the fourth stanza? What popular kind of program is this scene from? In what way does the line "Somewhere in Space, in an atmosphere of hate" tie together and bring to a strong climax all the scenes described? What commercial follows?

5. Explain the **irony** of the last five lines of the poem. In your explanation, take into account the meaning given to "love" (line 36) and the activities of the viewer.

6. Explain the **irony** of the title and of the first line of the poem.

As they stand between their individual rocket ships
Which have landed, appropriately, on some rocks
Somewhere in Space, in an atmosphere of hate
Where one tells the other to pull up his socks   30
And get going, he doesn't say where; they fade,
And an angel food cake flutters in the void.

I used to leave now and again;
No more. A lot of violence in American life
These days, mobsters and cops all over the scene.   35
But there's a lot of love, too, mixed with the strife,
And kitchen-kindness, like a bedtime story
With rich food and a more kissable depilatory.
Still, I keep my weapons handy, sitting here
Smoking and shaving and drinking the dry beer.   40

On our vast system of superhighways and in our powerful cars, we can travel with amazing speed and comfort. A journey that once would have taken a month now takes hours. What price do we pay for this benefit? Here is one answer.

DEFINITIONS AND EXPLANATIONS

needlepoint (line 5) Skillfully worked embroidery.

bereaved (line 8) Suffering from a serious loss as of love, hope, or happiness.

cynical (line 8) Questioning; pessimistic.

yews (line 8) A variety of evergreen trees.

columbines (line 9) A variety of especially lovely, often admired flowers.

abstract (line 15) Thought of in a general way apart from anything concrete, specific, or particular.

STUDY QUESTIONS

1. The centaur is a creature from ancient mythology with the upper torso of a man and the body of a horse. What comparable picture of a modern person does the title suggest? To what extent is this view justified?

2. What is the "creaking and enormous foot" (line 2) that crushes the clover? In what sense is it "enormous"?

3. What are some of the delicate sights and sounds mentioned that the driver misses as the car eats up the miles on the highway? What can you add? The moss is compared to needlepoint. Why is this an apt **metaphor**? What **personification** is used to describe the brook? In what sense are the yews "bereaved"?

4. What is the rich, intricate, and lovely world around the driver reduced to? What is the only impression that registers on the driver's mind? Why is space abstract to the driver?

5. Explain the last line. In the view of the speaker, what has been the effect of automobiles on the people who drive them?

Eight-Cylinder Man

FLORENCE RIPLEY MASTIN

He grinds the clover at its root
with a creaking and enormous foot.
In his circumference vast and dim
no small life has a place for him.
The needlepoint of curious moss   5
where delicate footprints cross,
the brook composing mountain blues,
the bereaved and cynical yews,
columbines dancing on a wall—
these he has never seen at all.   10

Speed is the only register
within his mind, and in that blur
of gas and gleaming chromium
he adds the swiftly mounting sum
of miles, a purely abstract space,   15
and passes summer face to face.

In order to understand nature better and to reshape it for human benefit, scientists analyze the things of nature; they take them apart. By looking at the parts and the way they work, science aims to understand the whole better. May something be lost by scientific analysis? See what Walt Whitman thinks and whether you agree or disagree with him.

DEFINITION

unaccountable (line 5)   Not explainable.

STUDY QUESTIONS

1. Who is the speaker of this poem? Where is the speaker when the poem opens (lines 1–5)? What is the speaker listening to? What is the speaker shown?

2. What is the effect of the lecture on the others in the audience? What is the effect on the speaker? What **repetition** reflects the speaker's mood? What does the speaker do? What is the result of the speaker's action upon his mood? Which alliterated phrase reflects the speaker's changed mood?

3. Which word in the poem suggests that the speaker subconsciously senses that the whole of a thing in nature is greater than the sum of its parts and that something hard to define is lost in the process of scientific analysis?

4. Do you agree or disagree with the point of view expressed in this poem? Why?

When I Heard the Learn'd Astronomer

WALT WHITMAN

When I heard the learn'd astronomer,
When the proofs, the figures, were ranged in columns
    before me,
When I was shown the charts and diagrams, to add,
    divide, and measure them,
When I, sitting, heard the astronomer where he lectured
    with much applause in the lecture room,
How soon unaccountable I became tired and sick,   5
Till rising and gliding out I wandered off by myself,
In the mystical moist night air, and from time to time,
Looked up in perfect silence at the stars.

In the story of the growth of modern civilization, the scientist is a giant who has wrought vast changes at an ever-accelerating pace. For a long time, the scientist was worshipped as a hero, a benefactor, a savior. Then, as a result of brilliant work in mathematics and nuclear physics, came a bomb, the atomic bomb. The bomb was something new. Its immediate destructiveness is terrible to contemplate. Worse even are its "residual qualities" of fallout and contamination, whose range is far beyond the intended target, whose effects are a threat to the very existence of the human race. Since Hiroshima, the scientist is viewed by some with something less than the former reverence.

DEFINITIONS AND EXPLANATIONS

Attila (title) Attila was a king of an ancient tribe of barbarians, the Huns. Called the Scourge of God, Attila launched destructive wars on the civilizations of central Europe and on Rome.

myth (line 1) Imaginary picture of a person.

specs (line 3) Eyeglasses; spectacles.

furtive (line 4) Secretive.

mortar-board cap (line 5) The academic cap worn by college professors and students on ceremonious occasions.

medieval gown (line 6) The black gown is worn along with the mortar-board cap. The cap and gown as a costume are a symbol of learning and of the highest achievements of civilized society.

abstractions (line 15) Principles; concepts.

residual (line 18) Describing what is left after a process is completed, as ash after a fire or fallout after an atomic explosion.

STUDY QUESTIONS

1. The mythical Professor Attila is described in the first two **stanzas** of the poem. Give the details of the professor's appearance, personal mannerisms, and behavior. What kind of person, in general, was this Professor Attila imagined to be?

2. "They didn't think it, eh professor?" (line 7). Who is "they"? What is it, exactly, that "they" didn't think?

3. What picture is given of the new Professor Attila in the third stanza? What do the professor's quoted words (lines 17–18) add to this real picture of him? What force does the **allusion** contained in the professor's name add to the real picture of him?

4. Sandburg typically gives much of his poetry a highly special flavor by mixing colorful slang expressions with highly literary language and by introducing broad humor in a very serious context. Give examples of each of these **antitheses** of style.

5. Do you feel that the atomic scientists responsible for the bomb deserve the fierce rebuke of this poem or not? Justify your answer. Has the work of other kinds of scientists posed similar problems?

6. Some people argue that the atomic bomb is a blessing in disguise. They say that atomic weaponry has made it impossible to win a worldwide war, that the world leaders know it, and that for that reason we have not had a third world war and probably will not have one. What do you think? What do you think Sandburg would say?

Mr. Attila
CARL SANDBURG

They made a myth of you, professor,
    you of the gentle voice,
    the books, the specs,
    the furtive rabbit manners
    in the mortar-board cap   5
    and the medieval gown.

They didn't think it, eh professor?
On account of you're so absent-minded,
you bumping into the tree and saying,
"Excuse me, I thought you were a tree,"   10
passing on again blank and absent-minded.

Now it's "Mr. Attila, *how* do you do?"
Do you pack wallops of wholesale death?
Are you the practical dynamic son-of-a-gun?
Have you come through with a few abstractions?   15
Is it you Mr. Attila we hear saying,
"I beg your pardon but we believe we have made some
    degree of progress on the residual qualities of the atom"?

In this poem, the speaker is on a train traveling at high speed in the night. The experience itself has many similarities to that of the automobile driver in "Eight-Cylinder Man." However, people react to similar experiences in diverse ways, as you will see in this poem.

DEFINITIONS AND EXPLANATIONS

Pullman (line 3) A railroad car with sleeping berths for overnight journeys.

bleak (line 10) Bare and desolate.

ravines (line 18) Long deep hollows in the earth's surface.

gullies (line 19) Channels; narrow ravines.

STUDY QUESTIONS

1. In which part of the U.S. is the train traveling? Why is this significant?

2. There are three kinds of **imagery** in this poem: visual (things seen), auditory (things heard), and kinesthetic (things felt in the muscles and nerves of the body). List several examples of each type.

3. Many of the lines suggest the high speed of the train. Give a few examples. The basic **meter** of the poem is **iambic trimeter.** How is that meter appropriate to the poem?

4. What are the speaker's main feelings? What creates those feelings?

5. In "Eight-Cylinder Man" and other poems that you have read in this unit, science and technology have been seen as being in conflict with nature. What is the view in this poem? Can you suggest examples of other aspects of science and technology or their products that might form the subject matter for poems with a view similar to that of "Night Journey"?

Night Journey
THEODORE ROETHKE

Now as the train bears west,
Its rhythm rocks the earth,
And from my Pullman berth
I stare into the night
While others take their rest.　　　5
Bridges of iron lace,
A suddenness of trees,
A lap of mountain mist
All cross my line of sight,
Then a bleak wasted place,　　　10
And a lake below my knees.
Full on my neck I feel
The straining at a curve;
My muscles move with steel,
I wake in every nerve.　　　15
I watch a beacon swing
From dark to blazing bright;
We thunder through ravines
And gullies washed with light.
Beyond the mountain pass　　　20
Mist deepens on the pane;
We rush into a rain
That rattles double glass.
Wheels shake the roadbed stone,
The pistons jerk and shove,　　　25
I stay up half the night
To see the land I love.

What is the final estimate that we should make of "progress," of the changes wrought by science and technology, of the resulting ecological problems? Looking at the whole picture, should we be optimistic or pessimistic? Carl Sandburg looked at one part of the complex picture in "Mr. Attila" and gave us his reaction. This excerpt tells you how Sandburg feels about the whole story of the workings of human intelligence.

DEFINITIONS AND EXPLANATIONS

parallels (line 13) The imaginary lines, parallel to the equator, drawn on a map to show distance from the equator (degrees of latitude).

meridians (line 13) The imaginary lines drawn around the earth, running through the North and South Poles, that show degrees of longitude.

wrangling (line 14) Quarreling angrily.

reciprocals (line 47) Interacting parts; things having corresponding but reversed actions.

STUDY QUESTIONS

1. The "wheel" mentioned in the opening four lines is metaphorical. It stands for something besides itself. Explain the **metaphor.**

2. Who is the speaker of the quoted statement in lines 5–8? What view of the human race is expressed?

3. Study the third **stanza** (lines 9–17). What is suggested about "the people" and their story by such **images** as "fog gray" and "smoke red" and "lost on parallels and meridians"? Why are the words "My heart was made to be broken" (line 17) spoken with a laugh?

4. Who are the speakers of the quoted words in the fourth **stanza** (line 18 and line 21)? How are they shown to be wrong?

5. The wheel is mentioned again in lines 34–36, this time literally. Why is the wheel important? How does Sandburg describe the creative process, the process of invention, in these lines and in lines 37–40?

6. Notice the series of **images** and the **rhythms** of lines 44–47. What word would you use to sum up the combined effect of these images and rhythms?

7. What kind of answer does the whole poem suggest to the last two questions— "Where to? what next?"

8. Some people find it easy to arrive at answers to difficult problems because they are not realistic. They oversimplify and see only what they wish to see in order to arrive at the answer they want. In this poem, Sandburg has tackled the difficult question of human destiny. Has he been realistic or not in arriving at his answer?

The Wheel Turns
from *The People, Yes*

CARL SANDBURG

The wheel turns.
The wheel comes to a standstill.
The wheel waits.
The wheel turns.

"Something began me
and it had no beginning: 5
something will end me
and it has no end."

The people is a long shadow
trembling around the earth,   10
stepping out of fog gray into smoke red
and back from smoke red into fog gray
and lost on parallels and meridians
learning by shock and wrangling,
by heartbreak so often and loneliness so raw   15
the laugh comes at least half true,
"My heart was made to be broken."

"Man will never write,"
they said before the alphabet came
and man at last began to write.   20
"Man will never fly,"
they said before the planes and blimps
zoomed and purred in arcs
winding their circles around the globe.

"Man will never make the United States of Europe   25
nor later yet the United States of the World,

continued

"No, you are going too far when you talk about one
    world flag for the great Family of Nations,"
    they say that now.

And man the stumbler and finder, goes on,   30
    man the dreamer of deep dreams,
    man the shaper and maker,
    man the answerer.
The first wheel maker saw a wheel, carried
in his head a wheel, and one day found his   35
hands shaping a wheel, the first wheel.
The first wagon makers saw a wagon, joined
their hands and out of air, out of what
had lived in their minds, made the first
wagon.   40
One by one man alone and man joined
has made things with his hands
beginning in the fog wisp of a dim imagining
resulting in a tool, a plan, a working model,
    bones joined to breath being alive   45
in wheels within wheels, ignition, power,
transmission, reciprocals, beyond man alone,
alive only with man joined.
            Where to? what next?

Unit Review : ECOLOGY

1. **Memorable lines** Continue to add to your collection of memorable or quotable lines. From the poems in this unit, select two passages of one line or several. The basis of your selection may be strength of image, music of line, depth of emotion, appeal of theme, or any combination of these. Write the passages in your notebook with title and author. Memorizing the lines will give you added pleasure.

2. Briefly **review the poems** in this unit. Then answer these questions.

   a. Name two poems that celebrate the beauty of nature in autumn.
   b. Which poem sees unity in the natural beauty of land and sea?
   c. Which poem would appeal especially to those who are concerned with the conservation of wildlife?
   d. Which poem would appeal especially to the supporters of public television?
   e. Some people see human science and technology as pure villain and nature as pure hero. Name one poem that suggests that such a view is an oversimplification.

3. Show your knowledge of **terms in poetry**. Here are five short passages from the poems in this unit. First, see if you can identify the passage by title and author. Then, choosing from the list of terms below, name the term applicable to the passage.

   metaphor   **anticlimax**
   iambic trimeter   **personification**
   kinesthetic imagery

   a. "Thy winds, thy wide grey skies!
      Thy mists that roll and rise!"
      (Title? Author? Term?)

   b. "The Maple wears a gayer scarf"
      (Title? Author? Term?)

   c. "One hangs lanterns on the wrecks that cling,
      Empty husks of locusts, to iron poles."
      (Title? Author? Term?)

   d. "Till one turns, without a word, and smacks
      His buddy flat with the flat of an axe,
      Which cuts down on the dialogue
      Some, but is viewed rather as normal than sad
      By me, as I wait for the next ad."
      (Title? Author? Term?)

e. "Full on my neck I feel
　　The straining at a curve;
　　My muscles move with steel,
　　I wake in every nerve."

　　(Title? Author? Term?)

4. Add to your **vocabulary**. Match the definitions in the right-hand column with the words in the left-hand column.

(1) sages	*a.* awkward
(2) myriads	*b.* appeased
(3) flagons	*c.* wise persons
(4) propitiated	*d.* convenient
(5) raucous	*e.* made insane
(6) deranged	*f.* containers for liquid
(7) gauche	*g.* countless numbers
(8) expedient	*h.* secretive
(9) expound	*i.* harsh-sounding
(10) furtive	*j.* explain

5. Poems and paintings Poets and painters are artists who have much in common. Study each of the reproductions of paintings that follow. Examine the image carefully. Just what do you see? What feelings does the image arouse in you? What mood or idea does the picture suggest? If a person or persons appear, try to flesh out in your mind their background and character. Is rhythm, metaphor, or symbol important in the picture? After you have studied each picture in this way, select the one that you associate most powerfully in your feelings with one of the poems in this unit. Be ready to discuss or write about your choice and the reasons for it.

Optional: Select one picture that inspires you to write your own poem and write the poem.

Express Train *Thomas Hart Benton. 1924. Whitney Museum, New York.*

Two Fighting Hummingbirds with Two Orchids   *Martin J. Heade. 1875.*
Whitney Museum, New York.

Blast Furnace—Number 2
Thomas Hart Benton. 1929.
Whitney Museum, New York.

The Great Wave at Kanagawa *Katsushika Hokusai. 1823–29. The Metropolitan Museum of Art, The Howard Mansfield Collection, Rogers Fund, 1936.*

The Beach *William Baziotes. 1955. Whitney Museum, New York.*

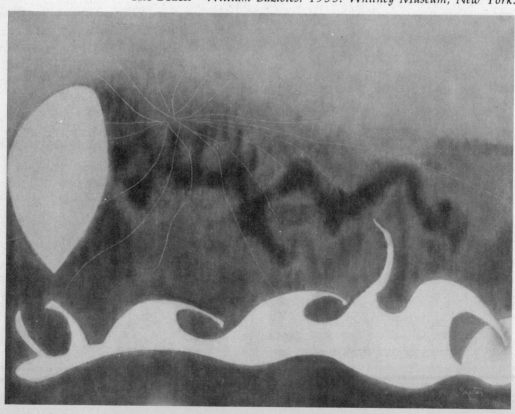

VALUES

"It is easier for a camel to go through
the eye of a needle, than for a rich man
to enter into the kingdom of God."

New Testament

"And now abideth faith, hope, charity, these three:
but the greatest of these is charity."

New Testament

"A crowd is not company, and faces are
but a gallery of pictures, and talk but a
tinkling cymbal, where there is no love."

Francis Bacon

"Beauty is truth, truth beauty,—that is all
Ye know on earth, and all ye need to know."

John Keats

As these quotations and many others from our prophets, poets, and sages illustrate, there is an ancient and universal human need for belief in great and basic "laws of life." We need values—moral, ethical, and spiritual convictions—to guide us and uplift us.

We need values to guide us in our everyday actions, choices, and decisions. We need values to give a deep meaning and purpose to our short and difficult existence. We need values for a sense of inner harmony and peace of mind. We need values to teach us how to live "the good life."

What about values in America? Americans have been a practical people, busy with material progress, with the production of wealth, with building, making, spending, with "getting ahead" and "keeping up with the Joneses." Just as surely as these tendencies have dominated American life, so has a sense of dissatisfaction gnawed at the American heart. Among our writers and thinkers and among ordinary people, there has been a sense of emptiness, of something missing. There has been a yearning for a new and better set of values.

What have our poets had to say?

In humanity's system of values, truth ranks at the top. Everybody will say that truth is good and right. How many will act that way? And there are more questions. Do people really want truth or do they prefer to be left alone, to be comfortable? Is truth, in any event, always good and right? Finally, do we know what truth is altogether?

STUDY QUESTIONS

1. In the first **stanza,** truth and untruth are represented by **symbols.** What are the symbols?

2. Which lines tell you how people have felt about the truth? What are the "night-years" (line 9)?

3. The character of truth is suggested in a **personification** in the second stanza. How is truth characterized?

4. A contrasting picture is given of the absence of truth in lines 16–21. Give a number of key words and phrases that help to sketch this picture.

5. The speaker has suggested a difficult choice, a dilemma. To find out where she stands, look carefully at the words of the last two lines. What does the speaker finally seem to be suggesting about the choice between truth and untruth?

6. The poet uses the music of **repetition** to give emotional intensity to her words. Give some examples.

7. Gwendolyn Brooks is a distinguished black poet. What comment may she be making to Americans in this poem about the racial problem?

8. In the next column is a poem entitled "Mirror" by Sylvia Plath. The "speaker" is a mirror. What is the mirror a **symbol** of? How does the woman in the poem feel about the mirror?

I am silver and exact. I have no
    preconceptions.
Whatever I see I swallow
    immediately
Just as it is, unmisted by love or
    dislike.
I am not cruel, only truthful—
The eye of a little god, four-
    cornered.   5
Most of the time I meditate on the
    opposite wall.
It is pink, with speckles. I have
    looked at it so long
I think it is a part of my heart. But it
    flickers.
Faces and darkness separate us over
    and over.

Now I am a lake. A woman bends
    over me,   10
Searching my reaches for what she
    really is.
Then she turns to those liars, the
    candles or the moon.
I see her back, and reflect it
    faithfully.
She rewards me with tears and an
    agitation of hands.
I am important to her. She comes
    and goes.   15
Each morning it is her face that
    replaces the darkness.
In me she has drowned a young girl,
    and in me an old woman
Rises toward her day after day, like
    a terrible fish.

Truth

GWENDOLYN BROOKS

And if sun comes
How shall we greet him?
Shall we not dread him,
Shall we not fear him
After so lengthy a   5
Session with shade?

Though we have wept for him,
Though we have prayed
All through the night-years—
What if we wake one shimmering morning to   10
Hear the fierce hammering
Of his firm knuckles
Hard on the door?

Shall we not shudder?—
Shall we not flee   15
Into the shelter, the dear thick shelter
Of the familiar
Propitious haze?

Sweet is it, sweet is it
To sleep in the coolness   20
Of snug unawareness.

The dark hangs heavily
Over the eyes.

This poem is among the most widely read and best known of all American poems. Why? In briefest form, it tells a dramatic story with interesting characters and a shocker of a surprise ending. It is stated in finely etched language. Above all, it is mind-boggling; it puzzles and makes the reader think and probe in dark corners.

DEFINITIONS AND EXPLANATIONS

sole to crown (line 3)   Foot to head.

Clean favored (line 4)   Having fine, handsome features.

imperially (line 4)   Majestically; aristocratically.

arrayed (line 5)   Dressed in fine clothing.

grace (line 10)   A sense of what is right and proper; charming and pleasing behavior.

in fine (line 11)   In conclusion.

STUDY QUESTIONS

1. Who are the speakers (look especially at lines 2, 13, 14) of the poem? What is their condition of life? Why do they curse the bread? What is the light they are waiting for?

2. Where do you imagine Richard Cory is coming *from* when he comes downtown? How does he act toward the people? How do they feel toward him? (Notice that line 11 says "we thought that he *was* everything" rather than "we thought that he *had* everything.")

3. Give all the key phrases that tell you something about Richard Cory's personality, background, and appearance, and explain them.

4. The picture of Richard Cory is given depth by the **diction** of the poem, the **connotations** of the carefully chosen words. For example, instead of "head to foot," the poet says "sole to crown." What is the **denotation** of "crown" in this use? What is its connotation? What

specific overall **image** is suggested by the connotation of "crown," "gentleman," "Clean favored," "imperially," "arrayed," "glittered," "king," "schooled," "grace," "In fine"? What bearing does this image have on the probable facts of Richard Cory's background and life?

5. The last line is a shocker because of its surprising content, which contrasts with everything that has been said before. How is the force of the shock added to by the **image**, the **diction**, the **rhythms**, and the **rhyme** of the line?

6. A startling **irony** underlies the poem. Despite their condition of life, the people worked on and waited for the light. Despite Richard Cory's condition of life—all the material and personal gifts he had—he chose to end his life with a bullet. What is your reaction?

7. What comment on values may the poem be making?

Richard Cory

EDWIN ARLINGTON ROBINSON

Whenever Richard Cory went down town,
We people on the pavement looked at him:
He was a gentleman from sole to crown,
Clean favored, and imperially slim.

And he was always quietly arrayed,   5
And he was always human when he talked;
But still he fluttered pulses when he said,
"Good-morning," and he glittered when he walked.

And he was rich—yes, richer than a king—
And admirably schooled in every grace: 10
In fine, we thought that he was everything
To make us wish that we were in his place.

So on we worked, and waited for the light,
And went without the meat, and cursed the bread;
And Richard Cory, one calm summer night,   15
Went home and put a bullet through his head.

In each new generation of young people, it seems that there are those who revolt against the values of the older generation. In recent years, some young people have sought more satisfying values in the form of a simpler, more natural way of life. They have expressed this yearning in their dress, in their hairstyles, in their eating habits, in their musical preferences. They have sought to work with their hands and some have even "returned to the soil" to meet their own needs by their own labor. That life-style and the values that govern it are not new, of course, as this poem about a member of a much older generation shows.

DEFINITIONS AND EXPLANATIONS

Lucinda Matlock (title) This is another poem from *Spoon River Anthology*. Remember that the speaker has died and is looking back on and evaluating her life.

Chandlerville (line 1) and **Winchester** (line 2) These are towns in western Illinois, the region in which *Spoon River Anthology* is set.

snap-out (line 2) Dancers formed two circles, an inner and an outer. They skipped by each other in opposite directions. At a signal, a young man would claim the girl of his choice by snapping her through the circle. The purpose of many such rural folk dances was courting.

medicinal weed (line 14) Many natural herbs and other plants have medicinal properties; others have been thought to have such properties, which they may or may not have. Most folk remedies are based on the use of such herbs and plants.

repose (line 17) Rest.

degenerate (line 20) Sunk to a lower level; deteriorated.

STUDY QUESTIONS

1. What are the two memories of her youth that stand out in Lucinda's mind? What do these show about her both as a young person and in her later years? How did she meet her future husband?

2. What is the evidence that Lucinda lived a simple and self-reliant life? What hardships and losses did she face? How does she seem to have reacted to these hardships and difficulties?

3. How do you explain Lucinda's "shouting" and "singing" (line 15)? Why does she say "that is all" (line 16)?

4. Apparently, the younger generation had feelings different from Lucinda's— "anger, discontent, drooping hopes" (line 19). How do you account for this change?

5. In the last line, Lucinda tells the younger people, "It takes life to love Life." What does she mean?

6. In the introduction to this poem, reference was made to the young people of today who have sought to return to a set of values similar to Lucinda's. However, what differences are there between Lucinda and these young people?

7. Have you read Thornton Wilder's famous play *Our Town?* How does the theme of that play compare with the theme of "Lucinda Matlock"?

Lucinda Matlock

EDGAR LEE MASTERS

I went to the dances at Chandlerville,
And played snap-out at Winchester.
One time we changed partners,
Driving home in the moonlight of middle June,
And then I found Davis.   5
We were married and lived together for seventy years,
Enjoying, working, raising the twelve children,
Eight of whom we lost
Ere I had reached the age of sixty.
I spun, I wove, I kept the house, I nursed the sick,   10
I made the garden, and for holiday
Rambled over the fields where sang the larks,
And by Spoon River gathering many a shell,
And many a flower and medicinal weed—
Shouting to the wooded hills, singing to the green valleys.   15
At ninety-six I had lived enough, that is all,
And passed to a sweet repose.
What is this I hear of sorrow and weariness,
Anger, discontent and drooping hopes?
Degenerate sons and daughters,   20
Life is too strong for you—
It takes life to love Life.

In many senses, Lucinda Matlock was a typical American. In one important sense, she was quite untypical. Americans characteristically set great store by "success," particularly the material success of money, power, and fame, and the status symbols that go with them. In the admiring picture he sketched of Lucinda, Masters was speaking out against the American ethic of success. In this poem, Ogden Nash speaks out on the same theme, but with his own unique voice.

DEFINITIONS AND EXPLANATIONS

Kindly Unhitch That Star, Buddy (title) In one of his essays, Emerson wrote, "Hitch your wagon to a star." The statement has become widely known and is used as a proverb. It is often interpreted to mean "Be ambitious for great success," though that was not quite what Emerson had in mind.

azalea (line 2) A beautiful flowering shrub.

celestial (line 3) Heavenly.

archangels (line 3) Angels of the chief rank.

cherubim (line 3) An order of angels of high rank. Note that the word is of Hebrew origin. The singular is "cherub" and the plural is formed by adding the suffix "im."

seraphim (line 3) An order of angels of high rank. Note that the singular is "seraph" and the plural is formed as in the case of "cherub."

process-servers (line 4) Low-level officers of a judicial court, who deliver summonses or other court orders.

bailiffim (line 4) A bailiff is an officer of the court, assistant to the sheriff. The actual plural of the word is "bailiffs."

sheriffim (line 4) The sheriff is the chief law enforcement officer of a county. The plural is "sheriffs."

Palm Beach (line 9) A Florida resort for the super-rich.

Ritz (line 9) A Parisian hotel, long known as one of the most elegant and expensive in the world.

STUDY QUESTIONS

1. Cite two lines that show you that Nash is writing about material success.

2. Which single line of the poem sums up most forthrightly what the poet thinks of success and the effects of success? In your own words, what does the line say?

3. Look at the first line again. In what way are the successes and failures really the same people? What alternative is there?

4. Explain the humor of the second line.

5. Explain the humor of the phrase "run-of-the-mill angels" (line 3).

6. The poem illustrates Nash's genius for finding startling **rhymes** in existing words and for fashioning rhymes out of nonexistent word forms and spellings. Give at least one example of each.

7. Give one example from the poem of those who seek success by saying "yes" and one example of those who seek success by saying "no."

8. Do you think Lucinda Matlock would have enjoyed reading this poem? Why or why not?

Kindly Unhitch That Star, Buddy

OGDEN NASH

I hardly suppose I know anybody who wouldn't rather be a success
    than a failure,
Just as I suppose every piece of crabgrass in the garden would much
    rather be an azalea,
And in celestial circles all the run-of-the-mill angels would rather be
    archangels or at least cherubim and seraphim,
And in the legal world all the little process-servers hope to grow up
    into great big bailiffim and sheriffim.
Indeed, everybody wants to be a wow,   5
But not everybody knows exactly how.
Some people think they will eventually wear diamonds instead of
    rhinestones
Only by everlastingly keeping their noses to their grhinestones,
And other people think they will be able to put in more time at Palm
    Beach and the Ritz
By not paying too much attention to attendance at the office but
    rather in being brilliant by starts and fits.   10
Some people after a full day's work sit up all night getting a college
    education by correspondence,
While others seem to think they'll get just as far by devoting their
    evenings to the study of the difference in temperament between
    brunettance and blondance.
Some stake their all on luck,
And others put their faith in their ability to pass the buck.
In short, the world is filled with people trying to achieve success,   15
And half of them think they'll get it by saying No and half of them
    by saying Yes,
And if all the ones who say No said Yes, and vice versa, such is the
    fate of humanity that ninety-nine per cent of them still wouldn't
    be any better off then they were before,
Which perhaps is just as well because if everybody was a success
    nobody could be contemptuous of anybody else and
    everybody would start in all over again trying to be a bigger
    success than everybody else so they would have somebody
    to be contemptuous of and so on forevermore,
Because when people start hitching their wagons to a star,
That's the way they are.   20

A sense of joy in being alive, a sense of being delighted to be one's self—these are states of mind that practically everybody seeks, but all too few achieve. What value or values may lead to that state of mind? Certainly one such value is beauty, in one of the many forms that beauty takes. Here, with a twinkle in her eye, Emily Dickinson tells of the effect on her mind of the beauty of nature during a glorious summer day and suggests to us the importance of nature's beauty in her value system.

DEFINITIONS AND EXPLANATIONS

tankards (line 2) Large drinking cups with handles.

inebriate (line 5) Made drunk; feeling exhilarated.

debauchee (line 6) A person who indulges the appetite for sensual pleasure to an extreme.

foxglove's (line 10) Of a plant that bears many thimble-shaped flowers on long stalks.

renounce (line 11) Give up; swear off.

drams (line 11) Small drinks of alcohol.

tippler (line 15) Drunkard.

STUDY QUESTIONS

1. This poem is an **extended metaphor,** in which the poet speaks of herself as though she were finding joy on a drunken spree. Give as many as you can of the words or phrases that help to build the metaphorical **image** of a drunk on a spree. Who are some of the speaker's "drinking" companions? What does mention of these companions add to the effect of the image?

2. What is really making the speaker feel so "high"? Mention some specifics.

3. The **extended metaphor** of this poem is unusual and joyously comic. Why?

4. The "spree" comes to its climax in the last **stanza.** What audience gathers to see the "drunkard"? Why is this audience humorously incongruous to the figurative meaning of the poem but appropriate to its literal meaning? Just how "high" does the drunkard finally feel?

5. Go back to "Lucinda Matlock" for a moment. Which lines tell you of a time that Lucinda was feeling a "high" similar to that of the speaker in this poem? Was she "drunk" on the same "beverage"?

6. Is this poem real to you? Have you ever felt intoxicated or exalted by any contact you have had with natural beauty? If so, when? Has some other form of beauty ever had this kind of effect on you? When?

7. Do you think the words of this poem could readily be used as the lyrics of a song? Why?

I taste a liquor never brewed

EMILY DICKINSON

I taste a liquor never brewed,
From tankards scooped in pearl;
Not all the vats upon the Rhine
Yield such an alcohol!

Inebriate of air am I,   5
And debauchee of dew,
Reeling, through endless summer days,
From inns of molten blue.

When landlords turn the drunken bee
Out of the foxglove's door,   10
When butterflies renounce their drams,
I shall but drink the more!

Till seraphs swing their snowy hats,
And saints to windows run,
To see the little tippler   15
Leaning against the sun!

As a basic value in life, beauty can act in several ways. Often, beauty serves people as an intense expression of their own feelings and experience. It is the high point of all the richness and joy that life has to offer. However, most of us have moments when we are feeling down —depressed and unhappy. At such times, beauty can be a welcome escape, a relief from the pain, sadness, or worry we are feeling. The beauty of music has probably provided you with such escape and relief, as it does for the speaker of this poem.

DEFINITIONS AND EXPLANATIONS

Beethoven (title)   Ludwig van Beethoven is regarded by many as the greatest of all composers of classical music, and his symphonies are among the supreme works of art of the world.

plausible   (line 4)   Acceptable; trustworthy.

benign (line 5)   Kindly.

scullions (line 8)   The lowest servants in the medieval castle, who did the rough work in the kitchen.

tranquil (line 10)   Serene; placid.

tortured (line 10)   Twisted; distorted.

rampart (line 14)   Protective wall of a castle or fort.

STUDY QUESTIONS

1. In the **apostrophe** in the opening lines, to whom or what does the speaker address her request? What is the request?

2. The speaker suggests that there are two worlds—the outside world of real life and the world created by the music. How does she feel about each of these worlds? Give two or three words or phrases from the poem that show her feelings about each world.

3. You probably know the famous fairy tale of "The Sleeping Beauty." In the tale, the whole castle is enchanted. Time stands still. There is no aging, no death. All is harmonious and peaceful. Cite all the words and phrases you can from the poem that suggest that the poet is comparing her experience with the music to the atmosphere of the enchanted castle in "The Sleeping Beauty." Which line tells you that the escape to the enchanted world cannot last?

4. Explain the **metaphor** in lines 9 and 10. Which flower best fits the **image?** Why?

5. The intricate **imagery** of this poem is woven into the strict confines of the **verse form** known as the **sonnet.** Determine the **rhyme scheme.** Is this an English sonnet or an Italian sonnet?

6. For Emily Dickinson, beauty is the expression of life. For Millay, in this poem, beauty is an escape from life. Whose vision of beauty appeals to you more? Why?

On Hearing a Symphony of Beethoven
EDNA ST. VINCENT MILLAY

Sweet sounds, oh, beautiful music, do not cease!
Reject me not into the world again.
With you alone is excellence and peace,
Mankind made plausible, his purpose plain.
Enchanted in your air benign and shrewd,   5
With limbs a-sprawl and empty faces pale,
The spiteful and the stingy and the rude
Sleep like the scullions in the fairy-tale.

This moment is the best the world can give:
The tranquil blossom on the tortured stem.   10
Reject me not, sweet sounds! oh, let me live,
Till Doom espy my towers and scatter them,
A city spell-bound under the aging sun.
Music my rampart, and my only one.

What makes life worthwhile? What values bring a sense of fulfillment and peace, a sense of deep and satisfying meaning to existence despite the pain, hardship, and struggle we all experience?
Richard Cory found no answer to these questions and could not go
on living. Lucinda Matlock found meaning in the everyday struggle
itself, in the challenges bravely met, win or lose. The speaker of Emily
Dickinson's poem saw beauty all around her and found her answer
in the sense of ecstasy inspired by this beauty. The speaker of Edna St.
Vincent Millay's poem saw everyday life as a painful experience from
which beauty provided temporary escape and forgetfulness. The
speaker in this poem sees both the hard painful struggle and the joy
of uplifting beauty. She sees life, as suggested by the title "Barter," as
an exchange, a trade. You pay the price of pain for the ecstasy of
beauty. Does the speaker profit from this barter? Does she get the
better of the bargain?

STUDY QUESTIONS

1. Three lines of the poem repeat the
"barter" theme of the title, almost as a
refrain. What are the three lines? What is
the "barter" or "trade" the speaker is pro-
posing? Cite a pair of lines that tells you
that the speaker is satisfied that she has
gotten the better of the trade.

2. Emily Dickinson reveled especially in
the beauty of nature and Edna St. Vincent
Millay in the beauty of music. Give lines
in which each of these two forms of beauty
is mentioned in this poem. Give lines
from this poem that cite three other forms
of beauty.

3. Of the forms of beauty mentioned in the
poem, which has most appeal for you personally? Why? Can you give two other
forms of beauty which you prefer that are
not mentioned in this poem? (Think of
actual examples.)

4. Notice the **simile** in line 8. To express
the beauty of music, an **image** is created
containing a shape (a curve) and a material (gold). Why is the shape appropriate?
Why is the material?

5. What is the **rhyme scheme** of the three
stanzas? How does this rhyme scheme fit
the mood of the poem?

Barter

SARA TEASDALE

Life has loveliness to sell,
  All beautiful and splendid things,
Blue waves whitened on a cliff,
  Soaring fire that sways and sings,
And children's faces looking up   5
Holding wonder like a cup.

Life has loveliness to sell,
  Music like a curve of gold,
Scent of pine trees in the rain,
  Eyes that love you, arms that hold,   10
And for your spirit's still delight,
Holy thoughts that star the night.

Spend all you have for loveliness,
  Buy it and never count the cost;
For one white singing hour of peace   15
  Count many a year of strife well lost,
And for a breath of ecstasy
Give all you have been, or could be.

The "work ethic" is one of the threads that has run through the fabric of the American system of values. According to the "work ethic," one of the greatest personal rewards comes from dedication to one's occupation or job. Fulfillment comes from enjoyment of one's work and from a sense of the job well done. Since most people expend the major part of their time and energy on their work career, it would seem important that they derive an inner satisfaction from it. Yet how many people do you know who find such fulfillment? How many people do you know whose job is only a means to earn a living rather than a goal in itself? Let's look at one case—the speaker in this poem.

EXPLANATION

ridge-pole (line 9) The main horizontal wooden beam acting as a support at the top of the upward slopes of the roof of a house.

STUDY QUESTIONS

1. In many lines of work, the worker handles particular materials and particular tools. The qualities of those materials and those tools may be important to the worker's reaction to the job. What material does the speaker in this poem work with? What tools are mentioned?

2. On the job, this carpenter experiences sights, sounds, and smells that are pleasurable. What are some of these sights, sounds, and smells?

3. The carpenter also derives a sense of fulfilling pleasure from the skills she executes with the tools. Mention several examples of these particular pleasures.

4. You are familiar with the expression "sitting on top of the world." Which line in the poem gives a picture of the carpenter "sitting on top of the world" both literally and figuratively? Explain.

5. The poet skillfully combines **rhythms** and word-sounds with word pictures to create rich and exact **images.** Give and explain one good example.

6. The poet has done a good job in writing the poem. Why does she say in the last line that doing the carpentry work is easier than writing about it? Is she serious or jesting?

7. Think of other lines of work in which the worker handles specific materials and tools and executes skills. Some examples are farmer, plumber, office worker, textile worker, steelworker, fruit and vegetable shopkeeper, car mechanic. Other examples will occur to you. Select one example. What pleasurable sights, sounds, and smells may be experienced by the worker? What are some of the skills whose execution may afford the worker pleasure? This poem is written by a woman. May housework, the traditional "trade" of women, afford rewards similar to those described in the poem?

Trades

AMY LOWELL

I want to be a carpenter,
To work all day long in clean wood,
Shaving it into little thin slivers
Which screw up into curls behind my plane;
Pounding square, black nails into white boards,   5
With the claws of my hammer glistening
Like the tongue of a snake.
I want to shingle a house,
Sitting on the ridge-pole in a bright breeze.
I want to put the shingles on neatly,   10
Taking great care that each is directly between two
    others.
I want my hands to have the tang of wood:
Spruce, Cedar, Cypress.
I want to draw a line on a board with a flat pencil,
And then saw along that line,   15
With the sweet-smelling sawdust piling up in a yellow
    heap at my feet.

That is the life!
Heigh-ho!
It is much easier than to write this poem.

The aim of a woodcarver is to bring out the natural beauty that is in the wood—the grain, the texture, the shape. In this poem about his wife, the poet has a similar aim. He wants to bring out in words the natural qualities of his wife as closely as he can without adornment, addition, or exaggeration. That is why he calls it, paradoxically, "Poem in Prose." But the poet is not just writing about his wife. He is making a statement about love as a value for living.

DEFINITION AND EXPLANATION

"Like the burl on the knife" (line 4)   A burl is a knot in a piece of wood. The line refers to the wooden handle on the knife.

freshening (line 22)   Invigorating.

STUDY QUESTIONS

1. What is the "mark" (line 3) that is on the poem? How is it like the burl on the knife (line 4)?

2. The speaker mentions "The well-swept room," "curtains and flowers," "candles and baked bread," "a cloth spread," "a clean house." Is he merely appreciating the fact that his wife is a good housekeeper? How does line 11 "Love's lovely duty" help to answer the question?

3. Explain the **metaphor** and **personification** in lines 21–24 and the mood created by these **images**.

4. "Wherever she is it is now" (line 25). What does the word "now" mean in this line? How does this line help to explain lines 30–31?

>   "My own life to live in,
>   This she has given me—"

5. In the last line, the poet paradoxically suggests that a person cannot *give* what his wife "has given" him. Why not?

6. The woodcarver must use tools skillfully to bring out the natural beauty of the wood, to help the wood make its own statement. Among the tools of the poet are **diction, imagery, rhythm,** and **rhyme.** How effectively has the poet used these tools to make his poem "plainly and honestly"?

Poem in Prose

ARCHIBALD MacLEISH

This poem is for my wife.
I have made it plainly and honestly:
The mark is on it
Like the burl on the knife.

I have not made it for praise.   5
She has no more need for praise
Than summer has
Or the bright days.

In all that becomes a woman
Her words and her ways are beautiful: 10
Love's lovely duty,
The well-swept room.

Wherever she is there is sun
And time and a sweet air:
Peace is there,   15
Work done.

There are always curtains and flowers
And candles and baked bread
And a cloth spread
And a clean house.   20

Her voice when she sings is a voice
At dawn by a freshening sea
Where the wave leaps in the
Wind and rejoices.

Wherever she is it is now.   25
It is here where the apples are:
Here in the stars,
In the quick hour.

The greatest and richest good,
My own life to live in,   30
This she has given me—

If giver could.

Is love the chief and best of values? If so, how do we know this? Does our head, our brain, our logic, our reason tell us? Or does our heart, our feelings, our instinct tell us?

DEFINITION

syntax (line 3) The rules of sentence structure.

STUDY QUESTIONS

1. The speaker makes comparisons between language and life which suggest that mechanical or logical rules don't help us to understand either one. Give the three examples from the poem of those comparisons.

2. Look at the second and third **stanzas**. What is really meant by each of these words: "fool," "Spring," "blood," "wisdom"?

3. Why does the speaker choose flowers to swear by? What is a "gesture" of the "brain," and why does the speaker consider it less than the "eyelids' flutter" (lines 11–12)?

4. Why does the speaker say "laugh" to his beloved (line 14)?

5. How is the theme of this poem similar to that of "Poem in Prose"? How is its emphasis different? Which appeals to you more?

6. In his own language style, as well as in his interpretation of life and love, E. E. Cummings ignores conventional rules as he sees fit. Does his style seem to you to help or hinder the force of this poem?

since feeling is first

E. E. CUMMINGS

since feeling is first
who pays any attention
to the syntax of things
will never wholly kiss you;

wholly to be a fool   5
while Spring is in the world

my blood approves,
and kisses are a better fate
than wisdom
lady i swear by all flowers. Don't cry   10
—the best gesture of my brain is less than
your eyelids' flutter which says

we are for each other: then
laugh, leaning back in my arms
for life's not a paragraph   15

And death i think is no parenthesis

One of the great things about love is the magical powers of communication that love gives to lovers. An exchange of glances or a touch of the hand can express worlds of meaning. Even when two lovers are far apart, the bonds of love can act like invisible telephone wires permitting them to hold conversations impossible for others. This poem is a dialogue between two lovers about a conversation they had on a "lovers' telephone."

STUDY QUESTIONS

1. Let us call the two lovers in the poem lover 1 and lover 2 and make sure we know who is saying what. Assume that the first speaker is lover 1. Which lines belong to lover 1, which to lover 2?

2. What physical objects act as the two ends of the "telephone"? Why are they an appropriate **symbol?**

3. Where was lover 1 during the telephone conversation? lover 2?

4. What testing and teasing about the "telephone" conversation takes place during the actual conversation recorded in the poem? How would you explain the teasing? What was actually said on the "telephone"?

5. What does the last line really say?

6. Assume that lovers 1 and 2 are husband and wife. Which is which? Can you prove it?

The Telephone

ROBERT FROST

"When I was just as far as I could walk
From here today,
There was an hour
All still
When leaning with my head against a flower   5
I heard you talk.
Don't say I didn't, for I heard you say—
You spoke from that flower on the window sill—
Do you remember what it was you said?"

"First tell me what it was you thought you heard."   10

"Having found the flower and driven a bee away,
I leaned my head,
And holding by the stalk,
I listened and I thought I caught the word—
What was it? Did you call me by my name?   15
Or did you say—
Someone said 'Come'—I heard it as I bowed."

"I may have thought as much, but not aloud."

"Well, so I came."

The title of this poem suggests that Edna St. Vincent Millay is going to disagree with the poetic statements about love by MacLeish, Frost, and E. E. Cummings that you have read. What can she have in mind?

EXPLANATION —————————————————————————————

nagged by want past resolution's power
(line 11) An acceptable paraphrase of this difficult line is: "frustrated by a need that cannot be filled despite strong determination."

STUDY QUESTIONS ———————————————————————————

1. The speaker begins with the statement "Love is not all" and goes on to list a number of practical needs that love does not satisfy. What are some of those needs?

2. Suddenly, the speaker switches from her practical point of view to a different one. At which pair of lines does this switch take place? Which character in an earlier poem in this unit do these two lines sharply remind you of?

3. Again, the speaker speculates about circumstances that might drive her to "trade" her love or its memory. What are the circumstances she mentions?

4. After reasonably recognizing all the practicalities and possibilities, the speaker tells us what she really feels. How does she feel?

5. In the light of the whole poem, does the speaker literally mean the opening statement? Explain. In the context of the whole poem, why does the last line have an especially strong impact?

6. Read the poem again carefully with this question in mind, and then answer it: Does the poem suggest anything to you about the probable future of the love relationship? That is, do enduring happiness and fulfillment in this relationship seem to be ahead, or do you see heartbreak and tears in the future? Explain.

7. What is the **verse form** of the poem? Justify your answer.

Love Is Not All

EDNA ST. VINCENT MILLAY

Love is not all: it is not meat nor drink
Nor slumber nor a roof against the rain;
Nor yet a floating spar to men that sink
And rise and sink and rise and sink again;
Love can not fill the thickened lung with breath, 5
Nor clean the blood, nor set the fractured bone;
Yet many a man is making friends with death
Even as I speak, for lack of love alone.
It well may be that in a difficult hour,
Pinned down by pain and moaning for release, 10
Or nagged by want past resolution's power,
I might be driven to sell your love for peace,
Or trade the memory of this night for food.
It well may be. I do not think I would.

The values we treasure help steer us through life. They shape our everyday decisions and choices and give meaning and direction to all the little things we do. The speaker in "Trades" seems to prefer the enjoyment of carpentry to making a lot of money or working to change society for the better. The speaker in "Barter" would give up everything for "loveliness." Sometimes, though, a person may be faced with a conflict in values. Then that person has to make the difficult decision of choosing one value over another.

STUDY QUESTIONS

1. On the surface, this poem narrates a simple incident. Why does the speaker stop? How does the horse react? What does the speaker see? What sounds does the speaker hear? How does the speaker feel about what he sees? Why does the speaker go on?

2. Look beneath the surface of the poem. What does this serene, secluded area—the woods, the frozen lake, the falling snow, the soft sounds—probably symbolize for the speaker? (What parallel might there be between the meaning of this setting for this speaker and the meaning of the Beethoven symphony for the speaker of Edna St. Vincent Millay's poem?) Why does the owner of the woods come into the speaker's mind?

3. What symbolic meaning may be suggested by lines 14 and 15? What are the "promises" and to whom might they have been made? What are the "miles to go" and the "sleep"?

4. An **image** that dominates this poem is captured in the words of lines 11–12: ". . . the sweep/Of easy wind and downy flake." That image is reflected in the sounds of the **rhyme scheme** that moves through the poem. What is the rhyme scheme? How is the rhyme scheme used to create an "easy" sweep from each **stanza** to the one that follows? What change is made in the last stanza to bring the flowing pattern to a gentle end? How is the ending neatly reinforced?

5. In reading the poem aloud, would you read the last two lines in the same way or would you read each line differently? Explain.

Stopping by Woods on a Snowy Evening

ROBERT FROST

Whose woods these are I think I know.
His house is in the village, though;
He will not see me stopping here
To watch his woods fill up with snow.

My little horse must think it queer   5
To stop without a farmhouse near
Between the woods and frozen lake
The darkest evening of the year.

He gives his harness bells a shake
To ask if there is some mistake.   10
The only other sound's the sweep
Of easy wind and downy flake.

The woods are lovely, dark, and deep,
But I have promises to keep,
And miles to go before I sleep,   15
And miles to go before I sleep.

Most of us do not like a person who brags and boasts, who is filled with a sense of self-importance. Most of us do find attractive the person who is modest and humble. Why is this? Is it just a matter of psychology or personality? Or is there some basic value involved? Is it somehow important for each of us to recognize how small and inconsequential we are? Is humility one of the laws of "the good life"? Is it true, as the Bible says, that the meek will inherit the earth?

STUDY QUESTIONS

1. The poet chose to write about blades of grass, not people, standing before God. Why? What point does he want to drive home by the choice of this particular **image**?

2. Why does the one blade of grass say "Memory is bitter to me" (line 13)?

3. Why does God feel that the humble blade of grass is the best one?

4. The humble blade of grass is, in the poem, rewarded in heaven for its virtue. What rewards are there for the humble person on earth? What rewards or benefits are there for human society at large in practicing humility?

The Blades of Grass

STEPHEN CRANE

In heaven,
Some little blades of grass
Stood before God.
"What did you do?"
Then all save one of the little blades   5
Began eagerly to relate
The merits of their lives.
This one stayed a small way behind,
Ashamed.
Presently, God said,   10
"And what did you do?"
The little blade answered, "Oh, my lord,
Memory is bitter to me,
For, if I did good deeds,
I know not of them."   15
Then God, in all His splendor,
Arose from His throne.
"Ah, best little blade of grass!" He said.

Can the human race survive? Doom seems to threaten on all sides. Mother Nature menaces us with prospects of giant earthquakes, a new ice age, a great meteor from outer space hitting the earth, the death of the sun. We endanger our own species by disturbing the delicate balance of the environment, by polluting the earth, air, and water. Atomic missiles capable of destroying all life are poised for firing at the press of a button. What anchor of hope or faith is there for human survival?

DEFINITIONS AND EXPLANATIONS

Epitaph (title) The inscription on a tombstone or the last words written in tribute to a dead person.

dike (line 1) A dam made to prevent flooding.

levee (line 1) An embankment or low wall built to prevent flooding.

estranged (line 3) Made hostile or alien.

disarray (line 4) Disorder.

scull (line 13) Row with one oar at the rear of a small boat, in the manner of a fish's tail.

STUDY QUESTIONS

1. What disaster has occurred? What are some of the specific results?

2. Which line tells you that this is not a local and specific disaster, but one symbolizing a universal disaster for the human race? From this point of view, what may the dike, the levee, the good fields, the cattle, the faithful ground, the tree, and the home be seen as representing?

3. What is the question the speaker asks in lines 5–8? In answering this question, why does the speaker repeat the word "no" (line 9)? What does the speaker see that makes her give this answer? How do lines 11 and 12 emphasize the point?

4. Why is man's face twisted? Why does he carry the "pocket full of seeds"? How do these last four words symbolically contrast with the rest of the poem?

5. In view of the outcome, why does the poet use the word "epitaph" in the title?

6. Why is this poem an expression of faith? What faith is expressed?

excerpt from *Epitaph for the Race of Man*

EDNA ST. VINCENT MILLAY

The broken dike, the levee washed away,
The good fields flooded and the cattle drowned,
Estranged and treacherous all the faithful ground,
And nothing left but floating disarray
Of tree and home uprooted—was this the day   5
Man dropped upon his shadow without a sound
And died, having labored well and having found
His burden heavier than a quilt of clay?
No, no. I saw him when the sun had set
In water, leaning on his single oar   10
Above his garden faintly glimmering yet . . .
There bulked the plough, here washed the
        updrifted weeds . . .
And scull across his roof and make for shore,
With twisted face and pocket full of seeds.

Despite all our advancement in knowledge, much of the universe and the meaning of our own life within it remains a mystery. What lies behind that veil of mystery? The speaker in this poem observes one of the wonders of nature—the remarkable autumn flight of migratory birds from the far north to warm southern climates. The speaker observes one of these birds flying unerringly through vast zones of empty sky as though there were signposts along the way. The speaker feels that in that flight he sees the hand of a Supreme Being at work.

DEFINITIONS AND EXPLANATIONS

Whither (line 1) Where.

fowler's eye (line 5) The eye of the hunter of wild fowl.

plashy brink (line 9) Water-splashed edge.

marge (line 10) Edge; bank.

billows (line 11) Great waves.

chafed ocean-side (line 12) The shore worn by the action of the waves.

STUDY QUESTIONS

1. Give a picture of what the speaker first sees.

2. Why is the air described as "desert" (line 15)?

3. What does the bird do as night comes?

4. What is the bird's destination? What will happen there?

5. What parallel does the speaker feel between himself and the bird on its flight? What comforting faith is inspired in the speaker?

6. The **diction** of this poem has an archaic Biblical flavor. What are some examples? Why is the diction appropriate to the statement the poem makes?

7. The **rhythms** of this poem beat strong and steady in the **meter,** in the use of the **quatrain** as **verse form,** and in the **rhyme scheme.** What is the rhyme scheme? Why are these strong and regular rhythms appropriate to the statement the poem makes?

To a Waterfowl

WILLIAM CULLEN BRYANT

Whither, 'midst falling dew,
While glow the heavens with the last steps of day,
Far, through their rosy depths, dost thou pursue
    Thy solitary way?

Vainly the fowler's eye   5
Might mark thy distant flight, to do thee wrong,
As, darkly seen against the crimson sky,
    Thy figure floats along.

Seek'st thou the plashy brink
Of weedy lake, or marge of river wide,   10
Or where the rocking billows rise and sink
    On the chafed ocean-side?

There is a Power, whose care
Teaches thy way along that pathless coast—
The desert and illimitable air,   15
    Lone wandering, but not lost.

All day thy wings have fanned,
At that far height, the cold, thin atmosphere;
Yet stoop not, weary, to the welcome land,
    Though the dark night is near.   20

And soon that toil shall end,
Soon shalt thou find a summer home, and rest,
And scream among thy fellows; reeds shall bend,
    Soon, o'er thy sheltered nest.

Thou'rt gone, the abyss of heaven   25
Hath swallowed up thy form, yet, on my heart
Deeply has sunk the lesson thou hast given,
    And shall not soon depart.

He who, from zone to zone,
Guides through the boundless sky thy certain flight,   30
In the long way that I must tread alone,
    Will lead my steps aright.

Many people yearn for the sustenance of a deep and simple faith. For some, that yearning is richly satisifed by the accounts and tales of the Bible, perhaps above all by the account of the creation in the Book of Genesis. James Weldon Johnson here retells that tale in the form of a sermon to a Southern congregation by a black minister. In its human simplicity, in its dramatic fireworks, and in its tenderness, this is a retelling to stir every heart.

EXPLANATION

cypress swamp (line 8) A variety of cypress tree known as the bald cypress grows liberally in Southern swamplands. Its widespreading roots can live under water. The roots produce knobs that extend above the water and supply the roots with air.

STUDY QUESTIONS

1. How does the first **stanza** immediately establish a bond with the human audience?

2. Why is a cypress swamp used in the comparison made in lines 5–8?

3. What are the three exciting actions that are described in the fourth stanza? How are the mountains then made?

4. What sharp contrast in **images** and mood is there between the sixth stanza (lines 34–41) and the seventh stanza (lines 42–50)?

5. Why is line 69 dramatic and appealing? What anticipation does the line evoke in the audience?

6. "Like a mammy bending over her baby" (line 85). Give several reasons explaining why this line has enormous emotional force in the poem.

7. How is man created?

8. Why is the last line powerful?

9. How does the "sermon" humanize religious faith?

The Creation

JAMES WELDON JOHNSON

And God stepped out on space,
And he looked around and said:
I'm lonely—
I'll make me a world.

And far as the eye of God could see   5
Darkness covered everything,
Blacker than a hundred midnights
Down in a cypress swamp.

Then God smiled,
And the light broke,   10
And the darkness rolled up on one side,
And the light stood shining on the other,
And God said: That's good!

Then God reached out and took the light in his hands,
And God rolled the light around in his hands   15
Until he made the sun;
And he set that sun a-blazing in the heavens.
And the light that was left from making the sun
God gathered it up in a shining ball
And flung it against the darkness,   20
Spangling the night with the moon and stars.
Then down between
The darkness and the light
He hurled the world;
And God said: That's good!   25

Then God himself stepped down—
And the sun was on his right hand,
And the moon was on his left;
The stars were clustered about his head,
And the earth was under his feet.   30
And God walked, and where he trod

continued

His footsteps hollowed the valleys out
And bulged the mountains up.

Then he stopped and looked and saw
That the earth was hot and barren.   35
So God stepped over to the edge of the world
And he spat out the seven seas—
He batted his eyes and the lightnings flashed—
He clapped his hands, and the thunders rolled—
And the waters above the earth came down,   40
The cooling waters came down.

Then the green grass sprouted,
And the little red flowers blossomed,
The pine tree pointed his finger to the sky,
And the oak spread out his arms,   45
The lakes cuddled down in the hollows of the ground,
And the rivers ran down to the sea;
And God smiled again,
And the rainbow appeared,
And curled itself around his shoulder.   50

Then God raised his arm and he waved his hand
Over the sea and over the land,
And he said: Bring forth! Bring forth!
And quicker than God could drop his hand,
Fishes and fowls   55
And beasts and birds
Swam the rivers and the seas,
Roamed the forests and the woods,
And split the air with their wings.
And God said: That's good!   60

Then God walked around,

And God looked around
On all that he had made.
He looked at his sun,
And he looked at his moon, 65
And he looked at his little stars;
He looked on his world
With all its living things,
And God said: I'm lonely still.

Then God sat down— 70
On the side of a hill where he could think;
By a deep, wide river he sat down;
With his head in his hands,
God thought and thought,
Till he thought: I'll make me a man! 75

Up from the bed of the river
God scooped the clay;
And by the bank of the river
He kneeled him down;
And there the great God Almighty 80
Who lit the sun and fixed it in the sky,
Who flung the stars to the most far corner of the night,
Who rounded the earth in the middle of his hand;
This Great God,
Like a mammy bending over her baby, 85
Kneeled down in the dust
Toiling over a lump of clay
Till he shaped it in his own image;

Then into it he blew the breath of life,
And man became a living soul. 90
Amen. Amen.

In *Hamlet*, a father gives advice to his son in a famous speech of which the best-known line is "This above all: to thine own self be true." In this poem, too, a father advises his young son. The father gives the son a set of guidelines and values to help his son steer through the problems, pains, uncertainties, and complexities of life. The father knows that there is no easy or simple formula for living, but he wants to suggest values that will help his son lead a meaningful, satisfying existence. Of these suggestions, the one the father feels is most important is "to thine own self be true."

DEFINITIONS AND EXPLANATIONS

loam (line 8)   A rich soil.

lucre (line 18)   Money.

thwarted (line 20)   Frustrated; defeated.

Pavlov (line 39)   The great Russian scientist who discovered the "conditioned response." In his most famous experiment, he trained a dog to expect food whenever a bell rang. He showed that the dog would salivate whenever the bell rang even when food no longer came with the ringing of the bell.

Michael Faraday (line 40)   A great British scientist who discovered electromagnetism. He showed that when a wire passed through a magnetic field, electricity flowed in the wire.

STUDY QUESTIONS

1. Cite the lines in which the father tells the son that courage or inner strength is important. What examples can you give of "storms" (line 4) and "sudden betrayals" (line 6)?

2. Cite the lines in which the father tells the son that gentleness, or compassion, is important. Explain the **metaphor** of the flower. Does this advice contradict the advice to "be steel; be a rock" (line 3)? Explain.

3. Cite the lines in which the father tells the son that it is important to have strong personal goals. What warning, however, does the father give right after this advice? What goals are suggested by the words "rich soft wanting" (line 14)?

4. Cite the lines in which the father tells the son that humility is important, that no one should think of himself or herself as perfect. What reason does the father give for the importance of humility?

5. Cite the lines in which the father tells his son "to thine own self be true." What are the "white lies" and "protective fronts" (line 30)? What does mention of these show about the father? In which lines does the father tell the son to cultivate his own personal individuality? his own natural talents and abilities?

continued

A Father Sees a Son Nearing Manhood
from *The People, Yes*

CARL SANDBURG

A father sees a son nearing manhood.
What shall he tell that son?
"Life is hard; be steel; be a rock."
And this might stand him for the storms
and serve him for humdrum and monotony   5
and guide him amid sudden betrayals
and tighten him for slack moments.
"Life is a soft loam; be gentle; go easy."
And this too might serve him.
Brutes have been gentled where lashes failed.   10
The growth of a frail flower in a path up
has sometimes shattered and split a rock.
A tough will counts. So does desire.
So does a rich soft wanting.
Without rich wanting nothing arrives.   15
Tell him too much money has killed men
and left them dead years before burial:
the quest of lucre beyond a few easy needs
has twisted good enough men
sometimes into dry thwarted worms.   20
Tell him time as a stuff can be wasted.
Tell him to be a fool every so often
and to have no shame over having been a fool
yet learning something out of every folly
hoping to repeat none of the cheap follies   25
thus arriving at intimate understanding
of a world numbering many fools.
Tell him to be alone often and get at himself

continued

A Father Sees a Son Nearing Manhood

6. Why does the father mention Shakespeare, the Wright brothers, Pasteur, Pavlov, and Michael Faraday? Does he expect the son to achieve greatness like these men?

7. In what sense will the son be "lonely" (line 42)?

8. Has this parent left out any advice that you think is important? What is it? Has this parent included any advice that you would prefer to omit? Explain.

9. Suppose this were advice to a daughter instead of a son. Would it have to be changed in any way? Explain.

and above all tell himself no lies about himself
whatever the white lies and protective fronts   30
he may use amongst other people.
Tell him solitude is creative if he is strong
and the final decisions are made in silent rooms.
Tell him to be different from other people
if it comes natural and easy being different.   35
Let him have lazy days seeking his deeper motives.
Let him seek deep for where he is a born natural.
    Then he may understand Shakespeare
    and the Wright brothers, Pasteur, Pavlov,
    Michael Faraday and free imaginations   40
bringing changes into a world resenting change.
    He will be lonely enough
    to have time for the work
    he knows as his own.

When we speak of love, we speak of it as though it were one thing but it comes in many forms. There is the love between sweethearts, between husband and wife, between brothers and sisters, between parent and child, between close friends. This poem is about a mother and her little daughter. It is the end of summer. They live in a house in a woodland setting near the ocean shore. They have lain down for an afternoon nap. The mother's head is full of half-drowsy thoughts and reveries about the little girl and the world in which she is growing up.

DEFINITIONS AND EXPLANATIONS

bittersweet (line 36)   A shrub that bears clusters of berries that turn bright orange.

ark (line 45)   The huge boat built by Noah to help two living creatures of every kind survive the Flood.

zebra fish (line 48)   Small tropical fish striped like a zebra. Zebra fish are among the common varieties kept in tropical fish tanks by hobbyists.

pheasant (line 54)   A woodland game bird with brilliant body feathers and long, sweeping tail feathers. It was once the fashion for ladies' hats to be decorated with pheasant tail feathers.

mulch (line 55)   A layer of fallen leaves, branches, and other debris on the surface of the soil.

STUDY QUESTIONS

1. As they lie in bed, the mother holds the child's pulse that "counts" her blood. What does the pulse really count? What **figure of speech** is this? Why does the mother hold the pulse?

2. As the mother and child lie in bed, the mother's mind drifts back and forth between the child and the world of nature outside. The mother seems haunted by **images** of uncertainty, pain, danger, catastrophe, and death, all of which she sees as a threat to her child. Cite several different passages that illustrate the mother's troubled thoughts.

3. What catastrophe does the mother think about in lines 45–49? What feeling does the thought of catastrophe leave her with?

4. The mother tries to shake off the mood and comforts herself and the child with a joke, a gesture, and a promise. What is the joke? What is the gesture? What is the promise?

5. What is the meaning of the title of the poem?

The Fortress

ANNE SEXTON

while taking a nap with Linda

Under the pink quilted covers
I hold the pulse that counts your blood.
I think the woods outdoors
are half asleep,
left over from summer   5
like a stack of books after a flood,
left over like those promises I never keep.
On the right, the scrub pine tree
waits like a fruit store
holding up bunches of tufted broccoli.   10

We watch the wind from our square bed.
I press down my index finger—
half in jest, half in dread—
on the brown mole
under your left eye, inherited   15
from my right cheek: a spot of danger
where a bewitched worm ate its way through our soul
in search of beauty. My child, since July
the leaves have been fed
secretly from a pool of beet-red dye.   20

And sometimes they are battle green
with trunks as wet as hunters' boots,
smacked hard by the wind, clean
as oilskins. No,
the wind's not off the ocean.   25
Yes, it cried in your room like a wolf
and your pony tail hurt you. That was a long time ago.
The wind rolled the tide like a dying
woman. She wouldn't sleep,
she rolled there all night, grunting and sighing.   30

continued

Darling, life is not in my hands;
life with its terrible changes
will take you, bombs or glands,
your own child at
your breast, your own house on your own land.   35
Outside the bittersweet turns orange.
Before she died, my mother and I picked those fat
branches, finding orange nipples
on the gray wire strands.
We weeded the forest, curing trees like cripples.   40

Your feet thump-thump against my back
and you whisper to yourself. Child,
what are you wishing? What pact
are you making?
What mouse runs between your eyes? What ark   45
can I fill for you when the world goes wild?
The woods are underwater, their weeds are shaking
in the tide; birches like zebra fish
flash by in a pack.
Child, I cannot promise that you will get your wish.   50

I cannot promise very much.
I give you the images I know.
Lie still with me and watch.
A pheasant moves
by like a seal, pulled through the mulch   55
by his thick white collar. He's on show
like a clown. He drags a beige feather that he removed,
one time, from an old lady's hat.
We laugh and we touch.
I promise you love. Time will not take away that.   60

Unit Review : VALUES

1. Memorable lines Continue to add to your collection of memorable or quotable lines. From the poems in this unit, select two passages of one line or several. The basis of your selection may be strength of image, music of line, depth of emotion, appeal of theme, or any combination of these. Write the passages in your notebook with title and author. Memorizing the lines will give you added pleasure.

2. Briefly **review the poems** in this unit. Then answer these questions.

a. Name a poem that emphasizes joy in the beauty of nature as a value for living and another poem that offers the beauty of art as an escape from the pain of life.

b. Name two poems about people who failed to find a set of values for satisfactory living.

c. Which poem is an expression of spiritual or religious faith?

d. Select the poem that seems to you the best statement of love as a value.

e. Which poem from this unit made the deepest impression on you personally?

3. Show your knowledge of **terms in poetry.** Here are five short passages from the poems in this unit. First, see if you can identify the passage by title and author. Then, choosing from the list of terms below, name the term applicable to the passage.

apostrophe	**metonymy**
imagery	**symbolism**
personification	

a. "Where the wave leaps in the
    Wind and rejoices"
    (Title? Author? Term?)

b. "I hold the pulse that counts your blood."
    (Title? Author? Term?)

c. "Sweet sounds, oh, beautiful music, do not cease!"
    (Title? Author? Term?)

d. "Pounding square, black nails into white boards"
    (Title? Author? Term?)

e. "And miles to go before I sleep."
    (Title? Author? Term?)

4. Add to your **vocabulary.** Match the definitions in the right-hand column with the words in the left-hand column.

(1) benign		*a.*	rest
(2) billows		*b.*	heavenly
(3) celestial		*c.*	give up
(4) estranged		*d.*	kindly
(5) lucre		*e.*	waves
(6) renounce		*f.*	money
(7) repose		*g.*	frustrated
(8) plausible		*h.*	serene
(9) thwarted		*i.*	acceptable
(10) tranquil		*j.*	made hostile

5. Poems and paintings Poets and painters are artists who have much in common. Study each of the reproductions of paintings that follow. Examine the image carefully. Just what do you see? What feelings does the image arouse in you? What mood or idea does the picture suggest? If a person or persons appear, try to flesh out in your mind their background and character. Is rhythm, metaphor, or symbol important in the picture? After you have studied each picture in this way, select the one that you associate most powerfully in your feelings with one of the poems in this unit. Be ready to discuss or write about your choice and the reasons for it.

Optional: Select one picture that inspires you to write your own poem and write the poem.

The Screen Porch
Fairfield Porter. 1964.
Whitney Museum, New York.

Tree Planting Group   *Grant Wood. 1937. Whitney Museum, New York.*

Dragon   *Leo Katz. 1966.*
Whitney Museum, New York.

Flower Market   *David Park. Whitney Museum, New York.*

The Lord Is My Shepherd
*Thomas Hart Benton.
1926. Whitney Museum,
New York.*

THE GIFT OUTRIGHT

The character of every nation is influenced by its geography, its land and its climate. Before there was an American nation, the land of America was here to give its character to the nation that would develop.

It was a new world, an ocean apart from Europe. It was vast. It was rich. It was infinitely varied with fertile plains, with rivers, lakes, and harbors, with mighty mountain ranges, with timberlands, with wildlife, with a wealth of natural resources, and with great oceans on its eastern and western shores.

What were later to be named Maine and California were here. The Deep South and the Dakotas were here. Texas, Pennsylvania, and New York were here. The Grand Canyon, the Great Lakes, the Everglades, Pike's Peak, and the Mississippi were here.

This land was the unique setting for the unique American nation. This land shaped the nation's history, ideas, and customs. Out of this land grew the nation's cities, towns, villages, farmlands, parks, highways, monuments.

The poems in this unit are about the land—"the gift outright"—and what has sprung from it.

The inauguration ceremony for President John F. Kennedy in 1961 was a moving and dramatic spectacle. Perhaps the most stirring moment of all came when Robert Frost, his white hair tossed by a cold winter wind, stood and recited this poem for the occasion. It will help you to understand the poem if you note that Frost seemed to have in mind a thought that appears in the poem only by suggestion. The thought was that the land of America was the one proper place for the development of the ideas and ideals of America. The land was like a great, rich farm for growing democracy and liberty, waiting only to be cultivated.

DEFINITIONS AND EXPLANATIONS

Outright (title)   Complete; without reservations.

deed (line 13)   A legal document stating a transfer of property.

deeds (line 13)   Acts of courage.

realizing (line 14) Coming into full reality.

unstoried (line 15)   Without a history.

artless (line 15)   Simple and natural.

unenhanced (line 15)   Not made greater or richer.

STUDY QUESTIONS

1. Before the American Revolution, in what sense was it true that "The land was ours . . . before we were her people" and that we possessed "what we still were unpossessed by"?

2. What were we "withholding" that "made us weak" (line 8)?

3. The usual idea is that people deal in land, owning it and transferring ownership by sale or gift. Explain carefully how that process is reversed in lines 9–13.

4. What play on words do you see in line 13?

5. Did we give ourselves to the land only once, or many times? Explain. What is suggested about the process of development of a democracy?

6. How were the land and we different when first "we gave ourselves outright" from what it and we are now?

7. Comment on the wording of the last line. Why is it especially strong?

8. According to the poem, what was the role of the land in the development of the American nation? What was the role of the people?

The Gift Outright

ROBERT FROST

The land was ours before we were the land's.
She was our land more than a hundred years
Before we were her people. She was ours
In Massachusetts, in Virginia,
But we were England's, still colonials,   5
Possessing what we still were unpossessed by,
Possessed by what we now no more possessed.
Something we were withholding made us weak
Until we found out that it was ourselves
We were withholding from our land of living,   10
And forthwith found salvation in surrender.
Such as we were we gave ourselves outright
(The deed of gift was many deeds of war)
To the land vaguely realizing westward,
But still unstoried, artless, unenhanced,   15
Such as she was, such as she would become.

In the following line, Robert Frost wrote suggestively not only of the American land as it stretches across the continent in space but also as it has stretched across the centuries in time.

"Such as she was, such as she would become."

This poem tells something of that story of changes in the land that have come with time. It tells especially of that important part of the land referred to in Frost's phrase "vaguely realizing westward."

STUDY QUESTIONS

1. Notice the phrase "flower-fed buffaloes of the spring." What are the **connotations** of these words? How is the impression of the buffalo created by this phrase different from the impression of the buffalo that many people have?

2. What has taken the place of the buffalo on the prairie lands? What has replaced the prairie grass? What other change has taken place?

3. What are the "Wheels and wheels and wheels" that "spin by" (line 7)?

4. In what two ways does the poet echo the sound of the **rhythm** of the wheels in lines 7 and 8?

5. Where does the poet use **repetition** of mournful phrases to express his feelings about what once was and is now gone?

6. This poem tells of the passing of the buffalo, the prairie grass, the Blackfeet and the Pawnees. How are they and all they represent still with us?

The Flower-Fed Buffaloes

VACHEL LINDSAY

The flower-fed buffaloes of the spring
In the days of long ago,
Ranged where the locomotives sing
And the prairie flowers lie low:—
The tossing, blooming, perfumed grass   5
Is swept away by the wheat,
Wheels and wheels and wheels spin by
In the spring that still is sweet.
But the flower-fed buffaloes of the spring
Left us, long ago.   10
They gore no more, they bellow no more,
They trundle around the hills no more:—
With the Blackfeet, lying low,
With the Pawnees, lying low,
Lying low.   15

Of all the varied lands in which the roots of the American nation took hold and flourished, New England was the first. The great ports and harbors, the rivers and forests, the biting winters, brilliant autumns, and lovely springs of New England first energized the farming, the fishing, and the industry of the region. The spirit of enterprise, independence, and freedom—all the basic traits of the American character—thrived there. It is difficult to capture the many facets of the land of New England in a poem. Amy Lowell does it by using the lilac as a centerpiece and symbol, the lilac which in May decorates every corner of New England with its color and fragrance.

DEFINITIONS AND EXPLANATIONS

Lilacs (title) A shrub that grows widely in New England, as well as elsewhere in the world. It is loved for the beauty and fragrance of its blooms, which grow in great heavy clusters or puffs in many shades of blue, lavender, purple, and white. In New England, the lilac blooms in May, wild, in front yards, and in gardens. Almost every house has some of its cut blooms in a vase.

orioles (line 9) Small birds with bright orange or yellow feathers with black markings.

flaunted (line 28) Showed off proudly.

Custom Houses (line 29) The buildings housing the customs offices, where taxes on imported goods are collected.

sandal-wood (line 30) A hard sweet-smelling wood from Asia, used in fine cabinetmaking.

quill (line 31) A large, stiff bird feather, commonly used years ago as a pen.

greenhouses (line 50) Buildings whose roofs and sides are made mostly of glass, used for the cultivation of delicate or out-of-season plants; hothouses.

Pashas (line 60) A Turkish title of high rank or honor.

reticent (line 62) Not given to much talking; silent; reserved.

candid (line 63) Honest; outspoken.

State Houses (line 82) The official buildings of the state government.

Charters (line 82) Legal documents founding some of the New England colonies and giving them a degree of self-government.

thrush (line 85) A large group of songbirds that includes the robin, the bluebird, and the woodthrush.

STUDY QUESTIONS

1. The poet chose the lilac as a **symbol** to represent New England itself and to express her own deep feelings about New England. It is a symbol appropriate in many ways. The lilac enabled the poet to offer many little exact scenes of New

continued

Lilacs

AMY LOWELL

Lilacs,
False blue,
White,
Purple,
Color of lilac,   5
Your great puffs of flowers
Are everywhere in this my New England.
Among your heart-shaped leaves
Orange orioles hop like music-box birds and sing
Their little weak soft songs;   10
In the crooks of your branches
The bright eyes of song sparrows sitting on spotted eggs
Peer restlessly through the light and shadow
Of all Springs.
Lilacs in dooryards   15
Holding quiet conversations with an early moon;
Lilacs watching a deserted house
Settling sideways into the grass of an old road;
Lilacs, wind-beaten, staggering under a lopsided shock of bloom
Above a cellar dug into a hill.   20
You are everywhere.
You were everywhere.
You tapped the window when the preacher preached his sermon,
And ran along the road beside the boy going to school.
You stood by pasture-bars to give the cows good milking,   25
You persuaded the housewife that her dish pan was of silver.
And her husband an image of pure gold.
You flaunted the fragrance of your blossoms
Through the wide doors of Custom Houses—
You, and sandal-wood, and tea,   30
Charging the noses of quill-driving clerks

continued

Lilacs

England nature found in association with the lilac. Give two examples that appeal to you as especially attractive or lovely. The lilac enabled the poet to give typical small scenes of everyday New England life and activity, past and present. Give two examples. The lilac enabled the poet to weave **allusions** to New England geography and history into her poem. Give two examples.

2. How was the lilac able to persuade "the housewife that her dish pan was of silver/ And her husband an image of pure gold" (lines 26–27)?

3. Note the passage about the Custom Houses and their clerks (lines 29–40). Why are Custom Houses significant in the story of New England? Why are the clerks called "Paradoxical" (line 37)?

4. Explain the **personification** in the **image** in lines 50–52.

5. What is suggested about the origin of the lilac in lines 58–60? What contrast is brought out in the lines that follow?

6. Explain in detail the **image** in lines 65–67? (How has the lilac become "friendly to a house-cat and a pair of spectacles"?)

7. Explain the meaning of the following **image:**

> "May is a full light wind of lilac
> From Canada to Narragansett Bay."
>   (lines 93–94)

8. The poem is written in **free verse,** but its marked **rhythms** are lyrical—songlike and lovely. What rhythmic **refrain** occurs three times in the poem? How are these lines made distinctive and emphatic? Give other examples of **repetition** that add to the haunting lyricism of the poem. Give two examples of lines whose musical quality is enhanced through **alliteration**.

When a ship was in from China.
You called to them: "Goose-quill men, goose-quill men,
May is a month for flitting,"
Until they writhed on their high stools   35
And wrote poetry on their letter-sheets behind the propped-up
    ledgers.
Paradoxical New England clerks,
Writing inventories in ledgers, reading the "Song of Solomon"
    at night,
So many verses before bed-time,
Because it was the Bible.   40
The dead fed you
Amid the slant stones of graveyards.
Pale ghosts who planted you
Came in the night-time
And let their thin hair blow through your clustered stems.   45
You are of the green sea,
And of the stone hills which reach a long distance.
You are of elm-shaded streets with little shops where they sell
    kites and marbles,
You are of great parks where everyone walks and nobody is at
    home.
You cover the blind sides of greenhouses   50
And lean over the top to say a hurry-word through the glass
To your friends, the grapes, inside.

Lilacs,
False blue,
White,   55
Purple,
Color of lilac,

continued

Lilacs

You have forgotten your Eastern origin,
The veiled women with eyes like panthers,
The swollen, aggressive turbans of jeweled Pashas.   60
Now you are a very decent flower.
A reticent flower,
A curiously clear-cut, candid flower,
Standing beside clean doorways,
Friendly to a house-cat and a pair of spectacles,   65
Making poetry out of a bit of moonlight
And a hundred or two sharp blossoms.

Maine knows you,
Has for years and years;
New Hampshire knows you,   70
And Massachusetts
And Vermont.
Cape Cod starts you along the beaches to Rhode Island;
Connecticut takes you from a river to the sea.
You are brighter than apples,   75
Sweeter than tulips,
You are the great flood of our souls
Bursting above the leaf-shapes of our hearts,
You are the smell of all summers,
The love of wives and children,   80
The recollection of the gardens of little children,
You are State Houses and Charters
And the familiar treading of the foot to and fro on a road it
      knows.
May is lilac here in New England,
May is thrush singing "Sun up!" on a tip-top ash-tree,   85
May is white clouds behind pine-trees

Puffed out and marching upon a blue sky.
May is green as no other,
May is much sun through small leaves,
May is soft earth,   90
And apple-blossoms,
And windows open to a South wind.
May is a full light wind of lilac
From Canada to Narragansett Bay.

Lilacs,   95
False blue,
White,
Purple,
Color of lilac.
Heart-leaves of lilac all over New England,   100
Roots of lilac under all the soil of New England,
Lilac in me because I am New England,
Because my roots are in it,
Because my leaves are of it,
Because my flowers are for it,   105
Because it is my country
And I speak to it of itself
And sing of it with my own voice
Since certainly it is mine.

From the Atlantic to the Pacific, the American landscape is rich with sights and scenes that are spectacularly beautiful or quietly lovely, sights that overwhelm the imagination or move the mind to thought. Among the sights whose majesty and grandeur almost defy words, none surpasses the Grand Canyon, carved by the Colorado River in northern Arizona. This poem expresses the impact of the Grand Canyon on the beholder.

EXPLANATIONS

Zeus (line 1) In Greek mythology, Zeus was the supreme ruler and mightiest of the gods. He wielded the thunderbolt as his weapon. His wife was Hera. Zeus delegated to his brother Poseidon the rule of the sea and to his brother Hades the rule of the underworld.

Titans (line 3) The Titans were a race of giant gods who made unsuccessful war on Zeus. One of the Titans was Atlas, whom Zeus forced to bear the world on his shoulders. Another was Prometheus, who angered Zeus by giving the gift of fire to humankind. Prometheus was chained to a mountain where a vulture came every day to gnaw at his liver.

Gods (line 4) Besides Zeus, Hera, Poseidon, and Hades, the important gods included Athene, Apollo, Hermes, Ares, and Aphrodite.

Heroes (line 4) Among the heroes whose fabled deeds were told by Homer and others were Odysseus (Ulysses), Achilles, Hercules, Theseus, Jason, and Perseus.

STUDY QUESTIONS

1. Nowhere in the poem does the speaker attempt to describe or depict the Grand Canyon. Why?

2. The speaker does give her reaction to the sight. In a few words, what is her reaction? What role does the speaker see for the Grand Canyon? Why?

3. What other spectacular sight in the American landscape might inspire a poem similar to this one in tone and style?

4. This poem is written in a verse form called the **cinquain,** which was first used by Adelaide Crapsey as a variation on the Japanese **haiku.** Students often find the cinquain an interesting form of poetry to try and one with which they achieve remarkable success. Use the sight you mentioned in answer to question 3 (or, if you prefer, any other topic), and write a cinquain of your own.

The Grand Canyon

ADELAIDE CRAPSEY

By Zeus!
Shout word of this
To the eldest dead!   Titans,
Gods, Heroes, come who have once more
A home!   5

As you know, there are oceans on either side of America. There are oceans in the middle of America, too. In our great agricultural states, the corn and wheat fields stretch as far as the eye can see, and when the wind blows, sealike waves ripple across the fields.

STUDY QUESTIONS

1. Sailors walk with a gait adapted to the rolling of the deck. Why would the boy walking through corn fields naturally walk with a similar gait?

2. What is the green "fire" referred to in line 4?

3. Why does the boy, who has never seen the sea and who is many hundreds of miles from it, taste "the bitter spray" and hear "the sea winds crying"?

4. What touch of **irony** is there in the dreams of the boy as compared to what probably were the dreams of his ancestor?

5. What does the poem tell about the land of America and its people?

6. Though the setting of this poem is a Kansas farm, it is sharp with the feeling of the sea. What are some of the **images** that help create this sea tone?

Kansas Boy
RUTH LECHLITNER

This Kansas boy who never saw the sea
Walks through the young corn rippling at his knee
As sailors walk; and when the grain grows higher
Watches the dark waves leap with greener fire
Than ever oceans hold. He follows ships, 5
Tasting the bitter spray upon his lips,
For in his blood up-stirs the salty ghost
Of one who sailed a storm-bound English coast.
Across wide fields he hears the sea winds crying,
Shouts at the crows—and dreams of white gulls flying. 10

The lives of many Americans are rooted in the land and change in a regular rhythm according to the seasons. But in each section of the country, the seasons are different, bring different conditions, create different feelings and moods, require different responses. This poem is about winter in the farmlands of Oregon.

STUDY QUESTIONS

1. What is the chief characteristic of the Oregon winter? Describe it in detail through references to the poem.

2. How are the farmhouses personified in lines 5–6?

3. What are the tasks the farmers have completed in preparation for winter?

4. What are the predominant smells in the farmhouses during winter?

5. How do the farm people spend their time?

6. What is the mood of Oregon winter as expressed by the poem? How does it compare to the mood of the winter you know?

7. Suppose an artist were to paint a picture depicting Oregon winter. What color or colors would predominate? What are some of the visual details that would appear in the picture?

Oregon Winter

JEANNE McGAHEY

The rain begins. This is no summer rain,
Dropping the blotches of wet on the dusty road:
This rain is slow, without thunder or hurry:
There is plenty of time—there will be months of rain.
    Lost in the hills, the old gray farmhouses   5
Hump their backs against it, and smoke from their chimneys
Struggles through weighted air. The sky is sodden with water,
It sags against the hills, and the wild geese,
Wedge-flying, brush the heaviest cloud with their wings.
    The farmers move unhurried. The wood is in,   10
The hay has long been in, the barn lofts piled
Up to the high windows, dripping yellow straws.
There will be plenty of time now, time that will smell of fires,
And drying leather, and catalogues, and apple cores.
    The farmers clean their boots, and whittle, and drowse.   15

American architecture has grown from the American soil as surely as its native plant life. The log cabin, the adobe house, the sod hut, the salt box, the Colonial house, the Cape Cod cottage, the California mission, the ranch house, the Pennsylvania Dutch house, the brownstone, the tenement, the skyscraper are examples. Of all these, no architecture is more distinctively American or more beautiful than the New England church. With the neat lines of its gleaming white clapboard sides, with its simple clean structure, with its characteristicly slim graceful spire rising to the sky, it is as much a part of the New England landscape as the rocky farmlands, the fresh streams, the hills and bays.

DEFINITIONS AND EXPLANATIONS

Meeting-House (title) A Quaker place of worship.

mad (line 1) Foolish; unreasonable.

portico (line 7) A porch with a roof supported by columns.

elegance (line 7) Dignity and tastefulness of style.

royals (line 17) Sails set high on the mainmast of a sailing ship. Royals are used to catch light breezes.

two-reef breeze (line 18) A breeze for which the sails have been taken in twice.

tea clipper (line 19) A clipper was a large, fast ocean-going sailing vessel used to transport freight. This one has carried tea and porcelain from the port of Canton in China to New England.

tacking (line 20) Sailing at an angle into the wind.

coolie (line 23) In China, formerly, a person doing heavy labor for little pay.

STUDY QUESTIONS

1. In the first **stanza**, the speaker catches sight of "the curve of a blue bay" and the "white church above thin trees." What are her emotions and reactions?

2. Notice lines 12–14. What strange attribute does the spire seem to have? What physical explanation is there for this? What comparison comes into the speaker's mind? How does her imagination extend this comparison specifically?

3. The comparison ends with "a Chinese coolie leaning over the rail/Gazing at the white spire." In what way does this seem to contradict what has gone before? How do you explain this contradiction psychologically?

4. What does the picture of the Chinese coolie gazing at the spire "With dull, sea-spent eyes" suggest to you?

Meeting-House Hill

AMY LOWELL

I must be mad, or very tired,
When the curve of a blue bay beyond the railroad track
Is shrill and sweet to me like the sudden springing of a tune,
And the sight of a white church above thin trees in a city square
Amazes my eyes as though it were the Parthenon.   5
Clear, reticent, superbly final,
With the pillars of its portico refined to a cautious elegance,
It dominates the weak trees,
And the shot of its spire
Is cool and candid,   10
Raising into an unresisting sky.

Strange meeting house
Pausing a moment upon a squalid hilltop.
I watch the spire sweeping the sky,
I am dizzy with the movement of the sky;   15
I might be watching a mast
With its royals set full
Straining before a two-reef breeze.
I might be sighting a tea clipper,
Tacking into the blue bay,   20
Just back from Canton
With her hold full of green and blue porcelain
And a Chinese coolie leaning over the rail
Gazing at the white spire
With dull, sea-spent eyes.   25

In the varied geography of America, Florida is unique, with its semi-tropical climate and lush native vegetation. Hundreds of years ago Ponce de León sought the fountain of youth there. Today many thousands of Americans live there, vacation there, retire there. Perhaps they wish to escape the harshness of winter. Perhaps, like Ponce de León, they hope to find health and long life in the warm and mild climate. Or perhaps they just want to revel in Florida's own particular kind of beauty.

DEFINITIONS AND EXPLANATIONS

Nomad (title)   A wanderer.

Exquisite (title)   Being highly sensitive; having exceptional awareness of beauty or perfection.

Meet (line 11)   Fitting; suitable.

STUDY QUESTIONS

1. What does the title tell you about the speaker?

2. What characteristic of the climate of Florida is brought out by the repeated phrase "immense dew"?

3. Which words and phrases suggest the tropical lushness of the scene?

4. What **image** is brought to your mind by the use of the word "angering" in the phrase "green vine angering for life" (line 4)? What **figure of speech** is this?

5. What is the emotional effect of the brilliant scene on the "beholder"?

6. In your opinion, what does the speaker mean when he says:

> "So, in me, come flinging
> Forms, flames, and the flakes of
>   flames." (lines 13–14)

7. In these last two lines of the poem, notice the strong **alliteration** of the *f* sound. This same sound weaves and intertwines through the rest of the poem, just as the shapes and colors of the Florida vegetation weave and intertwine. Give as many examples of this sound **repetition** as you can. Other words and phrases are repeated in the poem, again to suggest the rich intertwining growth. Give examples.

Nomad Exquisite

WALLACE STEVENS

As the immense dew of Florida
Brings forth
The big-finned palm
And green vine angering for life,

As the immense dew of Florida 5
Brings forth hymn and hymn
From the beholder,
Beholding all these green sides
And gold sides of green sides,

And blessed mornings, 10
Meet for the eye of the young alligator,
And lightning colors
So, in me, come flinging
Forms, flames, and the flakes of flames.

The attractions of the mild climate of the "sunbelt"—Florida, Southern California, Arizona, and similar regions of the country—have caused great changes in American population distribution and in the economy. Nevertheless, it is far from true that everybody feels the same way. For example, see what the speaker of this sonnet has to say.

DEFINITIONS AND EXPLANATIONS

Puritan (title)   The Puritans were among the earliest settlers of New England. They emphasized strictness in their moral and religious beliefs and simplicity, plainness, and even self-denial in their life-style. The Puritan heritage runs through the American character as an important strain.

austere (line 3)   Very simple; severe; lacking in richness or abundance.

immaculate (line 3)   Pure; without flaw or fault.

spate (line 7)   A flood.

fenced with stones (line 8)   This phrase refers to the same stone walls or "fences" that inspired Frost's "Mending Wall."

sheaves (line 10)   The bundles into which stalks of grain, corn, etc. are gathered and tied during the harvest.

STUDY QUESTIONS

1. What does the first line tell you about the heritage of the speaker and the depth to which she feels that heritage?

2. In line 2, notice the phrase "this richness." What does this reference tell you about the probable locale of the speaker as she writes the poem?

3. In your own words, what are some of the features of the landscape preferred by the speaker as described in lines 4–8?

4. To describe her Puritan preferences in geographical surroundings, the speaker dots her poem with such adjectives as "austere" and "immaculate." List five other adjectives from the poem that also reflect the speaker's preferences.

5. The speaker's preferences are also expressed in the colors and tints that are "painted" into the poem, the "pearly monotones." List as many of these colors and tints as you can.

6. Which characteristic of New England, as contrasted, for example, with Florida, is described in the last four lines of the poem?

7. Notice the **metaphor** in line 11 and the **similes** in lines 13 and 14. What is each of the three seasons compared to?

8. Is this an Italian or English **sonnet?** How do you know?

9. Which way does your own preference in climatic surrounding lean, toward that of "Nomad Exquisite" or "Puritan Sonnet"? Why?

Puritan Sonnet

ELINOR WYLIE

Down to the Puritan marrow of my bones
There's something in this richness that I hate.
I love the look, austere, immaculate,
Of landscapes drawn in pearly monotones.
There's something in my very blood that owns   5
Bare hills, cold silver on a sky of slate,
A thread of water, churned to milky spate
Streaming through slanted pastures fenced with stones.

I love those skies, thin blue or snowy gray,
Those fields sparse-planted, rendering meager sheaves;   10
That spring, briefer than apple-blossom's breath,
Summer, so much too beautiful to stay,
Swift autumn, like a bonfire of leaves,
And sleepy winter, like the sleep of death.

The lovely and historic Potomac River flows through the country-side that forms the boundary of Maryland, West Virginia, and Virginia. On the banks of the river, about 125 miles from Chesapeake Bay, where the river begins to become a wide tidal stream, our nation's capital was built amid a serene and majestic geographical setting. The great dome of the Capitol, built on a plateau that rises above the area, dominates the scene. Nearby stands the classically dignified Supreme Court. The Washington Monument and the Lincoln and Jefferson memorials are at water's edge. This setting, an unusual marriage of natural and architectural beauty, is the center of the nation's government and power. It is also an ideal symbol of America, its strength, its riches, and its historic dedication to human dignity and freedom. This poem, in a few simple strokes, captures the reality and the spirit of the nation's capital, the land and the architecture.

STUDY QUESTIONS

1. To express the physical beauty of the scene and its symbolism, Sandburg paints a picture in words. As the poem opens, what time of day does Sandburg choose for his painting? Which two words express the quality of the light? Why do you think Sandburg chose that time of day and that quality of light?

2. What colors appear in the painting? What **connotations** do these colors have for you?

3. What two physical features of the capital city appear in the painting? Why do you think Sandburg has chosen only these two features and why has he emphasized the setting of air, light, and sky rather than buildings or people?

4. What change in the scene takes place?

5. What might the "star" in the last line symbolize? What do you think is the meaning of the sentence "It's a long way across"?

Smoke Rose Gold

CARL SANDBURG

The dome of the capitol looks to the Potomac river.
  Out of haze over the sunset,
  Out of a smoke rose gold:
One star shines over the sunset.
Night takes the dome and the river, the sun and the smoke
  rose gold,   5
The haze changes from sunset to star.
The pour of a thin silver struggles against the dark.
A star might call: It's a long way across.

The land has shaped our history, and we have left the marks of our history on the land in memorials and monuments, none more famous than Gettysburg. What, however, does the shrine of Gettysburg, with its bronze and marble statues and tablets, mean to the thousands who visit there each year? Do they remember the terrible bloodshed? Do they feel the incredible courage? Do they thrill to the causes that were at stake? Or is their visit merely a day's outing, an idle social amusement, just something to do?

DEFINITIONS AND EXPLANATIONS

Gettysburg The Battle of Gettysburg took place on July 1, 2, and 3 in 1863. This Pennsylvania battleground marked the high point of Lee's invasion of the North and the turning point of the war. Two parallel ridges run south from Gettysburg—Seminary Ridge to the west and about a mile to the east across open fields, Cemetery Ridge. The Confederate Army took positions on Seminary Ridge, and the Union Army, under General Meade, took defensive positions along Cemetery Ridge. At the northern flank of Cemetery Ridge are two hills, Cemetery Hill and Culp's Hill. At the southern flank are two other hills, Little Round Top and Big Round Top. These hills, overlooking the Union forces on Cemetery Ridge, were strategically important to the Union defenses. On July 2, Southern troops attempted to take Little Round Top, but the defenses were reinforced at the last moment and the Confederate attack was repulsed, with sharpshooters of the 20th Maine Regiment playing a key role in the fierce fighting. An attack on the two hills to the north was also repulsed. An advance on the Union center gained ground but was finally repulsed. On July 3, Lee ordered a direct frontal attack across the open fields by the Virginians under General Pickett, with some support from other troops. Pickett's men lay behind Seminary Ridge ready

for their advance. Shortly after 1 P.M., Confederate cannons launched a withering barrage against the Union positions. The fire was returned by the Union artillery. After two hours, the barrage suddenly stopped. Pickett's men moved out and began their advance across the open fields. For a few moments, a strange hush fell across the battleground as the gray ranks, flags flying, marched forward. Then the Union artillery opened fire, blowing great holes in the exposed ranks. The Southerners kept coming until they advanced within range of murderous rifle fire. A few hundred survivors reached and charged the Union lines and fought hand to hand in a hopeless struggle. They died or surrendered or ran. The Battle of Gettysburg was over. When the artillery duels, the gunfire, the hand-to-hand combat, the attacks and counterattacks were done, Lee had lost 28,000 men, Meade 23,000.

Pickett's boulder (line 23)   A large granite rock, now marked with a plaque, stands at the high point of the charge of Pickett's men into the Union lines.

decalcomania (line 41)   More commonly known now as a "decal," a decalcomania is a design or print that can be transferred from the special paper on which it comes to some other surface.

continued

from *John Brown's Body*

STEPHEN VINCENT BENÉT

You took a carriage to that battlefield.
Now, I suppose, you take a motor-bus,
But then, it was a carriage—and you ate
Fried chicken out of wrappings of waxed paper,
While the slow guide buzzed on about the war   5
And the enormous, curdled summer clouds
Piled up like giant cream puffs in the blue.
The carriage smelt of axle-grease and leather
And the old horse nodded a sleepy head
Adorned with a straw hat. His ears stuck through it.   10
It was the middle of hay-fever summer
And it was hot. And you could stand and look
All the way down from Cemetery Ridge,
Much as it was, except for monuments
And startling groups of monumental men   15
Bursting in bronze and marble from the ground,
And all the curious names upon the gravestones. . . .

So peaceable it was, so calm and hot,
So tidy and great-skied.
            No men had fought   20
There but enormous, monumental men
Who bled neat streams of uncorrupting bronze,
Even at the Round Tops, even by Pickett's boulder,
Where the bronze, open book could still be read
By visitors and sparrows and the wind: 25
And the wind came, the wind moved in the grass,
Saying . . . while the long light . . . and all so calm . . .

continued

John Brown's Body

1. The speaker is recalling a visit to Gettysburg, years ago when he was young. How do you know this? What are some of the speaker's memories of the trip as suggested in lines 1–12? What do these memories tell you about the meaning of this memorial to the young visitor?

2. In lines 12–25, the speaker describes the former battlefield as he saw it. He uses such adjectives as "peaceable," "calm," "tidy." He refers to "the curious names upon the gravestones." He says:

> "No men had fought
> There but enormous, monumental men
> Who bled neat streams of uncorrupting
> bronze"

What ironic contrast is the poet suggesting between the terrible human reality of the battle and the meaning of the shrine to the speaker?

3. What is the message of the wind?

4. How is the **irony** of the poem brought to a climax in the last three lines?

5. In his address after the Battle of Gettysburg, Lincoln said:

> "But, in a larger sense, we cannot dedicate, we cannot consecrate, we cannot hallow this ground. The brave men, living and dead, who struggled here, have consecrated it far above our poor power to add or detract. The world will little note nor long remember what we say here, but it can never forget what they did here."

In your opinion, do the words of this poem affirm or deny the words of Lincoln? Explain.

6. How do you yourself feel about the monuments, shrines, and memorials that mark the American story on American land? Do they serve effectively to keep alive the meaning of great events and great persons in history, or are they empty, hollow gestures, mere commercial tourist attractions? If you can clarify your answers by reference to a visit you have made to such a memorial, Gettysburg or any other, do so.

"Pickett came
And the South came
And the end came,   30
And the grass comes
And the wind blows
On the bronze book
On the bronze men
On the grown grass,   35
And the wind says
'Long ago
Long
Ago.'"

Then it was time to buy a paperweight   40
With flags upon it in decalcomania
And hope you wouldn't break it, driving home.

Of the fruits that have sprung from our land, none is more phenomenal than our great cities. New York, Chicago, Boston, San Francisco, Los Angeles, Philadelphia, Detroit, Denver, Atlanta, New Orleans, Seattle, Dallas, Baltimore—each is a unique product of its own geography and location. Each is a great center of vitality, of culture, of commerce. Each is a marvel of achievement, a concentration of problems. This is the best known of all our city poems, about one of our greatest and most colorful cities, by one of our greatest poets.

EXPLANATION

Chicago (title) Chicago is located approximately at the center of the distribution of the nation's population and is ideally situated at the crossroads of the nation's industry, agriculture, and commerce. It has become the greatest livestock and meat packing center, the largest railroad center, and the most important grain market of the entire world. Its airport, O'Hare, is the busiest in the nation. It has even replaced New York in the boast of having the tallest building in the world, the Sears Tower. At the same time, especially during the Prohibition era, Chicago was notorious as the city where the czars of crime operated freely and corruption prevailed.

STUDY QUESTIONS

1. Chicago is personified at several points —in lines 4 and 5, line 10, line 11, lines 20 and 21. As what is the city personified in these lines? What characteristics of the city are suggested by these **personifications?** How are these same characteristics expressed in the style of the opening **stanza**—the **imagery,** the capitalized nouns and adjectives, the **line** lengths, the **rhythms.** What manner of delivery would you use to recite the stanza aloud? What other part of the poem has a style and an effect similar to that of the first stanza?

2. What problems of the city are mentioned? The poem was written a long time ago. If Sandburg were to write the poem today, to what extent would the list of problems be different?

3. "To those who sneer" the speaker would "give them back the sneer" (line 9). What is his answer to the critics of this city? What, in your opinion, is "the terrible burden of destiny" (line 19)?

4. Choose the city that you live in or one that you know well. Write a short **free-verse** poem in the style of the opening stanza of "Chicago" about your city.

Chicago

CARL SANDBURG

Hog Butcher for the World,
Tool Maker, Stacker of Wheat,
Player with Railroads and the Nation's Freight Handler;
Stormy, husky, brawling,
City of the Big Shoulders: 5

They tell me you are wicked and I believe them, for I have seen
    your painted women under the gas lamps luring the farm boys.
And they tell me you are crooked and I answer: Yes, it is true I
    have seen the gunman kill and go free to kill again.
And they tell me you are brutal and my reply is: On the faces of
    women and children I have seen the marks of wanton hunger.
And having answered so I turn once more to those who sneer at this
    my city, and I give them back the sneer and say to them:
Come and show me another city with lifted head singing so proud
    to be alive and coarse and strong and cunning.   10
Flinging magnetic curses amid the toil of piling job on job, here
    is a tall bold slugger set vivid against the little soft cities;
Fierce as a dog with tongue lapping for action, cunning as a savage
    pitted against the wilderness,
        Bareheaded,
        Shoveling,
        Wrecking,   15
        Planning,
        Building, breaking, rebuilding,
Under the smoke, dust all over his mouth, laughing with white
    teeth,
Under the terrible burden of destiny laughing as a young man
    laughs,
Laughing even as an ignorant fighter laughs who has never lost
    a battle,   20
Bragging and laughing that under his wrist is the pulse, and under
    his ribs the heart of the people,
        Laughing!
Laughing the stormy, husky, brawling laughter of Youth,
    half-naked, sweating, proud to be Hog Butcher, Tool Maker,
    Stacker of Wheat, Player with Railroads and Freight Handler
    to the Nation.

The speaker in this poem describes two scenes. The first is of sardine fishermen at work off the coast of central California, one of the prime sardine fisheries of the world. The second scene is of a city in the same region, seen from a mountaintop at night. The speaker sees an analogy between the two scenes, an analogy that leads him to a conclusion about the meaning of our big cities to the lives of the people within them.

DEFINITIONS AND EXPLANATIONS

Purse-Seine (title) A net used to entrap shoals of small fish such as the sardine. The cord from which the net is hung is strung with floats. The bottom of the net is strung with lead weights. When a shoal is sighted, the fishing boat runs the cord of the net around the shoal in a great circle, the weights carry the net down, and the fish are encircled in a wall of net. The net is pulled shut at the bottom by a drawstring called the purse line, and the fish are entrapped and ready to be hauled aboard the boat.

phosphorescence (line 2) The quality of shining or giving off light without heat. Dying fish and decaying wood are often phosphorescent.

galaxies (line 14) Clusters of millions of stars, like the Milky Way.

luminous (line 15) Bright; radiant.

insulated (line 17) Separated or shut off from.

STUDY QUESTIONS

1. How do the fishermen first spot the shoal of sardines?

2. Why is it a "great labor" to haul the net in (line 6)?

3. What two opposite words does the speaker use to describe his reactions to the scene of the trapped fish? Explain why he has these two reactions.

4. The speaker uses phrases of light and dark and brilliant color. What are some of them? In what way are the **connotations** and associations of these brilliant colors the opposite of their usual connotations and associations?

5. Explain this **metaphor.** (How is the night like walls?)

". . . the vast walls of night
   Stand erect to the stars." (lines 11–12)

6. As the speaker looks down on the city from a mountaintop at night, he sees a parallel to the fishing scene. What is the parallel? How is his reaction similar?

continued

The Purse-Seine

ROBINSON JEFFERS

Our sardine fishermen work at night in the dark of the moon;
daylight or moonlight
They could not tell where to spread the net, unable to see the
phosphorescence of the shoals of fish.
They work northward from Monterey, coasting Santa Cruz; off
New Year's Point or off Pigeon Point
The look-out man will see some lakes of milk-color light on the
sea's night-purple; he points, and the helmsman
Turns the dark prow, the motorboat circles the gleaming shoal and
drifts out her seine-net. They close the circle   5
And purse the bottom of the net, then with great labor haul it in.

       I cannot tell you
How beautiful the scene is, and a little terrible, then, when the
crowded fish
Know they are caught, and wildly beat from one wall to the other
of their closing destiny the phosphorescent
Water to a pool of flame, each beautiful slender body sheeted
with flame, like a live rocket
A comet's tail wake of clear yellow flame; while outside the
narrowing   10
Floats and cordage of the net great sea-lions come up to watch,
sighing in the dark; the vast walls of night
Stand erect to the stars.

       Lately I was looking from a night mountain-top
On a wide city, the colored splendor, galaxies of light: how could I
help but recall the seine-net
Gathering the luminous fish? I cannot tell you how beautiful the
city appeared, and a little terrible.   15

continued

The Purse-Seine

7. Read lines 16–18. What does the speaker think of the "interdependence" of the people in the cities? Why are the city people incapable of "free survival," according to the speaker?

8. In what way does the "verse" (that is, the speaker—an example of **metonymy**) keep "its reason" though "troubled or frowning"?

9. To what extent are your own feelings about the trapped sardines and the people in cities in agreement with the feelings of the speaker in this poem? What do you think the author of "Chicago" would say?

I thought, We have geared the machines and locked all together
    into interdependence; we have built the great cities; now
There is no escape. We have gathered vast populations incapable
    of free survival, insulated
From the strong earth, each person in himself helpless, on all
    dependent. The circle is closed, and the net
Is being hauled in. They hardly feel the cords drawing, yet they
    shine already. The inevitable mass-disasters
Will not come in our time nor in our children's, but we and our
    children   20
Must watch the net draw narrower, government take all powers—
    or revolution, and the new government
Take more than all, add to kept bodies kept souls—or anarchy,
    the mass-disasters.

            These things are Progress;
Do you marvel our verse is troubled or frowning, while it keeps
    its reason? Or it lets go, lets the mood flow
In the manner of the recent young men into mere hysteria,
    splintered gleams, crackled laughter. But they are quite
    wrong.   25
There is no reason for amazement: surely one always knew that
    cultures decay, and life's end is death.

In "The Purse-Seine," Robinson Jeffers expresses a not uncommon pessimistic attitude about our big cities. In this poem, Ogden Nash writes with his usual light, but sharp and witty, touch to express a different attitude about the city.

DEFINITIONS AND EXPLANATIONS

ditty (line 1)   A short, usually light, poem or song.

metropular (line 4)   This is a typical coined Nash word, for the sake of humorous rhyme. The actual word from which "metropular" is coined is *metropolitan*, which means "pertaining to a big city."

Sentimentalists (line 5)   People who tend to be influenced by unrealistic emotions.

urban (line 9)   Having to do with the city or city life; the opposite of rural.

W.C.T.U. (line 10)   The Women's Christian Temperance Union has favored the prohibition of the drinking of any alcoholic beverage.

marts (line 11)   Certain forms of words like *e'er* (ever), *o'er* (over), *ere* (before), *thee* (you) appeared commonly in older, traditional poetry. "Mart" for *market* is in that category. Used in a poem written in modern language and style, such words are humorously incongruous.

caucets (line 18)   Nash has humorously misspelled *corsets* to give the appearance of an exact rhyme with "faucets."

stoically (line 21)   Bearing pain or difficulty without showing any emotional reaction; unemotionally.

querulous (line 25)   Complaining.

queasy (line 25)   Particular as to taste or preference.

perpetually (line 32)   Continuously.

STUDY QUESTIONS

1. According to the first **stanza**, why is this kind of poem unpopular?

2. According to the second stanza, many people prefer nature and the natural to human-created things and institutions. How does Nash neatly puncture that belief?

3. How, according to the poem, do artists feel about the city? What practical argument does Nash bring up? How does he use **rhyme** to drive his point home?

4. What are some of the advantages of the city humorously suggested in lines 17–24? In these lines, **synecdoche** is used humorously. Give one or two examples.

5. What example of humorous **hyperbole** occurs in the next-to-last stanza?

6. When Nash uses the words "sissies" and "soft" in the last stanza, does he do so with **connotations** of approval or disapproval? Explain. What is the humor of the word "oft" in the last line?

7. The speakers of "Chicago," "The Purse-Seine," and "The City" have expressed three attitudes toward the cities that have grown up on our land. Which point of view do you personally prefer? Which of the poems did you like best for its language and style?

The City

OGDEN NASH

This beautiful ditty
Is, for a change, about the city,
Although ditties aren't very popular
Unless they're rural and not metropular.

Sentimentalists object to towns initially   5
Because they are made artificially,
But so is vaccination,
While smallpox is an original creation.

Artists speak of everything urban
As the W.C.T.U. speaks of rye and bourbon,   10
And they say cities are only commercial marts,
But they fail to realize that no marts, no arts.

The country was made first,
Yes, but people lived in it and rehearsed,
And when they finally got civilization down,   15
Why, they moved to town.

City people always want the most faucets
And the comfortablest caucets,
And labor-saving devices in their kitchenette,
And at the movies, armchairs in which to set.   20

Take country people, they suffer stoically,
But city people prefer to live unheroically;
Therefore city dentistry is less painful,
Because city dentists find it more gainful.

City people are querulous and queasy,   25
And they'd rather die than not live easy
And if they did die, they'd find fault
If they weren't put in an air-conditioned vault.

Yes, indeed, they are certainly sissies,
Not at all like Hercules or Ulysses,   30
But because they are so soft,
City life is comfortable, if not perpetually, at least oft.

Unit Review : THE GIFT OUTRIGHT

1. Memorable lines   Continue to add to your collection of memorable or quotable lines. From the poems in this unit, select two passages of one line or several. The basis of your selection may be strength of image, music of line, depth of emotion, appeal of theme, or any combination of these. Write the passages in your notebook with title and author. Memorizing the lines will give you added pleasure.

2. Briefly **review the poems** in this unit. Then answer these questions.

  a. Which poem raises questions about the significance of physical memorials and monuments?
  b. Which poem is a song of praise for the vitality of one of our great cities?
  c. Name two poems that are set in particular regions of our country.
  d. Which poem is about our nation's capital and what it symbolizes?
  e. Name two poems that express contrary attitudes or points of view.

3. Show your knowledge of **terms in poetry.** Here are five short passages from the poems in this unit. First, see if you can identify the passage by title and author. Then, choosing from the list of terms below, name the term applicable to the passage.

  allusion   **simile**
  hyperbole   **symbolism**
  personification

  a. "Lilacs in dooryards
      Holding quiet conversations with an early moon"
      (Title? Author? Term?)

  b. "And if they did die, they'd find fault
      If they weren't put in an air-conditioned vault."
      (Title? Author? Term?)

  c. "By Zeus!
      Shout word of this"
      (Title? Author? Term?)

  d. "Swift autumn, like a bonfire of leaves"
      (Title? Author? Term?)

  e. "A star might call: It's a long way across."
      (Title? Author? Term?)

4. Add to your **vocabulary.** Match the definitions in the right-hand column with the words in the left-hand column.

(1) candid	*a.* not talkative
(2) elegance	*b.* outspoken
(3) immaculate	*c.* dignity of style
(4) insulated	*d.* wanderer
(5) luminous	*e.* fitting
(6) meet	*f.* pure
(7) nomad	*g.* separated
(8) perpetually	*h.* bright
(9) reticent	*i.* unemotionally
(10) stoically	*j.* continuously

5. Poems and paintings Poets and painters are artists who have much in common. Study each of the reproductions of paintings that follow. Examine the image carefully. Just what do you see? What feelings does the image arouse in you? What mood or idea does the picture suggest? If a person or persons appear, try to flesh out in your mind their background and character. Is rhythm, metaphor, or symbol important in the picture? After you have studied each picture in this way, select the one that you associate most powerfully in your feelings with one of the poems in this unit. Be ready to discuss or write about your choice and the reasons for it.

Optional: Select one picture that inspires you to write your own poem and write the poem.

Spring on the Hillside   *Wanda Gag. 1936. Whitney Museum, New York.*

Merced River, Yosemite Valley   *Albert Bierstadt. The Metropolitan Museum of Art,*
Gift of the sons of William Paton, 1909.

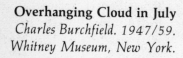

Overhanging Cloud in July
Charles Burchfield. 1947/59.
Whitney Museum, New York.

Midnight Ride of Paul Revere   *Grant Wood. 1931. The Metropolitan Museum of Art, Arthur H. Hearn Fund, 1950. Courtesy of Associated American Artists.*

Times Square Sector
Howard Cook. 1930.
Whitney Museum, New York.

GOOD TIMES—BAD TIMES

In his famous soliloquy, Hamlet thinks of the many bad experiences that outside circumstances can bring to people ("the slings and arrows of outrageous fortune") and of the frailties of our own flesh ("the thousand natural shocks that flesh is heir to"). He thinks of the disappointments we all experience—the broken hearts, the loss of loved ones, the loneliness—and he wonders whether it is better to be dead or alive. ("To be, or not to be: that is the question.") Hamlet was right, of course. There are bad times that are part of everyone's life.

However, there are also times of fun and joy, of satisfaction and fulfillment. There is growing up; there are holidays; there are singing, dancing, music; and there is love. There are good times that are part of everyone's life.

The poems in this unit are about some of the bad times, and some of the good times.

Of all our writers, Poe is the "champ" of the melancholy mood—of sad events and of the broken heart. His best-known poem in this vein is "Annabel Lee." Like that other great tragic love story, *Romeo and Juliet*, this is a tale of two people who are very young, who love with a love that seems made in heaven, whose love is assailed by forces outside them, and whose story ends in tragic death. In this poem, the story content is highly romantic and imaginative, with a mysterious, unreal quality. Its expression of melancholy is crystal clear, however. And its mood is achieved as much through the music of the words as through their meanings.

DEFINITIONS AND EXPLANATIONS

seraphs (line 11)   Angels.

coveted (line 12)   Envied.

highborn (line 17)   Of noble birth; belonging to the aristocracy or royalty.

kinsmen (line 17)   Relatives.

sepulchre (line 19)   Tomb.

dissever (line 32)   Cut apart; separate.

night-tide (line 38)   Nighttime.

STUDY QUESTIONS

1. Notice the curious "facts" of the story. When did the events take place? Where? Annabel Lee's family background is mentioned. What was it? What can you infer about the speaker's background? What was the physical cause of Annabel Lee's death? What does the speaker suggest was the real cause? In what ways are the speaker and Annabel Lee not separated? What kind of "facts" are these? What tone do they create?

2. Might this highly imaginative story have had a parallel in the poet's real experience? If so, what guesses can you make about some of the facts of that experience?

3. Notice some of the ways in which the melancholy mood is expressed through word-music. Which sound is repeated many times in the **end rhymes?** Give several examples of **internal rhyme.** Give several examples of word and phrase **repetitions.**

4. In keeping with the "facts" of the story, the **diction** of the poem creates a mood that is both melancholy and unearthly. List a number of phrases whose **denotation, connotation,** or **imagery** contributes to the mood.

5. How does the speaker cope with his loss?

continued

Annabel Lee

EDGAR ALLAN POE

It was many and many a year ago,
  In a kingdom by the sea,
That a maiden there lived whom you may know
  By the name of Annabel Lee—
And this maiden she lived with no other thought   5
  Than to love and be loved by me.

She was a child and *I* was a child,
  In this kingdom by the sea,
But we loved with a love that was more than love—
  I and my Annabel Lee—   10
With a love that winged seraphs of Heaven
  Coveted her and me.

And this was the reason that, long ago,
  In this kingdom by the sea,
A wind blew out of a cloud by night   15
  Chilling my Annabel Lee;
So that her highborn kinsmen came
  And bore her away from me,
To shut her up in a sepulchre
  In this kingdom by the sea.   20

The angels, not half so happy in Heaven,
  Went envying her and me:—
Yes! that was the reason (as all men know,
  In this kingdom by the sea)
That the wind came out of the cloud, chilling   25
  And killing my Annabel Lee.

continued

Annabel Lee

6. There is no physical description of the two lovers of the story. How do you visualize them in your imagination? Give as complete a description as possible.

7. How do you explain the deep and wide appeal of tales of young, pure love coming to a tragic end, as in "Annabel Lee" and *Romeo and Juliet?*

But our love, it was stronger by far than the love
   Of those who were older than we—
   Of many far wiser than we—
And neither the angels in Heaven above   30
   Nor the demons down under the sea,
Can ever dissever my soul from the soul
   Of the beautiful Annabel Lee:—

For the moon never beams without bringing me dreams
   Of the beautiful Annabel Lee;   35
And the stars never rise but I see the bright eyes
   Of the beautiful Annabel Lee;
And so, all the night-tide, I lie down by the side
Of my darling, my darling, my life and my bride,
   In her sepulchre there by the sea—   40
   In her tomb by the side of the sea.

"A nnabel Lee" tells an imaginary, highly romantic tale of the heart-break of love lost. However, that particular kind of bad time has its certain counterpart in real experience, as reflected by the words of the speaker of this poem. Here an answer is given to an important question: How does a person feel when he or she is separated from one who is dearly loved?

DEFINITION

desolate (line 3)   Lonely; dreary.

STUDY QUESTIONS

1. The speaker is addressing another person. In what sense is the speaker talking to the "you" of the poem? What was the probable relationship between the two people? What has probably happened to the "you"?

2. What can you infer from the poem about what had been the life-style of the two people?

3. What two specific experiences that the couple shared are mentioned? What do the phrases "more than music" and "more than bread" tell you about the relationship?

4. What has been the effect of the loss of the loved one on the mind and heart of the speaker? To what extent do you think this reaction is common among people who are separated from a loved one?

5. What is your guess about the future of the speaker in the face of the tragic loss?

6. Do you find this poem or "Annabel Lee" a more moving expression of the heart-break of love lost? Why?

Music I Heard with You

CONRAD AIKEN

Music I heard with you was more than music,
And bread I broke with you was more than bread;
Now that I am without you, all is desolate;
All that was once so beautiful is dead.

Your hands once touched this table and this silver,   5
And I have seen your fingers hold this glass.
These things do not remember you, beloved,—
And yet your touch upon them will not pass.

For it was in my heart you moved among them,
And blessed them with your hands and with your eyes;   10
And in my heart they will remember always,—
They knew you once, O beautiful and wise!

It is a bad time for lovers when one of the lovers loses the other. It is a bad time for lovers when not one or the other is lost, but love itself goes sour. Why may this happen? What is the result?

STUDY QUESTIONS _____

1. Look at the **image** in the first **stanza.** What are "boatloads of hands"? What work are they going to do? What feelings and associations does the image create for you? How are these feelings and associations continued in the images of the second and third stanzas?

2. In these three stanzas, the mood established by the images is expressed directly in such words as "granite," "bleak," "stuck," "rock," "raw," and "trapped." Give several words that continue the mood in the remainder of the poem.

3. The two important people in the poem are the speaker and the person spoken to. What was the probable relationship between the two at first? What then apparently began to happen? Why do you suppose they came to the Maine lobster town? What was the result of their visit? Which lines metaphorically summarize the result?

4. The poet ends many of his lines with **near-rhymes** arranged in no particular pattern. Examples of near-rhymes are "hands"-"islands," "bleak"-"stuck"-"rock." Give two other examples of near-rhymes. In what way is this technique suitable to the meaning of the poem?

5. In your opinion, who is worse off, the speaker of this poem or the speakers of "Annabel Lee" and "Music I Heard with You"?

Water
ROBERT LOWELL

It was a Maine lobster town—
each morning boatloads of hands
pushed off for granite
quarries on the islands,

and left dozens of bleak   5
white frame houses stuck
like oyster shells
on a hill of rock,

and below us, the sea lapped
the raw little match-stick   10
mazes of a weir,
where the fish for bait were trapped.

Remember? We sat on a slab of rock.
From a distance in time,
it seems the color   15
of iris, rotting and turning purpler,

but it was only
the usual gray rock
turning the usual green
when drenched by the sea.   20

The sea drenched the rock
at our feet all day,
and kept tearing away
flake after flake.

One night you dreamed   25
you were a mermaid clinging to a wharf-pile,
and trying to pull
off the barnacles with your hands.

We wished our two souls
might return like gulls   30
to the rock. In the end,
the water was too cold for us.

When a person has a painful experience, he or she will naturally feel depressed for a time. Eventually, the pain is forgotten and a more balanced outlook returns. Sometimes, in the face of a particularly painful experience, a depression results that goes beyond the original cause and takes on a life of its own. Such a depression will seek and find food everywhere to nurture and fatten itself. The normal case of a painful experience resulting in depression is reversed. The depression results in all experience seeming painful. That is a particularly bad time for the person so affected.

DEFINITIONS AND EXPLANATIONS

thicket (line 4) A thick growth of underbrush or small trees.

waning (line 5) The gradual decreasing of the visible face of the moon after it has become full.

assails (line 10) Attacks.

STUDY QUESTIONS

1. What experience has caused the speaker's depression? (Which lines answer the question?)

2. In her state of depression, the speaker sees examples all about her in nature to confirm the feeling that nothing good lasts. Give several of these examples. Would a happy person have the same reaction to these examples? Explain.

3. Look at the **image** in lines 11 and 12. Then close your eyes and let your imagination—your mind's eye—fill in the specific details of this image. What do you see?

4. What is the lesson that the speaker says "the swift mind" sees everywhere, "be-holds at every turn"? In line 9, the speaker says she has known this lesson always. Do you think that is so? Why?

5. The speaker asks to be pitied because her heart is slow to learn the lesson that "the swift mind beholds at every turn." What does she mean? In your opinion, why is her heart slow to learn the lesson?

6. Look into your crystal ball. What do you foresee in the future of the speaker?

7. Give several examples of effective **alliteration** in the poem. What is the **verse form**?

Pity Me Not

EDNA ST. VINCENT MILLAY

Pity me not because the light of day
At close of day no longer walks the sky;
Pity me not for beauties passed away
From field and thicket as the year goes by;
Pity me not the waning of the moon,   5
Nor that the ebbing tide goes out to sea,
Nor that a man's desire is hushed so soon,
And you no longer look with love on me.
This have I known always: Love is no more
Than the wide blossom which the wind assails,   10
Than the great tide that treads the shifting shore,
Strewing fresh wreckage gathered in the gales:
Pity me that the heart is slow to learn
What the swift mind beholds at every turn.

Earlier, you read a poem by Emily Dickinson that described the feeling of sheer intoxicated joy aroused by the beauty of a summer day. Everyone knows that new love or even infatuation creates the same kind of euphoria, or wild delight and joy in being one's self and in being alive. Everyone knows that such a time is a very good time, maybe the best of times.

EXPLANATIONS

Recuerdo (title)   This is the Spanish word for "I remember."

ferry (line 2)   For many years, a ferry has run from the tip of Manhattan to Staten Island in New York City. It is a scenic, romantic excursion on the water. The salt smell of the sea is in the air. Ocean-going vessels, the Statue of Liberty, the magnificent skyline of lower Manhattan, the wooded hills of Staten Island, the graceful bridges of the city are all part of the vista. Because of the loveliness of the ride and the low fare (for a long time only a nickel), it has been a favorite evening outing for young lovers.

STUDY QUESTIONS

1. State the mood of the lovers suggested by the first two lines. How had they spent the night? What did they eat?

2. Does the poem suggest that the lovers got off the ferry at any point during the evening? If so, what did they do?

3. Where are the lovers when dawn comes? How is the dawn described? Using your imagination, describe the scene in detail. (Where are the lovers exactly? What are they doing? What else do they, and you, see, smell, hear in the scene?)

4. What do the lovers do when they finally leave the ferry?

5. Why do you think the poet used the word "Recuerdo" instead of "I Remember" as the title?

6. As indicated by the title, the speaker is recalling the night in her memory. In your opinion, is it a long time later or fairly soon afterward? What is the mood of the speaker at the time she is remembering? What is your guess as to the place and situation of this remembering?

7. Note that Millay wrote "Pity Me Not" as well as this poem. What conclusions do you draw from this fact?

Recuerdo

EDNA ST. VINCENT MILLAY

We were very tired, we were very merry—
We had gone back and forth all night on the ferry.
It was bare and bright, and smelled like a stable—
But we looked into a fire, we leaned across a table,
We lay on a hill-top underneath the moon;   5
And the whistles kept blowing, and the dawn came soon.

We were very tired, we were very merry—
We had gone back and forth all night on the ferry;
And you ate an apple, and I ate a pear,
From a dozen of each we had bought somewhere;   10
And the sky went wan, and the wind came cold,
And the sun rose dripping, a bucketful of gold.

We were very tired, we were very merry,
We had gone back and forth all night on the ferry.
We hailed, "Good morrow, mother!" to a shawl-covered head,   15
And bought a morning paper, which neither of us read;
And she wept, "God bless you!" for the apples and pears,
And we gave her all our money but our subway fares.

Here is a poem in the form of a simple brief note from one person to another. You can read the poem at the surface level and you will surely enjoy it. For all its brevity and simplicity, it is alive, vivid, and somehow very down to earth. However, such a note does not occur in a vacuum. It involves two real people and the complexities of the relationship between them. Look beneath the surface. Begin to read the poem more carefully, and you will want to answer some intriguing questions about these two people and their situation.

EXPLANATION

This Is Just to Say   These words serve as both title and first line of the poem.

STUDY QUESTIONS

1. Who is the writer of the note? To whom is it addressed?

2. At what time of day did the eating of the plums probably take place? Why do you think the writer ate the plums? Where do you think the other person was at the time?

3. The **diction** of the poem is important. In what circumstances would a person usually begin a written message with the words "This is just to say"? Under what circumstances does a person say "Forgive me"? Is this such a circumstance? If not, why were the words used?

4. Why does the writer mention that the other person was probably saving the plums for breakfast and then go on to describe carefully how "delicious," "sweet," and "cold" they were?

5. What do you think was the real message intended by the writer? How do you think the other person will react to the note? What general conclusions do you draw about the two people and the relationship between them?

6. This poem consists of only 33 words, 26 of which are of one syllable, and all of which are as simple, direct, and ordinary as words can be. Yet the poem has a powerful impact on the feelings of most readers and often stirs heated differences of opinion as to what lies behind the words. How do you explain this?

7. You will find it fun to try writing a similar poem. First, think up a situation between any two people—for example, two friends, two members of a family, a doctor and a patient, two fellow students or a teacher and a student, a boss and an employee. In that situation, one writes a note to the other. Write the note as a skeleton-bare poem in the style of "This Is Just to Say." Try to make it a poem that will make the reader itch to put flesh on the skeleton.

This Is Just to Say

WILLIAM CARLOS WILLIAMS

I have eaten
the plums
that were in
the icebox

and which   5
you were probably
saving
for breakfast

Forgive me
they were delicious   10
so sweet
and so cold

Young people tend to be idealistic in their expectations, and sometimes they are rudely disappointed when reality turns out to be a little different from their dreams. This can be especially true in boy-girl relationships, when the difference between being "in love with love" and being in love becomes clear.

STUDY QUESTIONS

1. What had the girl who is the speaker in this poem hoped for? Has that hope been fulfilled?

2. The speaker expresses her state of mind in a **simile.** What is the simile? What is her state of mind? Why is she in this state of mind?

3. In view of the total statement made in the poem, how would you explain the hope the girl had?

4. What is your guess as to the age of the speaker? How deep is her disappointment? Do you think she has learned something from the experience? What?

5. What effect do you suppose all this is going to have on the boy?

6. How common do you feel the kind of experience described in this poem is? Is any permanent damage likely to be involved?

7. Why do you think the poet chose to title this poem "The Kiss"?

The Kiss

SARA TEASDALE

I hoped that he would love me,
  And he has kissed my mouth,
But I am like a stricken bird
  That cannot reach the south.

For though I know he loves me,   5
  To-night my heart is sad;
His kiss was not so wonderful
  As all the dreams I had.

For the young, who are just learning what the game of life is like, even love can have its difficulties, as the girl of "The Kiss" found out. This poem tells about a father's way of expressing his love for his little son, resulting in an experience that had a meaning different for the child from the meaning it had for the father.

STUDY QUESTIONS

1. About how old is the boy in the poem? How do you know?

2. Perhaps the waltz was triggered by something the mother said. What might that have been?

3. What does the poem tell you about the father himself and about his feelings toward his son? (In arriving at your answer, be sure to include what you learn from line 10 and line 14 and the answer you gave to question 2.)

4. Describe the dance and its various effects on the boy.

5. Consider the feelings of the three people during the incident. How did the boy feel? How did the father feel? How did the mother feel? Why didn't she interfere?

6. The speaker is not the boy, but the boy grown to manhood and remembering. How does he now view his father? (How does the title help you to answer this question?) What may have brought this memory into the speaker's mind?

7. You know the speaker's childhood background. What kind of man has he grown to be?

My Papa's Waltz

THEODORE ROETHKE

The whiskey on your breath
Could make a small boy dizzy;
But I hung on like death:
Such waltzing was not easy.

We romped until the pans   5
Slid from the kitchen shelf;
My mother's countenance
Could not unfrown itself.

The hand that held my wrist
Was battered on one knuckle;   10
At every step you missed
My right ear scraped a buckle.

You beat time on my head
With a palm caked hard by dirt,
Then waltzed me off to bed   15
Still clinging to your shirt.

A bad time that practically everyone goes through is the so-called awkward age—the year or so when childhood is gone and adolescence has not quite arrived. Though the suffering of this stage of life is very real and very serious for the poor victim, it also has its humorous side. Having all been through it, we know that the difficult stage is temporary and the suffering will not last. We can all enjoy this portrait of a thirteen-year-old girl, written with a balanced mixture of sympathetic understanding and appropriately light humor.

DEFINITIONS AND EXPLANATIONS

wit (line 2) The ability to make clever talk.

Wednesday matinées (line 3) Afternoon performances in the theater are traditionally given on Wednesdays.

misses' clothing (line 3) Girls of a certain age usually look forward to moving from the children's clothing department to the misses' clothing department.

Sara Crewe (line 7) A once-popular children's book, written chiefly for girls, by Frances Burnett, also author of *Little Lord Fauntleroy.*

movie magazine (line 7) Some teenagers are fascinated by gossip and tales of glamour about the lives of the movie stars. *Movie Magazine* has been published for that audience.

anomalous (line 17) Not normal; not fiting together; incongruous.

chrysalis (line 19) The cocoon stage of a moth.

STUDY QUESTIONS

1. The first line of the poem states the theme. What is the theme?

2. According to lines 2–4, what are some characteristics of the life-style of the more mature girl, who has passed through the awkward age?

3. Of the activities and interests mentioned in lines 5–8, which belong to childhood? Which belong to the older teenager?

4. What is the chief characteristic of "thirteen" suggested in the second **stanza?**

What are the "masks" and "disguises" referred to in line 15?

5. What is the understood subject of the sentence in line 20? Explain. (How does it relate to the preceding pair of lines?)

6. What is the reason "thirteen" cannot be "quite recalled—/Not even with pity"?

7. Do you feel that this is a true portrait? Is the tone of the poem light or serious? To what extent do boys pass through a similar stage?

Portrait of Girl with Comic Book

PHYLLIS McGINLEY

Thirteen's no age at all. Thirteen is nothing.
It is not wit, or powder on the face,
Or Wednesday matinées, or misses' clothing,
Or intellect, or grace.
Twelve has its tribal customs. But thirteen   5
Is neither boys in battered cars nor dolls,
Nor *Sara Crewe*, or movie magazine,
Or pennants on the walls.

Thirteen keeps diaries and tropical fish
(A month, at most); scorns jumpropes in the spring;   10
Could not, would fortune grant it, name its wish;
Wants nothing, everything;
Has secrets from itself, friends it despises;
Admits none to the terrors that it feels;
Owns half a hundred masks but no disguises;   15
And walks upon its heels.

Thirteen's anomalous—not that, not this:
Not folded bud, or wave that laps a shore,
Or moth proverbial from the chrysalis.
Is the one age defeats the metaphor.   20
Is not a town, like childhood, strongly walled
But easily surrounded; is no city.
Nor, quitted once, can it be quite recalled—
Not even with pity.

There is a side to life, which most of us come to know sooner or later, that is perhaps the worst of all bad times. That side is when death or maiming strikes suddenly, unexpectedly, meaninglessly, wastefully. At such a time, the uncertainty and unpredictability that is part of all experience takes a form so fierce and so intense as to be very nearly overwhelming.

DEFINITION AND EXPLANATION

"Out, Out—" (title) In Shakespeare's tragic play, Macbeth is told the unwelcome and unexpected news of his wife's death. He speaks the following famous lines, from which the title of this poem is taken.

"To-morrow, and to-morrow, and
   to-morrow
Creeps in this petty pace from day to day
To the last syllable of recorded time;
And all our yesterdays have lighted fools

The way to dusty death. Out, out, brief
   candle!
Life's but a walking shadow, a poor
   player,
That struts and frets his hour upon
   the stage
And then is heard no more. It is a tale
Told by an idiot, full of sound and fury,
Signifying nothing."

rueful (line 19) Mournful.

STUDY QUESTIONS

1. The speaker is an onlooker at the scene. Is he a member of the family or someone else? What is the setting?

2. Look at the first nine lines, in which the speaker watches the boy at work, fixes his attention elsewhere for a moment, and then has his attention redrawn to the boy and the buzz saw. How do the very first words foreshadow danger? What close observations does the onlooker make as he watches the boy at work? Where does his attention then wander? Why is his attention again drawn back to the boy? How does this sequence of events affect the strength of the sense of danger created by the opening words of the poem? How does line 9 reinforce the suspense? Nowhere in these lines is the boy ever mentioned! Why?

3. What wish does the speaker express in lines 10–11? Do you think he thought of the wish at that moment or later?

4. Who is the "they" in line 10 and the "them" in lines 13 and 14? What happened when the sister announced supper? What was the boy's reaction in the first instant? How do you explain that reaction? What was his next reaction? What was "spilling"? What great fear does the boy have?

5. Describe the scene at the boy's death, beginning at line 28.

6. Macbeth's reaction to his wife's tragic death was that life was very short, a "brief candle," and meaningless, "a tale told by an idiot." What is the reaction to this tragic death as expressed in the last two lines of the poem?

7. Do you know people who have experienced the untimely, tragic loss of a loved one? How did they cope?

"Out, Out—"

ROBERT FROST

The buzz saw snarled and rattled in the yard
And made dust and dropped stove-length sticks of wood,
Sweet-scented stuff when the breeze drew across it.
And from there those that lifted eyes could count
Five mountain ranges one behind the other   5
Under the sunset far into Vermont.
And the saw snarled and rattled, snarled and rattled,
As it ran light, or had to bear a load.
And nothing happened: day was all but done.
Call it a day, I wish they might have said   10
To please the boy by giving him the half hour
That a boy counts so much when saved from work.
His sister stood beside them in her apron
To tell them "Supper." At the word, the saw,
As if to prove saws knew what supper meant,   15
Leaped out at the boy's hand, or seemed to leap—
He must have given the hand. However it was,
Neither refused the meeting. But the hand!
The boy's first outcry was a rueful laugh,
As he swung toward them holding up the hand,   20
Half in appeal, but half as if to keep
The life from spilling. Then the boy saw all—
Since he was old enough to know, big boy
Doing a man's work, though a child at heart—
He saw all spoiled. "Don't let him cut my hand off—   25
The doctor, when he comes. Don't let him, sister!"
So. But the hand was gone already.
The doctor put him in the dark of ether.
He lay and puffed his lips out with his breath.
And then—the watcher at his pulse took fright.   30
No one believed. They listened at his heart.
Little—less—nothing!—and that ended it.
No more to build on there. And they, since they
Were not the one dead, turned to their affairs.

Tragic death can strike the infant, the child, the youth, the young adult. It is hard to say which is the worst for those who are bereaved. This poem tells how a young mother attempts to cope with the death of her husband.

STUDY QUESTIONS

1. How many children are there in this family? What are their names and approximate ages?

2. According to the first line, the mother is speaking to the children. Is she really? Explain.

3. What seems to be the economic status of the fatherless family? What kind of thoughts chiefly occupy the mother's mind? How do her thoughts reflect both her feeling for her dead husband and her feeling for the living children?

4. Why does the mother say the following?

"Anne, eat your breakfast;
Dan, take your medicine"

5. What emotion is the mother expressing in the last line? How is she dealing with this emotion?

6. What feelings do you have toward this mother? How do you guess the family will fare?

Lament

EDNA ST. VINCENT MILLAY

Listen, children:
Your father is dead.
From his old coats
I'll make you little jackets;
I'll make you little trousers   5
From his old pants.
There'll be in his pockets
Things he used to put there,
Keys and pennies
Covered with tobacco;   10
Dan shall have the pennies
To save in his bank;
Anne shall have the keys
To make a pretty noise with.
Life must go on,   15
And the dead be forgotten;
Life must go on,
Though good men die;
Anne, eat your breakfast;
Dan, take your medicine;   20
Life must go on;
I forget just why.

For some children, summer can be a joyous time of the family together, of vacation at shore or country, of games and sports, of relaxation and fun. For a child, time hardly exists, and the delicious summer seems to last forever. But that is an illusion. Summer ends. The child grows up. For the adult, time moves faster and faster. The adult remembers the seemingly endless summer of childhood, sadly.

DEFINITIONS AND EXPLANATIONS

pizzicato (line 5) The plucking of the strings of a violin or other stringed instrument with the fingers instead of running the bow across the strings.

auburn (line 5) Reddish brown (referring here to suntan).

sloops (line 12) Small, one-masted sailboats.

gramophone (line 19) A hand-wound record player of years ago.

Bye Bye Blues Lindy's Coming (line 21) These are the titles of two popular songs of the 1920's.

wantonly (line 25) Freely, unrestrainedly; wastefully.

familial (line 25) Belonging to or involving the family.

chidingly (line 26) In the manner of scolding or rebuking.

sacks (line 27) Plunders; loots; lays waste.

STUDY QUESTIONS

1. The remembered summer is remembered mainly by sound. List the sounds that are recalled in the speaker's memory.

2. Through the named sounds, a clear picture of the remembered setting is suggested. Tell everything you can about that setting. For example: What is the locale? What people are present? What sort of house do they probably occupy? How spacious are the grounds?

3. This is a poem of sounds, not only of sounds named but also of the musical sounds in the words themselves. There are **onomatopoetic** words, such as "humming," "mumbling," "whirring." Give several other onomatopoetic words from the poem. There is **alliteration**. Give several examples. There is **repetition** of words and syllables and letter sounds. Give several examples. Do you feel that an overall emotional tone is expressed by these word sounds? What is it?

4. Notice the words "Hear" and "listen" repeated in lines 17 and 18. To whom is the speaker addressing these words? What is their purpose?

5. Who is saying "Time's Up" in lines 23 and 24? The same sentence is picked up in line 26 with a different meaning. What is the new meaning?

6. Why are the children mute and their clamor unvoiced (line 27)? What feeling is the speaker expressing when she says that the "unvoiced clamor sacks the summer air"?

7. What is the real feeling expressed in the question asked in the last line of the poem?

8. Do you have a vivid memory of a delightful and innocent time from your childhood that you recall with a mixture of pleasure in the memory and painful sorrow at time's passing? What is the memory?

Summer Remembered

ISABELLA GARDNER

Sounds sum and summon the remembering of summers.
The humming of the sun
The mumbling in the honey-suckle vine
The whirring in the clovered grass
The pizzicato plinkle of ice in an auburn   5
uncle's amber glass.
The whing of father's racquet and the whack
of brother's bat on cousin's ball
and calling voices call-
ing voices spilling voices . . .   10

The munching of saltwater at the splintered dock
The slap and slop of waves on little sloops
The quarreling of oarlocks hours across the bay
The canvas sails that bleat as they
are blown. The heaving buoy bell-   15
ing HERE I am
HERE you are HEAR HEAR

listen listen listen
The gramophone is wound
the music goes round and around   20
BYE BYE BLUES   LINDY'S COMING
voices calling   calling   calling
"Children!   Children!   Time's Up
Time's Up"
Merrily sturdily wantonly the familial voices   25
cheerily chidingly call to the children   TIME'S UP
and the mute children's unvoiced clamor sacks the summer air
crying Mother   Mother   are you there?

Everybody gets blue once in a while. Sometimes this melancholy mood comes as a result of some small disappointment; sometimes, perhaps, as a result of natural rhythms of emotional ups and downs. Maybe we even enjoy feeling sorry for ourselves occasionally. We can all use a little sympathy once in a while, even if we have to give it to ourselves! The fact that we all experience these periods of emotional downs probably accounts, at least in part, for the existence and enduring popularity of the form of American music known as "Blues." This music both expresses and gives relief to the melancholy mood. Here is a poem that is about being blue and is itself a piece of Blues music.

STUDY QUESTIONS

1. Try reading the whole poem aloud to make it sound like a Blues song. You will have to experiment with vocal expression and intonation. Try several readings until you are satisfied that your vocal expression and intonation are in the Blues manner.

2. Notice the words used to describe the blues in the first line—"sad old weary." What tone is established by this choice of words?

3. What specific effects of feeling blue are given in the first **stanza?** How do you explain these effects? Specifically, is it true that "Nobody cares about you/When you sink so low"?

4. Is the speaker seriously contemplating suicide? How do you know?

5. Look up the words of any popular Blues song, old or new. How do they compare to the words of "Too Blue"? Try fitting the words of "Too Blue" to a Blues tune that you know or an original one you can improvise yourself. What is the real message of this poem and of Blues music?

Too Blue

LANGSTON HUGHES

I got those sad old weary blues.
I don't know where to turn.
I don't know where to go.
Nobody cares about you
When you sink so low.   5

What shall I do?
What shall I say?
Shall I take a gun and
Put myself away?

I wonder if   10
One bullet would do?
Hard as my head is,
It would probably take two.

But I ain't got
Neither bullet nor gun—   15
And I'm too blue
To look for one.

Nothing has wider appeal to our emotions than our popular songs and music. We all listen to our own favorites of past and present on radio and record player. If we can, we sing them or play them. We remember for a long time the words and tunes of songs from different periods of our lives. Why? The sound is a pleasure in itself, a form of relaxation and entertainment. More, these songs are a release for us; they give expression to our own inexpressible longings, joys, sorrows, angers, hopes. They make us aware that we are not alone in these feelings. This poem is about the greatest form of American music, and it helps explain what the music says and does for us.

EXPLANATION

Jazz Fantasia (title) Two of the great forms of native American music, jazz and Blues, originated in the South from the folk music of the slaves brought here from Africa. Jazz is thought to have originated specifically in New Orleans, which certainly became the world capital of jazz. The early jazz musicians did not play from written scores, and in their improvisations, they gave full and free expression to deeply felt emotions and moods. Among the great names of jazz are Louis Armstrong and Duke Ellington. A fantasia is a musical composition of no fixed form or a medley of tunes.

STUDY QUESTIONS

1. What musical instruments do the jazzmen of this group use?

2. What specific emotions and moods does the speaker urge the jazzmen to reflect in their music? Why does the speaker so urge them?

3. Select lines at which you think certain instruments would predominate. Where would the saxophone predominate? the drums and traps? the trombone?

4. The poem reflects in its own sounds the sounds of the music it is written about. Give several examples of **onomatopoeia** and **alliteration** so used. Give ex- amples of **rhythms** in these **free-verse** lines so used.

5. Repeat for this poem the experiment in reading aloud for musical effect that you tried with "Too Blue."

6. How do you explain the wide and deep appeal that jazz, Blues, rock, and other forms of popular music have had for the American audience? What is your own favorite song? Why?

7. What similarities are there between the appeal of songs and the appeal of poetry? What differences are there?

Jazz Fantasia

CARL SANDBURG

Drum on your drums, batter on your banjoes,
sob on the long cool winding saxophones.
Go to it, O jazzmen.

1

Sling your knuckles on the bottoms of the happy
tin pans, let your trombones ooze, and go husha-
husha-hush with the slippery sand-paper.

2

Moan like an autumn wind high in the lonesome treetops, moan
soft like you wanted somebody terrible, cry like a racing car slipping away from a motorcycle cop, bang-bang! you jazzmen, bang
altogether drums, traps, banjoes, horns, tin cans—make two
people fight on the top of a stairway and scratch each other's eyes
in a clinch tumbling down the stairs.

3

Can the rough stuff . . . now a Mississippi steamboat pushes up the
night river with a hoo-hoo-hoo-oo . . . and the green lanterns
calling to the high soft stars . . . a red moon rides on the humps of
the low river hills . . . go to it, O jazzmen.

4

There is a mood that is the opposite of being blue. It doesn't have a color name, but it is a time when we are full of the joy of being alive, when we are happy with everything and everyone around us, and, above all, delighted to be ourselves. In this tiny gem of a poem, the speaker's own gladness is so bright it shines on us.

DEFINITION

tulip tree (line 5)   A tree of the magnolia family, with large, tulip-shaped, greenish-yellow blossoms.

STUDY QUESTIONS

1. What is the "going-home sun"? Suggest several ways in which this first line by **image** and **connotation** creates an opening note of gladness and brightness.

2. What is the actual effect on the speaker's eyes that is described in the second line? How does this line continue the note of brightness and gladness?

3. What is the "rough stick" of line 3? How do lines 3 and 4 suggest the presence of bright light? How is near-rhyme used within the **image** of these lines to add to the note of lively, sharp brightness?

4. What does the speaker see as he comes close to home (lines 5–7)? How are these lines emphasized by the **stanza** arrangement? What feelings are suggested to you by the stanza?

5. What does the speaker do? What are the feelings that lie behind this action?

6. This very short spare poem tells you directly and suggests a good deal more indirectly about the two people. Tell everything you know about them.

7. Explain the title.

The Fact
DAVE ETTER

The going-home sun
smiles my railroad eyes.

I run a rough stick
across the last picket fence.

Under our tulip tree   5
you wait in the yellow dust
smoothing a lilac dress.

I touch my arms, my chest,
watch my moving feet.

I have to know it's me,   10
really me, always.

When we are in a supremely happy mood, laughter comes easy. We are ready to see pleasant humor all about us. The speaker of this poem looks at his toes, has a little joke about them, and shares it with us.

EXPLANATIONS

In Extremis (title) This Latin phrase means "at the extremity or far end"; it is commonly used more specifically to mean "near death."

j'accuse (line 13) These French words for "I accuse" were the dramatic title of an essay by the French writer Émile Zola, which was of historical importance in the famous Dreyfus case.

STUDY QUESTIONS

1. The title is a pun, a play on the two meanings of the Latin phrase. Explain the pun. How is it carried into the poem?

2. In what well-known way were his toes the speaker's "best friends once" (line 4)? What does he humorously suggest have replaced the toes as close friends?

3. Explain the humor, also involving puns, of lines 11 and 12.

4. How are the toes humorously personified in line 13? What is their accusation?

Why does the speaker hide them in his shoes? How does the **rhyme** add to the humor of the final **couplet**?

5. Are toes an especially suitable subject for good-natured humor such as this? Why? Can you suggest any other part of the body or item of dress or other everyday object that would be a good subject for humorous exaggeration?

In Extremis

JOHN UPDIKE

I saw my toes the other day.
I hadn't looked at them for months.
Indeed, they might have passed away.
And yet they were my best friends once.

When I was small, I knew them well.   5
I counted on them up to ten
And put them in my mouth to tell
The larger from the lesser. Then

I loved them better than my ears,
My elbows, adenoids, and heart.   10
But with the swelling of the years
We drifted, toes and I, apart.

Now, gnarled and pale, each said, *j'accuse!*—
I hid them quickly in my shoes.

Unit Review : GOOD TIMES—BAD TIMES

1. Memorable lines Complete your collection of memorable or quotable lines. From the poems in this unit, select two passages of one line or several. The basis of your selection may be strength of image, music of line, depth of emotion, appeal of theme, or any combination of these. Write the passages in your notebook with title and author. Memorizing the lines will give you added pleasure.

2. Briefly **review the poems** in this unit. Then answer these questions.

  a. Name the one "good time" poem that you liked best.
  b. Name the one "bad time" poem that affected you most deeply.
  c. Name a poem in which the age of the speaker is directly related to the problem.
  d. Name a poem in which the speaker is relating a memory.
  e. Name a poem in which the "sound effects" are especially important.

3. Show your knowledge of **terms in poetry.** Here are five short passages from the poems in this unit. First, see if you can identify the passage by title and author. Then, choosing from the list of terms below, name the term applicable to the passage.

alliteration	**onomatopoeia**
internal rhyme	**personification**
near-rhyme	

  a. "For the moon never beams without bringing me dreams"
     (Title? Author? Term?)

  b. "white frame houses stuck
     like oyster shells
     on a hill of rock"
     (Title? Author? Term?)

  c. "Pity me not because the light of day
     At close of day no longer walks the sky"
     (Title? Author? Term?)

  d. "Sweet-scented stuff when the breeze draws across it."
     (Title? Author? Term?)

  e. "The whirring in the clovered grass"
     (Title? Author? Term?)

4. Add to your **vocabulary**. Match the definitions in the right-hand column with the words in the left-hand column.

(1)	anomalous	*a.*	envied
(2)	assails	*b.*	separate
(3)	auburn	*c.*	dreary
(4)	coveted	*d.*	attacks
(5)	desolate	*e.*	decreasing
(6)	dissever	*f.*	not fitting together
(7)	familial	*g.*	reddish brown
(8)	sacks	*h.*	belonging to the family
(9)	waning	*i.*	wastefully
(10)	wantonly	*j.*	plunders

5. Poems and paintings Poets and painters are artists who have much in common. Study each of the reproductions of paintings that follow. Examine the image carefully. Just what do you see? What feelings does the image arouse in you? What mood or idea does the picture suggest? If a person or persons appear, try to flesh out in your mind their background and character. Is rhythm, metaphor, or symbol important in the picture? After you have studied each picture in this way, select the one that you associate most powerfully in your feelings with one of the poems in this unit. Be ready to discuss or write about your choice and the reasons for it.

Optional: Select one picture that inspires you to write your own poem and write the poem.

Dust, Drought and Destruction *William C. Palmer. 1934. Whitney Museum, New York.*

The Silent Seasons—Fall
Will Barnet. 1967.
Whitney Museum, New York.

String Quartette   *Jack Levine. The Metropolitan Museum of Art,*
Arthur H. Hearn Fund, 1942.

Still Life   *Harley Perkins. 1926. Whitney Museum, New York.*

Self-Portrait
*Bradley Walker Tomlin. 1932.
Whitney Museum, New York.*

285

FINAL REVIEW

Study the pictures that follow as you studied those in each Unit Review. Your teacher will give you the follow-up assignment.

Good Evening Mr. Smallweiner, Sr. *Tommy Dale Palmore. 1971. Whitney Museum, New York.*

Family *Charles H. Alston. 1955. Whitney Museum, New York.*

√ **Office in a Small City** *Edward Hopper. 1953. The Metropolitan Museum of Art, George A. Hearn Fund, 1953.*

Anatomical Painting
Pavel Tchelitchew. 1945.
Whitney Museum, New York.

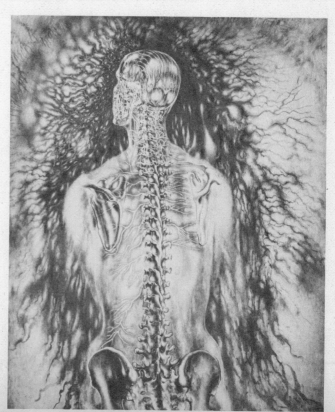

War Series: Beachhead   *Jacob Lawrence. 1947. Whitney Museum, New York.*

Indian Encampment   *Unknown American artist. c. 1850–75.*
Whitney Museum, New York.

Family Portrait *Marisol. 1961. Whitney Museum, New York.*

The Untilled Field *Peggy Bacon. 1937. Whitney Museum, New York.*

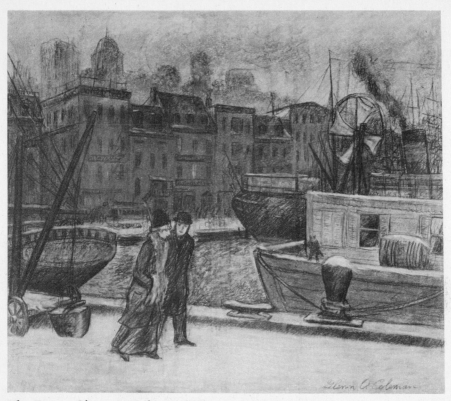

The Pier *Glenn O. Coleman. Whitney Museum, New York.*

Portrait of a Living Room
Dorothy Varian. 1944. Whitney Museum, New York.

Glossary of Terms in Poetry

Alliteration is the repetition of initial consonant sounds. Alliteration occurs in such names as Woodrow Wilson, Charlie Chaplin, Billy Budd, Simple Simon, Greta Garbo, and in such common expressions as "safe and sound," "rags to riches," "tip to toe," "do or die." The repetitions create a design or pattern of sounds that lends emphasis to the words and is memorable to the ear. In poetry, alliterated sounds blend artistically with other sounds, with word meaning, with **image** to create the total meaning effect of the poem. The following stanza from Coleridge's "The Rime of the Ancient Mariner" tells how the mariner's ship has been sailing before a brisk fresh wind and is suddenly totally and helplessly becalmed. It is a fine illustration of the artistic use of an interplay of alliterative sounds.

> "The fair breeze blew, the white foam flew,
>   The furrow followed free;
>   We were the first that ever burst
>   Into that silent sea."

Other examples are

> "The blazing brightness of her beauties beam"
>
> Edmund Spenser

> "Man's inhumanity to man.
>   Makes countless thousands mourn!"
>
> Robert Burns

> "Ay, they heard his foot upon the stirrup
>   And the sound of iron on stone
> And how the silence surged softly backward,
>   When the plunging hoofs were gone."
>
> Walter de la Mare

Allusion is a brief reference to a person, a place, an event, or to well-known words. An allusion may be drawn from history, literature, geography, the Bible, mythology, or any other area of knowledge. The author expects the reader to recognize the allusion and get the full meaning suggested by the brief word or phrase. For example, suppose a newspaper editorial says that a new law will open a Pandora's box. If you know the story of Pandora from Greek mythology, you know that the editorial is saying that the new law will let loose many unforeseen and unmanageable problems and difficulties. In the stanza below, from a poem about the spider, full understanding of the lines depends on an understanding of the allusion to Euclid, the "father" of plane geometry.

"He does not know he is unkind,
He has a jewel for a mind
And logic deadly as dry bone
This small son of Euclid's own."

Robert P. Tristram Coffin

The full meaning of the following lines depends on the allusions to Austerlitz and Waterloo, two crucial, bloody battles of the Napoleonic Wars.

"Pile the bodies high at Austerlitz and Waterloo.
Shovel them under and let me work—
I am the grass; I cover all."

Carl Sandburg

Ambiguity is the presence of two or more possible meanings or interpretations. A simple and familiar form of ambiguity is the *pun*, in which the double meaning of a word is played on for humorous effect. "What has four wheels and flies? A garbage truck." Shakespeare played on the meanings of words at a somewhat higher and sometimes more serious level. In *Romeo and Juliet*, Mercutio, a light-hearted person, lies mortally wounded and says, "Ask for me tomorrow, and you shall find me a *grave* man." Othello, insanely jealous of his wife Desdemona, decides to kill her by suffocating her with a pillow as she lies sleeping. First, he lowers the light of the lamp by her bedside; then, after giving her the kiss of death, he places the pillow on her face to snuff out her life. These two actions are accompanied by the words, "Put out the light, and then put out the light." In poetry, titles, single words, lines, the identity of the speaker, even the circumstances, can be ambiguous. Too, ambiguity can be regarded as a general characteristic of poetry because meaning in poetry is often multileveled, suggested, and open-ended. In this sense, poetry simply parallels real experience in which meaning is more often ambiguous than it is clear and simple, which is why we have so much difficulty in learning from history, making good laws, and finding clear-cut answers to personal problems and the problems of society.

Analogy is a comparison between two things that are actually alike in many respects. For example, an analogy is often made between the way electricity flows through a wire and the way water flows through a pipe. An analogy is a *literal* comparison as opposed to the **figurative** comparisons made in **simile, personification,** and **metaphor.** When scientists perform experiments on laboratory animals to learn about human beings, they are depending on analogies between humans and animals to draw conclusions applicable to both.

Anapestic foot. See **Meter.**

Anticlimax is the deliberate leading up to a big letdown, for the sake of humor or **irony,** as in the following examples:

> "See how the world its veterans rewards!
> A youth of frolics, an old age of cards."
>
> Alexander Pope

> "And there, there overhead, there, there hung over
> Those thousands of white faces, those dazed eyes,
> There in the starless dark, the poise, the hover,
> There with vast wings across the canceled skies,
> There in the sudden blackness, the black pall
> Of nothing, nothing, nothing—nothing at all."
>
> Archibald MacLeish

Antithesis is the placing together of contrasting ideas, often for the sake of **irony,** as in the following example:

> "O God! that bread should be so dear,
> And flesh and blood so cheap!"
>
> Thomas Hood

Apostrophe is the addressing of words to someone absent or something nonhuman as if it were present or human. The following are examples:

> "Thou, too, sail on, O Ship of State!
> Sail on, O Union, strong and great!"
>
> Henry Wadsworth Longfellow

> "O wind, rend open the heat,
> cut apart the heat,
> rend it to tatters."
>
> H. D.

> "O black and unknown bards of long ago,
> How came your lips to touch the sacred fire?"
>
> James Weldon Johnson

Assonance is the repetition of vowel sounds, as in the expression "fit as a fiddle" and in the following examples:

> "The greatest and richest good,
> My own life to live in,
> This she has given me—
>
> If giver could."

Archibald MacLeish

The following passage is an example of a rich, musical interlacing of assonance with **alliteration** and **consonance** and other **sound effects.**

> "How to keep—is there any any, is there none such, nowhere
> known some, bow or brooch or braid or brace, lace,
> latch or catch or key to keep
> Back beauty, keep it, beauty, beauty, beauty . . . from
> vanishing away?"

Gerard Manley Hopkins

Blank verse is poetry written in lines of **iambic pentameter** without **rhyme.** (Blank verse should not be confused with **free verse.**) What is generally recognized as the greatest poetry of the English language—the tragedies of Shakespeare and the epics of John Milton—is written in blank verse. Some memorable examples follow.

> "A mind not to be chang'd by place or time.
> The mind is its own place, and in itself
> Can make a heaven of hell, a hell of heaven."

John Milton

> "A dungeon horrible on all sides round
> As one great furnace flamed; yet from those flames
> No light; but rather darkness visible
> Served only to discover sights of woe,
> Regions of sorrow, doleful shades . . ."

John Milton

> ". . . Besides, this Duncan
> Hath borne his faculties so meek, hath been
> So clear in his great office, that his virtues
> Will plead like angels, trumpet-tongued, against
> The deep damnation of his taking-off"

William Shakespeare

In this book, Robert Frost's "'Out, Out'—" is written in blank verse.

Cacophony is a combination of sounds that are harsh and grating in effect. The poet will deliberately make use of cacophonous sounds to support an unpleasant mood, idea, or **image,** as in the following examples:

"The old South Boston Aquarium stands
in a Sahara of snow now. Its broken windows are boarded.
The bronze weathervane cod has lost half its scales.
The airy tanks are dry."

Robert Lowell

"Bent double, like old beggars under sacks,
Knock-kneed, coughing like hags, we cursed through sludge."

Wilfred Owen

"The buzz saw snarled and rattled in the yard."

Robert Frost

Cinquain. The cinquain is a poem of five lines consisting, respectively, of two, four, six, eight, and two syllables. This **verse form,** probably suggested by the Japanese **haiku,** was originated by the American poet Adelaide Crapsey. Her poem "November Night" is an example of the simple delicacy of the cinquain.

"Listen . . .
With faint dry sound,
Like steps of passing ghosts.
The leaves, frost-crisped, break from the trees
And fall."

Connotation is the overtone of meaning suggested by a word or words beyond their dictionary meaning. For example, the words "horse" and "steed" denote the same animal. However, "steed" has romantic and historical connotations that "horse" does not. Words like "doubloon," "corsair," and "cutlass" have connotations that "coin," "sail ship," and "knife" do not. The connotations of "filet mignon" and "champagne" are different from those of "steak" and "beer." Snakes and turtles are both reptiles; the connotations of "snake" and "turtle" are entirely different. Connotation is an important resource of the poet in creating a language of rich multidimensional meaning to parallel the complexity of human feeling and human experience.

Consonance is the repetition of final consonant sounds, as in such expressions as "la<u>st</u> but not lea<u>st</u>," "fir<u>st</u> and foremo<u>st</u>," "par<u>k</u> and lo<u>ck</u>," "o<u>dds</u> and en<u>ds</u>," and in the following examples from poetry:

"I saw his cropp<u>ed</u> haircut go under.
I leap<u>t</u>, and my steep body flash<u>ed</u>"

James Dickey

"Our throats were tight as tourniquets,
Our feet were bound with splints, but now,
Like convalescents . . ."

Karl Shapiro

Couplet is a pair of rhyming lines. The most widely used couplet is the heroic couplet, written in **iambic pentameter.** An entire poem can consist of couplets, or a couplet may occur only occasionally, or it may occur in a single instance in a poem, usually for emphasis, as in the last two lines of the **English sonnet.** Geoffrey Chaucer introduced the heroic couplet into English poetry, most notably in his *Canterbury Tales.* Another English poet, Alexander Pope, used the heroic couplet to create memorable, often quoted, proverb-like lines.

"And, spite of pride, in erring reason's spite,
One truth is clear, Whatever is, is right."

"Hope springs eternal in the human breast:
Man never is, but always to be blest."

As a very young girl, the American poet Edna St. Vincent Millay wrote the fine poem "Renascence" in couplets of **iambic tetrameter.**

"The world stands out on either side
No wider than the heart is wide;
Above the world is stretched the sky—
No higher than the soul is high."

Dactylic foot. See **Meter.**

Denotation is the dictionary meaning of a word, the thing or situation the word specifically refers to. The words "you" and "thou" have the same denotation, but the **connotations** have different flavors. The word "home" denotes the place where you live but has strong emotional connotations. In ordinary language—prose—the stress in word use is on denotation, in poetry, on connotation.

Diction is the careful choice of words, or the special vocabulary, employed by the poet. Diction may be employed to suit the character of the speaker, the mood or tone of the poem, or to create other effects desired by the poet. In the following lines, Ogden Nash mixes highly formal language and slang for humorous effect.

"And I shall even add to it by stating
unequivocally and without restraint
That you are much happier when you are happy
than when you ain't."

In the following lines from a poem by Philip Booth, the speaker is stopped in his automobile by the gates of a railroad crossing and watches and counts as the cars of a long freight train rattle by. The words of the poem are entirely the names seen on the cars, the types of cars, and the speaker's counting, as the train flashes by.

> "B & M boxcar,
> boxcar again,
> Frisco gondola,
> *eight-nine-ten*
> Erie and Wabash,
> Seaboard, U.P.,
> Pennsy tank car,
> *twenty-two, three"*

The diction of these lines captures the speaker's visual experience; their **rhythm,** the speaker's auditory experience.

Dramatic monologue is a poem in which the speaker, a specific person other than the poet, is talking to one or more listeners who are present, but not heard from. In this book, the following poems are examples of the dramatic monologue or variations of it: "The Unknown Citizen," "To James," and "Recuerdo." The dramatic monologue is not to be confused with the **soliloquy,** in which a specific person, other than the poet, is thinking aloud, putting his or her inner thoughts into words. The soliloquy is not addressed to another character, simply made available to the audience or reader. "Summer Remembered," "Patterns," and "American Rhapsody (4)" are examples of the soliloquy form.

End rhyme. See **Rhyme.**

English sonnet. See **Sonnet.**

Euphony is a combination of sounds that are pleasant and smooth in effect. The poet makes use of euphonious sounds to support a pleasant or sensual mood, idea, or **image,** as in the following examples:

> "Fluxions of yellow and dusk on the waters
> Make a wide dreaming pansy of an old pond in the
> night."

Carl Sandburg

> "With jellies soother than the creamy curd,
> And lucent syrops, tint with cinnamon;
> Manna and dates, in argosy transferred
> From Fez; and spicéd dainties, every one,
> From silken Samarcand to cedared Lebanon."

John Keats

Extended metaphor. See **Metaphor.**

Figurative language (Figure of Speech) is a way of using words so that they mean something other than what they seem to say, and in which the intended meaning is clear. If a person says, "My heart is broken," everyone will understand that these words are not to be taken literally to mean what they say. Everyone will understand that the words mean "I am deeply sad." Other common and readily understood examples of figurative language occur in such statements as: "They were sweating blood." "It was raining cats and dogs." "All hands on deck." "A new broom sweeps clean." The poet uses fresh, original figures of speech to make powerful use of language, to enrich and extend meaning. The important figures of speech or forms of figurative language include **simile, metaphor, personification, synecdoche, metonymy, hyperbole, paradox, apostrophe, irony.**

Free verse is poetry that is written in a loose **rhythm** instead of **meter** (regular rhythm) and usually has no **rhyme.** The lines of free verse vary greatly in length. Although the "Psalms" and the "Song of Solomon" of the King James Bible are written in a form resembling free verse, free verse did not become established in poetry until relatively recently. Walt Whitman, with his *Leaves of Grass*, introduced free verse to American poetry, after which it became firmly established as a poetic form in the writing of such poets as Amy Lowell, Carl Sandburg, and E. E. Cummings.

Haiku, sometimes spelled hokku, is a poetic form that originated in Japanese literature, consisting of a total of seventeen syllables divided into three lines of five, seven, and five syllables respectively. The haiku is typically simple and delicate, as in the following example:

> "All the world is cold . . .
> My fishing-line is trembling
> In the autumn wind"

> Buson

Hyperbole is deliberate exaggeration to emphasize a truth, as when a person says, "You could have knocked me over with a feather," and in the following examples from poems:

> "And my fingertips turned into stone
> From clutching immovable blackness."

> James Dickey

> "And I will luve thee still, my dear,
> Till a' the seas gang dry."

> Robert Burns

Iambic foot. See **Meter.**

Imagery (Image) is the use of words to recreate the sense impressions of actual experience. Verbal imagery most often is visual, but imagery also includes words of sound, smell, taste, and feel. The following lines about racing yachts present precise visual images of the scene:

> "Mothlike in mists, scintillant in the minute
>
> brilliance of cloudless days, with broad bellying sails
> they glide to the wind tossing green water
> from their sharp prows while over them the crew crawls
>
> ant-like . . ."
>
> William Carlos Williams

Sound images dominate the following stanza:

> "The ice was here, the ice was there,
> The ice was all around:
> It cracked and growled, and roared and howled
> Like noises in a swound!"
>
> Samuel Taylor Coleridge

The sight and feel of the tropical sun beating down on a becalmed ship come alive in the following stanza:

> "All in a hot and copper sky,
> The bloody Sun, at noon,
> Right up above the mast did stand,
> No bigger than the Moon."
>
> Samuel Taylor Coleridge

Imagery may be *literal*, directly describing sense experiences, as in the following lines:

> "Under our tulip tree
> you wait in the yellow dust
> smoothing a lilac dress."
>
> Dave Etter

Imagery is also often the strength of the figurative comparisons of **simile, metaphor,** and **personification,** as the similes of the following lines illustrate:

> "Our dried voices, when
> We whisper together
> Are quiet and meaningless
> As wind in dry grass
> Or rats' feet over broken glass
> In our dry cellar."
>
> T. S. Eliot

Good readers of poetry must be alert to images and respond to them sensitively. Good readers of poetry will not only see, hear, feel, taste, and smell the sense impressions of the poem but will add to them whatever is consistent to make the image even more complete. For example, readers of the last two lines of the passage by T. S. Eliot on page 301 will not only hear the sound of the rats' feet brushing the glass, but also they will be in the dark gloom of the cellar, see the scurrying grey forms and the vague shapes of discarded junk in the dark, and smell the dusty, mouldy cellar smell. An important part of the richly suggested meaning of poems is grasped by the readers' active and exact response to both the literal and **figurative** images.

Internal rhyme. See **Rhyme.**

Irony may occur in two forms. In its verbal form, it is the use of words to mean the opposite of what they say. If the weather has been wet and cold for days and someone says, "Well, another perfect day," the words are used ironically, as everyone will understand. When Siegfried Sassoon, in a poem about war, writes "Does it matter?—losing your sight? . . ./There's such splendid work for the blind," he is writing ironically. The second form of irony is dramatic irony or irony of situation. The contradiction between the outward and inward circumstances of Richard Cory's life is dramatic irony. The contradiction between Bert Kessler's view of the death of the bird he shot and his own death is ironic. In Randall Jarrell's poem "Losses," it is ironic that death-dealing bombers are tenderly given girls' names. In Carl Sandburg's "Mr. Attila," the contradiction between the professor's harmless appearance and personal behavior and his work on the atom bomb is ironic. Emily Dickinson pinpoints the irony of a blindly conformist society in "Much Madness is divinest Sense." Verbal irony sometimes takes specific forms as in **paradox, antithesis,** and **oxymoron.**

Italian sonnet. See **Sonnet.**

Line. In ordinary language, or prose, words are written or printed according to the meaning or thought. The main divisions or units, therefore, are sentences or paragraphs. Line beginnings and endings have no significance; they are determined mechanically by fixed margins on the page. In poetry, patterns of sound are important, and line beginnings and endings are determined by patterns of sound. The line is a basic unit of the pattern of sound. In traditional or regular poetry, each line has a fixed number of syllables and a fixed **meter,** or arrangement of those syllables. If **rhyme** is present, it reinforces the sound pattern established by the line. In **free verse,** the pattern of sound is reflected in a loose or irregular **rhythm,** and the number of syllables in a line varies. More often than not, the thought divisions of a poem do not correspond to the line endings. In reading poetry aloud, it is important to read according to meaning, and not make a full stop at the end of each line unless the thought requires it. The music of the sound pattern will make itself felt through the thought pattern.

Lyric. A lyric is a short songlike poem expressing personal feelings. Portions of many poems have lyrical or songlike qualities. A good example of a lyric is Ben Jonson's "Drink to Me Only with Thine Eyes," which so easily lent itself to the famous melody that was later written to go with the words.

Metaphor is usually defined as an implied comparison (no "like" or "as" is used, as they are in **simile**) between two unlike things. Real understanding of metaphor needs a fuller explanation. Look at a commonly used metaphorical statement. One student says to another, "The exam was a piece of cake." Obviously this is not a literal statement. The exam does not actually consist of a piece of cake. Moreover, the purpose of the speaker is not to tell anything about the factual substance of the exam. The purpose is to convey some specific essential characteristic of the exam realized in the experience of the speaker. In that experience, the exam was of such character as to be pleasantly and easily disposed of, "eaten up." The image of the piece of cake being so eaten is used to express the character of the exam in the experience of the speaker. From this example, we can learn that the purpose of a metaphor is to convey the speaker's feelings about a specific essential characteristic of a real thing. That purpose is accomplished by presenting an **image** of another and a different thing that vividly expresses the characteristic and the speaker's perception of it. To put this another way, a metaphor has two terms: a *literal* thing and a **figurative image** that brings out a feeling about the *literal* thing. The following examples of common metaphors will illustrate.

"Life is a bowl of cherries."

"We drove over a washboard road."

"The angry cop came up to us, breathing fire."

The writer of a metaphor works with two terms in mind. The first term is the original literal thing the writer wants to tell us something about. In the examples we have looked at, these are the exam, life, the road, the cop. The second term is the imaginative image that conveys the writer's feeling about some characteristic of the original term: eating a piece of cake, a bowl of cherries, a washboard, a dragon breathing fire. It is important to notice that the writer of the metaphor does not always spell it out completely. For example, "piece of cake" is only part of the image. It is necessary to complete the image by seeing a person pleasantly munching on a piece of cake and disposing of it quickly and easily. "Breathing fire" is only part of the image, and it is necessary to see the fierce and threatening dragon that is breathing fire. Moreover, the formula "*a* is *b*" does not always occur. The phrase "washboard road" condenses the formula. The good reader of poetry must be alert to the facts that the presence of a metaphor is not always spelled out and that a full figurative image is given only through the suggestion offered by a part of the image. Here is one example of a metaphor from a poem in this book.

"Kneeling in snow by the still lake side,
Rising with feet winged, gleaming, to glide."

In these lines from "The Skater of Ghost Lake," the poet metaphorically compares ice skates to wings on the feet. The imaginative image suggests the speed and flowing grace with which the skater moves. From the suggestion of the word "winged," the reader must complete the picture of the graceful, easy strides of the skater and get the feeling of the sudden power the skates have given to the skater. The metaphor is highly condensed. The lines do not say "her skates were wings." Skates are not even mentioned. The good reader, however, will see the complete metaphor as it is suggested in the phrase "feet winged." Most metaphors are brief. Sometimes, however, a single metaphor will be developed through many lines or even through a whole poem. Such **extended metaphors** occur in several of the poems in this book. For example, in "Underwater," the comparison of the sea beneath the surface to a cathedral is extended through much of the poem. In "To James," the comparison of life to a footrace is the thrust of the whole poem.

Meter. English words are made up of units of sound called syllables. The core of every syllable is a vowel sound. When English words of two or more syllables are spoken, one syllable is accented by raising the pitch and volume of voice slightly and holding the sound slightly longer, as in the following examples (− = accented, ˅ = unaccented):

tŏ dāy
yēs tĕr dăy
tŏ mōr rŏw

One-syllable words are accented or not according to meaning.

Ī ăm bŏss.
Ĭ ām bŏss.
Ĭ ăm bōss.

In ordinary speech, there is an irregular and usually accidental pattern of accented and unaccented syllables which lends speech a degree of rhythmic sound. In **free verse,** the pattern of accented and unaccented syllables is arranged to create a freely flowing, but definite, **rhythm.** In traditional poetry, words are arranged in a fixed pattern of accented and unaccented syllables called meter. Meter has two fixed units. The first unit is the **foot,** or pattern of accented and un-accented syllables followed in the poem. The basic feet are the following:

Examples	*Name of foot*	*Name of meter*
ĭn-sīst		
dĭ-vīde	**iamb**	**iambic**
rĕ-mōve		
pōr-tĭon		
ār-rŏw	**trochee**	**trochaic**
fūl-lў		
cŏn-tră-dīct		
ĭn-tĕr-rūpt	**anapest**	**anapestic**
ăs-cĕr-tāin		
stīm-ŭ-lăte		
āp-pĕt-ĭte	**dactyl**	**dactylic**
yēs-tĕr-dăy		

The second unit is the **line,** measured by the number of feet in it.

monometer (one foot)
dimeter (two feet)
trimeter (three feet)
tetrameter (four feet)
pentameter (five feet)
hexameter (six feet)
heptameter (seven feet)
octameter (eight feet)

The meter most commonly used is iambic and the most common line length is pentameter. The following are some examples of metric patterns from poems in this book.

Iambic tetrameter
"Ŏ beaūtĭfūl fŏr spācioŭs skīes"

Iambic trimeter
"Fŏr āmbĕr wāves ŏf grāin"

Iambic pentameter
"Thĕ wōrk ŏf hūntĕrs ĭs ănothĕr thīng"

Iambic dimeter
"Yoŭr grīef ănd mīne
Mŭst īntĕrtwīne"

Trochaic tetrameter
"Sūrgeŏns mūst bĕ vērў cārefŭl"

The purpose of the foregoing discussion is to provide a brief introduction to meter. It is not necessary to have this technical knowledge to understand and appreciate a poem fully. Nor should meter have any more than a background function in the reading of a poem aloud. Poems should be read according to meaning and not in a singsong patter that seeks to stress the meter.

Metonymy is a figure of speech in which the name of a thing is substituted for the name of something closely associated. When we ask, "Have you read Shakespeare?" we are substituting the name of the author for his works. When we say, "The pot is boiling," we are substituting the name of the container for the liquid contents. Other common examples of metonymy are "old salt" for sailor, "the crown" for a king, and "the oval office" for the President. In the following lines, "coroner," an official associated with death, is substituted, in an example of metonymy that is also **understatement,** for mass killing in war.

> "One simple thought, if you have it pat,
> Will eliminate the coroner"
>
> Ogden Nash

Near-rhyme. See **Rhyme.**

Octet. See **Sonnet.**

Onomatopoeia. Some words that name sounds also imitate the sound they name in their own sound. This quality is called onomatopoeia. Examples of onomatopoetic words are "cock-a-doodle-doo," "quack," "hiss," "buzz," "bang." Onomatopoetic effects can also be gained by **alliteration** or other combinations of sounds in words that are not themselves onomatopoetic, as in the following examples:

> "The moan of doves in immemorial elms,
> And murmuring of innumerable bees."
>
> Alfred, Lord Tennyson

> "I heard them blast
> The steep slate-quarry, and the great echo flap,
> And buffet round the hills, from bluff to bluff."
>
> Alfred, Lord Tennyson

> "Crisp is the whisper of long lean strides"
>
> William Rose Benét

Oxymoron is a concise **paradox** in which two successive words seemingly contradict each other: "living death," "successful failure," "thunderous silence," "sweet sorrow."

Paradox is a seeming contradiction that reveals an underlying truth, as in the following examples:

"Yet each man kills the thing he loves"

Oscar Wilde

"The only way to get rid of a temptation is to yield to it."

Oscar Wilde

"The more things a man is ashamed of, the more respectable he is."

George Bernard Shaw

Usually there is an underlying **irony** in paradox, as in the paradox in the poem about Grampa Schuler's youth and old age.

Personification is a special kind of **metaphor** in which an idea, object, or animal is given human characteristics. The tendency to personify is deeply rooted in us. The ancient Greeks personified various aspects of nature in their humanlike gods. We refer to "Mother Nature" and "Old Man River." In the following lines, gasoline pumps are personified as basketball players:

"Flick stands tall among the idiot pumps—
Five on a side, the old bubble-head style,
Their rubber elbows hanging loose and low."

John Updike

Pun. See **Ambiguity.**

Quatrain is a **stanza** of four lines. It is the most common stanza form in English poetry, often used in ballads and long narrative poems. Well-known poems written in quatrains are Coleridge's "The Rime of the Ancient Mariner," Gray's "Elegy in a Country Churchyard," and Fitzgerald's "The Rubaiyat of Omar Khayyam," the last of which includes the following familiar quatrain:

"A Book of Verses underneath the Bough,
A Jug of Wine, a Loaf of Bread—and Thou
Beside me singing in the Wilderness—
Oh, Wilderness were Paradise enow!"

Poems in this book written in quatrains include "The Skater of Ghost Lake," "Incident," "Atomic," "Richard Cory," "I taste a liquor never brewed," and "Water."

Refrain is a line that is repeated in a poem for musical and mood effect. In Millay's "Recuerdo," the line "We were very tired, we were very merry" occurs as a refrain at the beginning of each **stanza.**

Repetition. See **Sound effects.**

Rhyme is the repetition of the sounds of the final accented syllables of two or more words. This repetition usually occurs at the ends of lines **(end rhyme).** Sometimes the repetition occurs within a line **(internal rhyme).** Examples of rhyming words are "June"–"moon," "nation"–"inflation," "relax"–"attacks," "through"–"blue." End rhymes can be arranged in various patterns, called the **rhyme scheme.** The letters of the alphabet are used to code the rhyme scheme. A **couplet,** two rhyming lines, is coded *aa:*

> "Indeed, everybody wants to be a wow,   *a*
> But not everybody knows exactly how."   *a*
>
> Ogden Nash

A **quatrain** in which alternating lines rhyme is coded *abab:*

> "Whenever Richard Cory went down town,   *a*
> We people on the pavement looked at him: *b*
> He was a gentleman from sole to crown,   *a*
> Clean favored, and imperially slim."   *b*
>
> Edwin Arlington Robinson

A variety of more intricate rhyme schemes is possible. The rhyme scheme of the following **stanza** of six lines is *abcbdd:*

> "Life has loveliness to sell—   *a*
> All beautiful and splendid things,   *b*
> Blue waves whitened on a cliff,   *c*
> Climbing fire that sways and sings,   *b*
> And children's faces looking up   *d*
> Holding wonder like a cup."   *d*
>
> Sara Teasdale

Internal rhyme creates an especially rich musical effect.

> Ah, distinctly I <u>remember</u> it was in the bleak <u>December</u>   *a*
> And each separate dying <u>ember</u> wrought its ghost upon
>   the floor.   *b*
> Eagerly I wished the <u>morrow</u>; vainly I had sought
>   to <u>borrow</u>   *c*
> From my books surcease of <u>sorrow</u>—sorrow for
>   the lost Lenore   *b*
>
> Edgar Allan Poe

Sometimes poets use rhymes that are not perfect, but approximate. Such rhymes are called **near-rhymes.** Near-rhymes include **assonance** ("mix"–"tick," "how"–"loud") and **consonance** ("just"–"last," "mend"–"band") and words with various other kinds of sound similarity. The following are examples of near-rhyme.

"Wherever she is it is now.
    It is here where the apples are:
    Here in the stars,
    In the quick hour."

                    Archibald MacLeish

"Your feet thump-thump against my back
    and you whisper to yourself. Child,
    what are you wishing? What pact
    are you making?"

                    Anne Sexton

"For the lime-tree is in blossom
And one small flower has dropped upon my bosom."

                    Amy Lowell

"The whiskey on your breath
    Could make a small boy dizzy;
    But I hung on like death:
    Such waltzing was not easy."

                    Theodore Roethke

Rhythm is all around us and within us. There is rhythm in the rising
and setting of the sun, in birth and death, in the flow of tides, in the
coming and going of the seasons. There is rhythm in the beating
of our hearts, in our breathing, in our sleeping and waking, in our
walking. There is rhythm in music, in dance, in painting, in architecture. Too, there are rhythms in the sounds of language to reinforce the moods, ideas, and images expressed by the words of poems.
Poets use the repetitions of **alliteration, assonance, consonance,
rhyme,** and other kinds of repetition, to create rhythms. In traditional verse, poets use **meter,** a fixed pattern of accented and unaccented syllables in lines of fixed length, to create rhythm. In **free
verse,** poets use an arrangement of lines of irregular length to create
loosely flowing rhythms or cadences, reinforced by other kinds of
repetitions and patterns of **sound effects.** The following passage
illustrates the way the rhythms of free verse reflect the mood of
sorrow and mourning in a poem about the death of Lincoln.

"When lilacs last in the dooryard bloom'd,
    And the great star early droop'd in the western sky
        in the night,
    I mourn'd, and yet shall mourn with ever-returning spring.

    Ever returning spring, Trinity sure to me you bring,
    Lilac blooming perennial and drooping star in the west,
    And thought of him I love."

                    Walt Whitman

The stricter, pounding rhythms of lines that are metrical and rhymed can also be strongly effective in reinforcing the mood and meaning of the words of a poem.

> "It matters not how strait the gate,
> How charged with punishments the scroll,
> I am the master of my fate;
> I am the captain of my soul."
>
> William Ernest Henley

Sestet. See **Sonnet.**

Simile is a figure of speech similar to **metaphor** in which an imaginative image is used to express a feeling about an essential characteristic of a literal thing. Since the words "like" or "as" are used in a simile, this figure of speech is usually more apparent than metaphor. In the following simile, the poet compares the houses in a village on the Maine coast to oyster shells to express the hard, cold, lifeless, unattractive appearance of the houses.

> "White frame houses stuck
> like oyster shells
> on a hill of rock"
>
> Robert Lowell

The poet views children's faces as a cup full to the brim with the wonder of innocence in the following simile:

> "And children's faces looking up
> Holding wonder like a cup."
>
> Sara Teasdale

The swift movement of a hammer gives the impression that the forked claws move with the darting speed of the tongue of a snake.

> "With the claws of my hammer glistening
> Like the tongue of a snake."
>
> Amy Lowell

Simile is usually defined as the expressed comparison of two unlike things. More accurately, simile uses an imaginary image that expresses the poet's feeling about some characteristic of a literal thing. Robert Lowell's simile uses oyster shells to express his feeling about the houses as lifeless, hard, and cold.

Soliloquy. See **Dramatic monologue.**

Sonnet is an important, traditional form of poem, which conforms to a strict structure. A sonnet consists of fourteen lines of **iambic**

pentameter and has one of two **rhyme schemes.** The **Italian** or Petrarchan sonnet rhymes *abbaabbacdcdcd* (sometimes *cdecde*). The **English** or Shakesperean sonnet rhymes *ababcdcdefefgg* (three **quatrains** of alternating rhyme and a concluding **couplet**). The English sonnet often follows a structure in which the first eight lines **(octet)** develop the statement of a problem and the last six lines **(sestet)** lead to the resolution of the problem, a resolution that is finalized in the concluding **couplet.** The most famous sonnets are in the sonnet sequence of Shakespeare. Elizabeth Barrett Browning's "Sonnets from the Portuguese" is another noteworthy sequence of love sonnets. Among American poets, Edna St. Vincent Millay is most noted for her sonnets, including the sonnet sequence "Epitaph for the Race of Man."

Sound effects. Sound is important in our spoken language. When we are angry, we shout. When we speak words of tender love, we whisper. When we are excited, we raise the pitch of our voices; when sad, we lower the pitch. When we give commands, we use short, crisp emphatic words, carefully stressing every syllable. The human voice has been described as the most complex and remarkable of all musical instruments. We make some sounds, the vowels, using only various shapes of our open mouths through which the vibrations of our vocal chords are projected. We make the consonant sounds by using various combinations of positions of tongue, teeth, lips, and palate to form an amazing variety of sound-producing openings or partial openings. For such consonants as p, t, s, f, k, we use only expelled breath. For b, d, z, v, g, j, l, m, we use the vibrations of our vocal chords. Some sounds can be held indefinitely—all the vowel sounds and l, m, n, s, r. Some sounds can only be uttered and finished—d, t, b, k, g. Some sounds are soft and liquid—l, r, m. Some sounds are hard and explosive—k, b, d. The poet makes artistic use of all the aspects of the sound effects of speech to reinforce the mood and meaning of the words. He uses **rhythm, rhyme, assonance, consonance, alliteration, repetition.** Too, the poet uses other combinations of sound which somehow have a musical effect that intensifies meaning but are as hard to define or explain as music itself is. Here are some examples.

"The world is charged with the grandeur of God.
  It will flame out, like shining from shook foil;
  It gathers to a greatness, like the ooze of oil
Crushed. ... ."

                                        Gerard Manley Hopkins

"When the hounds of spring are on winter's traces,
  The mother of months in meadow or plain
Fills the shadows and windy places
  With lisp of leaves and ripple of rain"

                                        Algernon Charles Swinburne

"Not in vain the distance beacons. Forward, forward
  let us range,
Let the the great world spin forever down the ringing
  grooves of change."

Alfred, Lord Tennyson

"A poem should be palpable and mute
  As a globed fruit,

Dumb
As old medallions to the thumb"

Archibald MacLeish

Stanza. In a metrical poem, the stanza is the largest unit of **rhythm.** Each stanza contains a fixed number of lines and a fixed **rhyme scheme** that is usually repeated in all the other stanzas. For example, "Richard Cory" consists of four **quatrains** in **iambic pentameter** with lines of alternating rhymes: *abab cdcd efef ghgh.* In **free verse,** the poem may be divided into stanza sections determined by the poet according to mood, idea, rhythmic pattern, or other factor.

Symbol. We often use concrete objects as symbols for larger ideas or feelings. A snake symbolizes evil, snow symbolizes purity, and a dove symbolizes peace. In poetry, a word or a phrase used as a symbol stands for more than it says. Sometimes, a whole poem is symbolic and stands for more than it says. In "The Great Scarf of Birds," the flock and its movement seem to symbolize the awesome and mysterious ways of nature. The poem "Underwater" may symbolize the violence that lurks in the dark recesses of the human psyche, of which we are ashamed when it is exposed to the light. The scene in "heaven" in "The Origin of Baseball" symbolizes the feeling of disorder and frustration in human affairs. In "Water," the cold Maine water symbolizes the failure of love. General characteristics of poetry are its suggestiveness and its indirectness which make possible the expression of complex feelings and experiences in a few words. Symbolism like **metaphor, imagery, ambiguity,** and **allusion** is a powerful instrument for the expression of large worlds of meaning in a few words.

Synecdoche is a figure of speech in which a part of a thing is spoken of as representing the whole thing. When we use "pigskin" for football and when we speak of "heads" of cattle, we are using synecdoche. In the line "May God thy gold refine" from "America, the Beautiful," the word "gold" is used to stand for all the material wealth of which it is but one part.

Trochaic foot. See **Meter.**

Understatement is a form of **irony** or humor that depends on deliberately representing something as much less than it really is. Mark Twain's remark is a well-known example: "The reports of my death are greatly exaggerated."

Verse form is any one of a number of fixed traditional patterns of a whole poem. The **sonnet** is the best known of these. The limerick is a familiar form used mainly for light verse. The nine-line Spenserian **stanza** and the **quatrain** written in lines of **iambic tetrameter** with various **rhyme schemes** (*abcb, abab*) are other traditional verse forms.

Index of Authors

Index of Titles